THE HEART OF

HEBREW HISTORY

THE HEART OF
HEBREW HISTORY

A Study of the Old Testament

H. I. HESTER

Head of the Department of Religion, William Jewell College, 1926-1961
Vice President, Midwestern Baptist Theological Seminary, 1961-1965

BROADMAN PRESS
Nashville, Tennessee

ISBN: 0-8054-1217-4

Forty-Second Printing, 1980

DEWEY DECIMAL CLASSIFICATION: 221.95
SUBJECT HEADING: BIBLE. O.T.—
HISTORY OF BIBLICAL EVENTS

AUTHOR'S FOREWORD

In 1948 the author of this volume was invited by the Education Commission of the Southern Baptist Convention to prepare a textbook ,on the Old Testament for use by college students. The need for a new text seemed to be urgent and almost universal. The first edition appeared in 1949.

Before undertaking the task the writer wanted the opinions of other teachers of the Bible in our leading colleges. Accordingly a questionnaire was sent to instructors in more than fifty representative colleges asking for suggestions and recommendations. Replies were received from a large number of these teachers. The suggestions received were exceedingly helpful. Naturally not all of these suggestions could be followed in preparing a text. However, the writer has been guided by these recommendations and has sought to produce as nearly as possible the kind of book which these teachers feel is needed.

The task of producing a textbook is not an easy one. The writer does not claim to have measured up to the ideal. Indeed, he, more than any one else, is aware of the imperfection in the product of his labors. There is some comfort, however, in realizing that no writer can prepare a text that will be ideally suited to every other teacher.

Since the book is intended primarily for students on the freshman and sophomore level it could not be exhaustive or technical. While some attention has been given to background materials such as geography and antiquities, the chief purpose of the writer has been to present the leading facts in the history of the Hebrew people as given in the Old Testament. As far as possible these have been put in narrative form with an effort to preserve the element of human interest which is such an integral part of the memorable stories of the Old Testament. I have given only limited consideration to the critical problems of the Old Testament because of the conviction that the study of these matters should be reserved for more advanced students.

The author is indebted to many friends who have been helpful in this undertaking. To all who have assisted in various ways the author hereby expresses sincere appreciation.

The adoption of this book as a text by so many schools has made it necessary to produce other editions more frequently than was anticipated. The author is deeply gratified that the book appears to be meeting a real need in our colleges for a serviceable text book in the study of the Old Testament.

REVISED EDITION

Minor changes and corrections in the text have been made from time to time. With this printing the book has been substantially revised and brought up to date. The chapter on Biblical Archaeology has been enlarged so as to include the latest discoveries. Helpful suggestions in the revision have been made by college teachers of Religion who have used the text for several years. The teachers at Baylor University have been especially helpful. Dr. Roy Lee Honeycutt, Jr., Professor of Old Testament, and Dr. William H. Morton, Professor of Biblical Archaeology at Midwestern Baptist Theological Seminary, have given valuable assistance in the revision. To all of these the author expresses his sincere gratitude.

H. I. Hester

CONTENTS

MAPS

Chapter 1

THE BOOK WE STUDY

1. Introduction. 2. A Big Book. 3. Written by the Hebrews. 4. Meaning of the Word Bible. 5. Nature of Its Contents. 6. How It Was Written. 7. Divinely Inspired. 8. Miraculously Preserved. 9. Ancient Manuscripts. 10. Some of the Translations. 11. Influence of the Bible. 12. The Bible Today. 13. Why One Should Study the Bible. 14. How To Study the Bible.

CHAPTER I

The Book We Study

1. Introduction.

Nearly every young person today knows at least something of the Bible. It is such a significant and important book, has had such a vital part in the making of our nation, and is so often quoted that all of us have some idea of its general character. Many of us have become familiar with parts of it by our experiences in the program of our churches. Parents, Sunday School teachers and other friends have told us some of its charming stories and have taught us some of its familiar precepts. However, the large majority of people have but a very limited knowledge of this remarkable book because their study of it has been unorganized. Too often we have "dipped into" it here and there without any plan to see it as a whole, or to appreciate it as a remarkable library of history, literature and religion.

2. A Big Book.

We should understand that the Bible is a very big book. In reality it is a large collection of books — sixty-six in number. These books, written by many different authors over a long period of time, contain many kinds of literature such as history, laws, prophecy, poetry, biography and letters. To gain a thorough knowledge of it will require years of study. However, it is possible for the college student, with one year in a well-planned course, to gain a basic understanding of it. This study should be a delightful and rewarding experience.

Before attempting to study the contents of the Bible we should become acquainted with some of the important facts about the book itself. Such knowledge will make our study much more meaningful.

3. Written by the Hebrews.

The Bible is the book of the Hebrew people. With the single exception of Luke, who wrote the Gospel of Luke and the book of Acts, every other writer who contributed to this volume was of the Hebrew race. Almost all of the events and experiences recorded in the Bible had to do with the Hebrew people. To be sure, numbers of other peoples are mentioned in the Old Testament, but only incidentally. It is true that after the death of Jesus the New Testament records the story of how Christianity worked its way out of the strict limits of Jewish life and assumed international importance, but it is to be noted that it was the Jews themselves who crossed these frontiers and gave their teachings to other races.

4. Meaning of the Word Bible.

The word Bible comes from the Greek word *biblos* which at first meant the bark of the papyrus plant. The word was later used to designate the pith of papyrus plants from which writing material was made. Still later the word was applied to the writings themselves, that is, the scrolls or sheets of paper. In this sense it meant a book. Through Latin usage the word came over into the English language as Bible. Hence, this volume consisting of many smaller books is known as the Bible or *the* Book.

5. Nature of Its Contents.

The Bible has two main divisions called the Old Testament and the New Testament. The word testament means covenant or will. Hence the meaning is old and new covenant, or more specifically, the covenant of God with his people before Christ, and the new covenant made possible through Christ. The Old Testament closes with the period previous to the birth of Christ. The New Testament begins with the events connected with the birth of Christ and closes about the end of the first Christian century.

There are sixty-six books in the Bible. Thirty-nine of these are included in the Old Testament and twenty-seven in the New Testament. In reality, the Bible is a great library consisting of these sixty-six books. Several different classifications of these books have been made. The Jews have one for the Old Testament, and others have been used by different scholars. For the sake of brevity and convenience we may divide the Old Testament into three divisions. (1) The seventeen historical books: Genesis, Exodus, Leviticus, Numbers, Deuteronomy, Joshua, Judges, Ruth, I Samuel, II Samuel, I Kings, II Kings, I Chronicles, II Chronicles, Ezra, Nehemiah, and Esther. (2) The sixteen books of prophecy, usually called the "major" and "minor" prophets: Isaiah, Jeremiah, Ezekiel, Daniel, Hosea, Joel, Amos, Obadiah, Jonah, Micah, Nahum, Habakkuk, Zephaniah, Haggai, Zechariah, Malachi. The first four mentioned are called the "major" prophets and the other twelve, "minor" prophets. (3) The following books of poetry make up the third section: Job, Psalms, Proverbs, Ecclesiastes, Song of Solomon, and Lamentations.

The New Testament books may be classified as follows: (1) The four gospels, Matthew, Mark, Luke, John; (2) One book of history,

Acts; (3) Twenty-one epistles or letters. Thirteen of these were written by Paul: I Thessalonians, II Thessalonians, Galatians, Romans, I Corinthians, II Corinthians, Philippians, Colossians, Philemon, Ephesians, I Timothy, Titus, II Timothy. Eight of these are classified as general letters: Hebrews, James, Jude, I Peter, II Peter, I John, II John, III John; (4) One apocalyptic book, the Revelation.

6. How It Was Written.

There is a wide difference of opinion as to the time when the different books of the Bible were written. Many competent scholars believe that the earliest books were written around 1300 B.C. and that the New Testament was completed about 100 A.D. Thus it may be said that these sixty-six books were written during a period of some fourteen hundred years. It is generally held that there were about thirty authors. The Old Testament was written in the Hebrew language, except some small sections written in the Aramaic tongue. The writers of the New Testament used Greek. These men used finely prepared sheepskin, vellum, and the material known as papyrus, which was something like our paper. Their writings were preserved, not in the form of a book as we have them today, but in a scroll or long strip of papyrus rolled at either end. These were used sparingly, were closely guarded and were carefully preserved.

7. Divinely Inspired.

Christian people regard these writings as divinely inspired. Of course there are various theories as to the meaning of inspiration. In fact this subject is so important that a great many books have been written to explain it. We may say that in general there are three views of inspiration. (1) One extreme view, held by some liberal scholars, is that these original writers were inspired only in the sense that any writer is inspired when producing his best work. By this view Shakespeare, Browning, Goethe, Tennyson or any other were equally inspired and consequently their works have the same value. (2) Another extreme view, held by some ultra-conservative scholars, is that these writers were inspired to the degree that every minute detail of their work was automatically directed, even to the extent of proper spelling. In other words the writers were mechanically directed by a higher force and they were absolutely infallible. (3) There is a third view held by the majority of Bible students which comes in between these two. "Holy men of God spoke as they were moved by the Holy Spirit." These writers were men of ability and holy life and were "inbreathed" or inspired by God to write. The Holy Spirit directed them as they wrote the message of God. They were the instruments used for this important service, and yet they were men who were conscious of what they were doing and whose individuality is revealed in their writings. They were aware of divine leadership and because of this fact their writings have divine sanction and authority. It is the word of God, and as such it has a value and an authority which can be claimed for no other writing. Through the centuries Christian people have accepted the Bible as the word and revelation of God. It is authoritative and final and is sufficient for all the needs of men in spiritual matters.

8. *Miraculously Preserved.*

Each book of the Bible was written for some specific and immediate purpose. However, its value and use would not be exhausted with this particular occasion. The book would be needed for other situations, so it would be preserved. Usually they were highly prized and carefully guarded. When one considers the fact that the writings of some thirty men were kept through a period of more than 1000 years of changing fortunes, it seems nothing less than miraculous. Indeed we can not refuse to believe that God had a part in preserving these precious writings. The limits of space will not permit us to discuss here the story of how these books were kept from destruction and were later gathered into the volume of the Old Testament and the New Testament. Two or three facts ought to be mentioned. There were other writings similar in nature to the books of both Testaments written during these years. Some of these have been kept and are found in certain versions of the Bible like the Vulgate, which is the official Bible of the Roman Catholic Church. From all these books written during these years certain ones were selected and later were recognized as the Bible. These selected ones which met the test were included in the list known as the *canon* of the scriptures. Scholars are almost unanimously agreed that this process of selection was completed by about 400 A.D. Since that time the Bible has consisted of these selected books. The most remarkable thing in the history of literature is the fact that these sixty-six books, written by thirty or more men in different situations over a period of more than 1000 years, constitute one great book in which there are no contradictions or inconsistencies. Indeed, the marvel is that these various books, arranged in their present form, make up a volume which is marked by complete unity and through which one great purpose runs.

9. Ancient Manuscripts.

We do not have today the original manuscript of any of the books of either the Old Testament or the New Testament. These original manuscripts have long since perished. Every student is shocked when he first learns this fact. However, this feeling of disappointment soon disappears when he discovers that this fact does not affect the authenticity of these books as they now appear in our Bible. Ancient peoples guarded such precious documents with the greatest care. Copies were made from the originals as accurately as humanly possible and were distributed to various parts of the world at that time. No part of these sacred writings was allowed to be without many witnesses. We have abundant evidence that the writings we now have are substantially the same as in the days of the first Christian century.

We do have certain very old manuscripts of the books of both Testaments. While they are not the originals they are old enough to be very accurate copies. Of course, these are of inestimable value. They are to be found in various libraries of the world and are guarded with the greatest care.

Up to 1947-48 the oldest known manuscript of the Old Testament was dated at 900 A.D. The famous Dead Sea Scrolls (1947-48) date back to the first or second Christian century. These scrolls thus have tremendous significance in the study of the Old Testament text. Altogether there are some 1700 manuscripts of the Hebrew Scriptures in existence, but most of these are of comparatively late dates.

We can mention only three of the important manuscripts of the New Testament. The oldest of these is the Vatican Codex which is dated around 350 A.D. This Codex is in the Vatican Library in Rome. It has nearly 800 pages, 10x10½ inches and contains practically all of the Old and New Testaments. The Sinai Codex, dated about 375 A.D., is next to the Vatican Codex in importance. It is now in the British Museum. The Alexandrian Codex consisting of 776 pages, and containing practically all of our Bible goes back to about 425 A.D. It also is in England. In addition to these three there are several other important manuscripts which we need not name here. All of these ancient manuscripts have priceless value as surviving witnesses of the works of the inspired writers of old.

10. Some of the Translations.

The Old Testament, written in the Hebrew language, naturally was used by the Jews. About 275 B.C. when the Jews, along with other peoples of the Roman world, began to use the Greek language they felt that their scriptures ought to be in the spoken language of the day. So the famous Septuagint, the Old Testament in Greek, was produced. This was a monumental achievement and is the first translation of any part of the Bible into another tongue. The New Testament was written at a time when Greek was the universal language. Naturally then the New Testament writers used the Greek language. But as time passed and Christianity became the religion of other rates the need for new translations arose. About 200 A.D. the lesser known Peshito, a translation into the Syrian language, was made. Perhaps the most famous and influential of all these versions was the one made by Jerome near the end of the fourth Christian century. It was made in Latin, and after considerable controversy gradually became the standard used by European peoples. As the Roman Catholic Church grew in power and came to be the predominant expression of Christianity in Europe (400 A.D. to 1400 A.D.) this Latin Version was used exclusively. One can easily see the vast influence it exerted upon the entire world for a thousand years or more. With the rise of the English people there was a demand for the Bible in their language. The first real attempt at an English translation, made against almost unbelievable opposition, was that by John Wycliffe, a great scholar and opponent of the Roman Catholic Church. This important work appeared in 1380. It was most influential and was the forerunner of a number of other translations which appeared later. There were several translations which were called Reformation Versions — Tyndale's 1525, Coverdale's 1535, the Great Bible 1539, and so on. The most famous translation of the Bible ever made was the one produced during the reign of King James of England and called the King James or Authorized Version. This translation appeared in 1611 and, beyond doubt, has exerted a greater influence on the English speaking race, and on the world, than any other ever made. As time passed and earlier manuscripts of the New Testament were discovered, and the language used in the King James Version became obsolete, scholars felt the need of a new version. So after prolonged study and diligent labor the English Revised Version was produced in 1885. The American Revised Version appeared in 1901. Since then a number of translations in so-called "modern speech" have been produced. The new Revised Standard Version (N.T. 1946, O.T. 1952) has proved quite popular and may enjoy increasing usage, but only time can tell. In the meantime the King James Version continues to be the translation favored by millions of people.

The Bible has been translated into many other languages. In whole or in part it has appeared in more than eleven hundred languages and dialects. Today there is scarcely a tribe or group of people anywhere which does not have at least a part of this unique Book in its own speech.

11. Influence of the Bible.

The great men and women of history have known and appreciated the Bible. Queen Victoria said, "This book is the secret of England's greatness." Gladstone, the grand old man of Great Britain, told the secret of his life when he said, "My daily advisor and comfort is the impregnable Rock of the Holy Scriptures." Listen to Jefferson's estimate of the Book: "I have said and always will say, that the studious perusal of the Bible will make better citizens, better husbands, and better fathers." The rugged Andrew Jackson said, "The Bible is the rock on which our republic rests." Our great Lincoln knew and loved the Bible. His words are: "I am profitably engaged in reading the Bible. Take all of this upon reason that you can, and the balance on faith, and you will live and die a better man." Significant is the testimony of Theodore Roosevelt. "Almost every man who has by his life work added to the sum of human achievements of which the race is proud — has based his life work largely upon the teaching of the Bible." The great commoner, W. J. Bryan, speaking of the Bible, said "There is not a community which cannot be purified, redeemed and improved by a better knowledge and larger application of the Bible to daily life." The late Woodrow Wilson, son of a minister, bears weighty testimony: "I am sorry for the men who do not read the Bible daily. I wonder why they deprive themselves of the strength and the pleasure. I should be afraid to go forward if I did not believe that there lay at the foundation of all our schooling and all of our thought this incomparable and unimpeachable Word of God." Its beneficent influence on human history is incalculable. It has been the inspiration of the great movements for human betterment in the past 2000 years. In every field of worthy human endeavor the influence of this Book is clearly distinguishable.

Its characters and its teachings have been the theme of the world's greatest art. A visitor to the famous art galleries of the world will discover that the majority of the masterpieces are Biblical in theme.

There are more than 2600 recognized works of art with Christ as the center. The world has no finer productions than those of Michelangelo, Raphael, Van Dyck, Rubens, Murillo, Leonardo da Vinci, Hoffman and scores of others whose best works are based on Biblical themes.

In the realm of music also it has been the supreme source of inspiration. Many musicians have become famous because of their masterpieces with Biblical background and theme. Handel's "Messiah" and Mendelssohn's "Elijah" will suffice to illustrate this statement.

To recount the influence of the Bible on the literature of the world would require volumes. Some of the world's greatest writings were produced by men whose very soul was saturated with the truths of the Scriptures. Wordsworth, Shakespeare, Tennyson, Browning, and scores of others reflect its style, its language, and its truths in their works. No other book has inspired so many writers. No other book is so often quoted. No other book is so valued by lovers of literature.

The influence of the Bible on education is likewise incalculable. Through the centuries this remarkable book has stimulated scholars, has inspired the founding of schools, and has helped to dissipate the darkness of ignorance.

As one looks back upon the history of the past 2000 years he must conclude that most of the benefits of civilization have followed the circulation of the Bible among the peoples of the earth. It is truly the "forerunner of civilization."

Its usefulness is not altogether in the past, though some may so declare. Voltaire is said to have boasted that the next century would witness the disappearance of the Bible. But history has not vindicated his prophecy. Its message is still vital, and is applicable to our day. In every generation men will need the message of this timeless book.

It is still the best interpreter of history. It is still our best guide to moral standards. It has the only solution to our puzzling social, economic and international problems. It alone teaches an ideal social order, the fatherhood of God and the brotherhood of men. It stimulates worthy aims; it strengthens the will. It furnishes hope to men in dark despair. It teaches men to worship a loving God. It reveals our need of a Redeemer. It tells us all we know of God. It still pictures a suffering Saviour who loves all men and yearns for them to come into a knowledge of the truth.

The Bible has a part to play in the life of the modern world. In a broadcast to the nation the famous American scientist Dr. Robert A.

Millikan, closed with these remarkable words: "I suspect that the future progress of the human race will be determined by the circulation of the Bible."

> "We search the world for truth; we cull
>   The good, the pure, the beautiful,
> From graven stone, and written scroll,
>   From all old flower fields of the soul;
> And, weary seekers of the best,
>   We come back laden from our quest,
> To find that all the sages said
>   Is in the Book our mothers read."
>   *John Greenleaf Whittier.*

12. The Bible Today.

What a treasure Christian people have in the Bible! And yet how limited and fragmentary is our knowledge of it. But today as never before it is possible for every eager student to have a knowledge of the Bible. Within the past century the best scholarship has been busy with the study of this book. The physical features of all lands, but of Palestine especially, have been studied and reproduced with such great care that it is now possible to understand these and their bearing on the writing of the Bible as never before. The science of archaeology has done much to make the Bible a living book today. The scholars who have labored patiently and persistently in uncovering the remains of ancient civilizations in the Holy Land and other ancient countries have given a new meaning to the Bible. The discoveries of the archaeologists are serving to vindicate the divine record in more than one instance. For example, a few years ago the scholarship of the world was practically unanimous in its judgment that Luke was completely in error in his account of the census at the time of the birth of Jesus. But now the discoveries which have been made vindicate Luke and show that he was giving the facts in his account. A century ago there were more than five hundred words in our Greek New Testament unlike any other words in the Greek language known at that time. But since then the many papyrus scraps and documents found and translated have shown abundant use of words spoken and used by the ordinary people of the first Christian century. In these papers nearly all these five hundred words have been found. They were used in good taste among the people of that day and the writers of our New Testament were not using a new type of Greek, "Ecclesiastical Greek," but were following the ordinary custom of using the language of the day. All this has greatly illumined the study of the New Testament. Many other illustrations of the contribution of the archaeologists might be mentioned, but suffice it to say that all such discoveries are making an invaluable contribution to our understanding of the scriptures.

It is only fair to say here also that the work of the critic has been an aid in our understanding of the Bible. Not all criticism is bad. Some of it is. But the reverent, honest student who has applied the ordinary methods of critical study to our Bible has put us under obligation to him. The Bible has nothing to fear from honest investigation. It is said that one breath of honest criticism would destroy the Koran, the sacred book of the Mohammedans. But not so with our Bible. We welcome open investigation of it. This does not hurt, but helps. It shows its integrity and worth. As a result of all these efforts we can know the facts and circumstances connected with the writing of our Bible as never before.

In the light of these facts every Christian ought to know this great book, then follow its teachings, and then teach it to others.

> Lamp of our feet, whereby we trace
> Our path when wont to stray;
> Stream from the fount of heavenly grace
> Brook by the traveler's way.
>
> Word of the everlasting God,
> Will of his glorious Son;
> Without thee how could earth be trod
> Or heaven itself be won?
>
> Lord, grant us all aright to learn
> The wisdom it imparts;
> And to its heavenly teaching turn
> With simple, child-like hearts.
>
> *Bernard Barton.*

13. Why One Should Study the Bible.

There are several reasons why every person should study this marvelous book. (1) No other book has so permeated all areas of our life, our literature and our speech. It is such an integral part of our thinking and our culture that one can not claim to be an educated person without a knowledge of it. (2) Because of the character of its contents. Its laws are indispensable in human society. Its history is authentic. Its poetry is unsurpassed in quality and beauty. Its stories and parables are among the greatest masterpieces in literature. (3) Because the Bible is concerned with the highest area of life. It operates in the realm of the intellectual and the spiritual. It deals with our desires, our ideals, our hopes, our motives, our conduct. The quality of our character is determined by our response to it. Its effect on us is unlike that of any other book. (4) Because it is the book of religion. It is the one authentic record of God's effort to reveal Himself to men. It contains the full and complete teachings of the one adequate and final religion for mankind. If religion is the highest and most important area of life then a working knowledge of this supreme book of religion is essential to the life of every intelligent person.

14. How To Study the Bible.

Of course the same rules that apply to the study of any book must be used in the study of the Bible. It is read and studied with a view to learning facts and mastering its contents. There is no mystery nor magic secret involved. We gain a mastery of it by the usual route of diligent study and effort.

A few practical suggestions may be helpful to the student in his efforts to gain a working knowledge of this remarkable book.

(1) It should be studied historically, since much of it is history. A full understanding of any part of the Bible can be had only by placing that part in its proper historical setting. The first step with every student is a thorough acquaintance with Biblical history.

(2) The student who would become proficient in the field where so many facts are involved must necessarily do a certain amount of memory work. Many important details must be mastered. This may not be easy but there is no substitute for it.

(3) Since each book in the Bible is a unit in itself, it is suggested that a book by book study be made. In such a study the student must get the main facts about the book — the author, date and purpose — before making a detailed study of the book itself.

(4) When the student has acquired a knowledge of the main historical events and basic facts in the Bible he may desire to enter the larger field of interpretation. The guidance of an experienced teacher will be of great assistance in this undertaking.

(5) There are certain "helps" or additional books which every student should use. In addition to his study Bible he should have

a good Bible dictionary, a set of authoritative maps, a complete concordance, and one or more good commentaries.

(6) Every student should approach his task with a prayer for the guidance and illumination of the Holy Spirit in his work, for only under his direction are we able to find in this wonderful book the things which are there for our enjoyment and the enrichment of our individual lives.

Chapter II

THE OLD TESTAMENT WORLD

1. Introduction. 2. Extent of Old Testament World. 3. Palestine. 4. Names. 5. Location. 6. Size. 7. Climate. 8. Variety of Physical Features. 9. Plant Life. 10. Animal Life. 11. Natural Divisions. 12. Cities of Palestine. 13. Location of Cities. 14. General Plan. 15. Walls. 16. Gates. 17. Streets. 18. Some Biblical Cities.

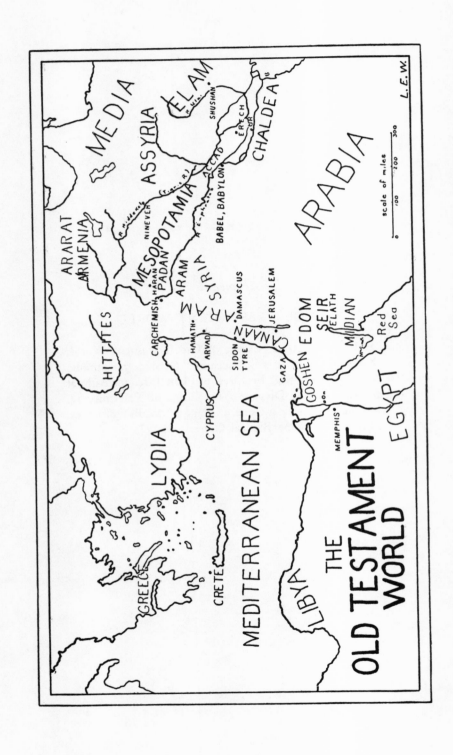

THE OLD TESTAMENT WORLD

MEDIA

ELAM

ASSYRIA

CHALDEA

ARABIA

ARARAT
ARMENIA

MESOPOTAMIA

HITTITES

ARAM

SYRIA

NINEVEH

CARCHEMISH

HARAN

PADAN

ACCAD

BABEL, BABYLON

ERECH

UR

SHUSHAN

HAMATH

ARVAD

SIDON

TYRE

DAMASCUS

CANAAN

JERUSALEM

GAZA

EDOM

SEIR

ELATH

MIDIAN

Red
Sea

GOSHEN

MEMPHIS

EGYPT

LIBYA

LYDIA

CYPRUS

MEDITERRANEAN SEA

CRETE

GREECE

scale of miles

0   100   200   300

L.E.W.

CHAPTER II

The Old Testament World

1. Introduction.

An intelligent study of history necessitates an understanding of geography. Old Testament history covers a period of nearly twenty centuries and involves an area of territory which was occupied by several important nations. It is necessary, therefore, for the student of the Old Testament to be familiar with the geography of the ancient world. He should know the names, location and extent of these ancient lands. A general acquaintance with the geographical features of these countries, particularly of Palestine, will make the study of the Old Testament much easier and more illuminating.

2. Extent.

The territory in which the events of Old Testament history took place is somewhat circumscribed in the light of our modern world. The whole world known to these people contained less than one-half the land area of the United States, and fully one-third of this was desert. In general it consisted of the territories of ancient Mesopotamia (modern Iraq), Syria, Palestine, and Egypt. Palestine, the real homeland of the Hebrews, was the little land in which most of the events recorded in the Old Testament occurred. Because this was their homeland and because of its unique geographical features, we are considering it in some detail in this chapter.

This Old Testament world started at the head of the Persian Gulf in the east. Beginning at this point and moving in a northwesterly direction up the valley between the Tigris and Euphrates rivers one comes to the boundaries of the land of Aram, the land of the ancient Hittites. Turning southward the traveler enters Syria passing through the beautiful valley between the Lebanon and anti-Lebanon mountains. Continuing southward he may take one of several routes through Canaan or Palestine into the land of Egypt, which lies southwest of Canaan with the Mediterranean Sea as its northern boundary. This route, which has been followed by travelers from time immemorial, was aptly described by Dr. J. H. Breasted, the noted Egyptologist, as the "Fertile Crescent." The territory traversed by this route is crescent shaped and includes ancient lands which encircled the triangular shaped Arabian desert on its eastern, northern and western sides.

Ancient Mesopotamia extended from the Persian Gulf to the foothills of the Taurus mountains, a distance of some six hundred miles. In this fertile valley were: (1) The old country of the Chaldees from which Abraham started his long journey; (2) Ancient Babylon whose famous king Hammurabi lived around 1900-1700 B.C.; (3) The great city of Nineveh which was the capital of the conquering Assyrian kings; and (4) The city of Haran, at which Abraham first stopped on his way to Canaan. It is estimated that ancient Mesopotamia once had a population of more than 15,000,000 people.

Syria occupied the territory around the Lebanon and anti-Lebanon mountains. It lay between the Mediterranean Sea on the west and the desert on the east, immediately north of Palestine. Damascus was its chief city, though other great cities such as Tyre, Sidon, Karkar, Carchemish, Kadesh, Aleppo and Hamath existed here.

Southwest of Palestine in the continent of Africa was the fabulous land of Egypt which, because of the fertile Nile valley, was the granary of antiquity. The Nile river makes the land of Egypt. This mighty river which originates in the heart of Africa flows northward a distance of 4,000 miles and empties into the Mediterranean Sea. At the southern end the valley of the Nile is narrow, but it broadens out as it goes northward. Near Cairo the river spreads out to form the famous Delta which is about 13,000 square miles in area. The valley is hemmed in by the arid desert on either side. Then as now, Egypt was the Nile valley.

Because the Nile regularly overflows its banks leaving a deep deposit of rich soil, this valley was famous for its agricultural products, particularly its grain, vegetables, grapes and other fruits, especially the date palm. At different times in her long history prior to the Christian era the Egyptian people developed a remarkable civilization. It was at several times one of the important empires of ancient times. Large commercial enterprises flourished and the fame of Egypt was known afar. The great pyramids, together with many remarkable archaeological treasures found by excavators, show something of the wealth and splendor of this ancient land. The most glorious period of her history was the period of Rameses II (1292-1225 B.C.).

3. Palestine.

Inasmuch as most of the experiences of the Hebrew people recorded in the Old Testament took place in the land of Canaan, their legitimate homeland, and since this little land is so unique in its geographical features, which had a very important influence on the Hebrew people, we are to study the geography of this land somewhat in detail. A working knowledge of the chief features of this land where so many familiar and important events occurred is indispensable to the student of the Old Testament.

4. Names.

Through the centuries this little territory has had a number of names. In earliest Bible times it was called Canaan, or lowlands. Later on it came to be called Palestine, a term probably derived from the word Philistia. It was the territory promised to Abraham and his descendants and hence is often referred to as the "Land of Promise." Since the time of Christ it has become a holy land to millions of people (Jews, Mohammedans, and Christians) and is thus frequently called the "Holy Land."

5. Location.

It is located in southwest Asia, and forms the southern part of the eastern shore of the Mediterranean Sea. Some of its boundaries have varied at different times, of course, but one may speak of it as being bounded on the west by the Mediterranean Sea, on the north by the countries of the Lebanon Mountains (usually Syria), on the east by the Arabian desert and on the south by that arid, semi-desert territory known as the Negeb or south country.

In a sense the land was isolated from the rest of the world. The deserts on the east and south, the mountains on the north, and the sea (without a single good harbor) on the west, practically separated it from the outside world. In the hills of western Palestine was the real home of the Hebrews and here they were really isolated from the other nations of the world. And yet in another sense it was centrally situated. It was on the highways of the nations. All travel, whether for trade, warfare or pleasure, between the great nations of the East and Egypt on the south, passed through this land. From earliest times along these lowland travel routes have passed the great caravans of travellers. But in her highlands as their secure home the Hebrews had a retreat from world events that were being enacted within the boundaries of their country. Thus the Hebrews were near to and yet aloof from the great stream of world activity. Because of this they could be a spectator of the world's conflict and not its victim. They could have a seclusion that would encourage undisturbed communion with God, and at the same time could observe God's providences in dealing with other nations.

6. Size.

Usually the student of the Bible is amazed to discover how small the country is. It is so famous and has exerted such a powerful influence in history that one would expect it to be large in area. Its total area is only 10,000 square miles, about one seventh the size of the State of Missouri, or about one third the area of the State of South Carolina. It is divided into two distinct sections by the Jordan River which runs the entire length of the country from north to south. Western Palestine extends from Dan in the north to Beersheba in the south, a distance of about one hundred forty-five miles. This western section varies in width from twenty miles in the north to ninety miles in the south, thus giving Western Palestine an area of about 6,000 square miles. Eastern Palestine is about one hundred miles long and averages about forty miles in width, thus having an area of about 4,000 square miles. The physical features of this country are the most unique of any land on the globe. No other country has such great diversity within such small compass. It is a world in miniature for everything is there — the seething gorge, the snow-capped mountain, the wide-sweeping valley, the elevated plain, the rolling table land. It is the "multum in parvo" of all lands. It has a wide diversity in temperature, plants, animals, products, industries and habits of people. In a sense the whole earth is epitomized in this little land. The Hebrew people were chosen and set apart as a peculiar people to be the medium of a divine message to all the world, and this land, peculiarly fitted, was chosen as their home, the place where they could be prepared to carry out their unique mission.

7. Climate.

One of the most unique features of Palestine is its climate. It is as diverse as are the physical features of the country. In the low coastal plains and in the Jordan valley it is extremely hot at times. Mt. Hermon in the north towers 9,200 feet above sea level and remains covered with snow for most of the year. In the western highlands, the real home of the Hebrews, the climate is temperate and equable. The chief things to note about its climate are, the temperature, the winds and the rainfall.

The temperature varies according to the elevation and exposure of the land. It varies between one section and another, also between summer and winter and even between day and night. In general it may be said that the mean annual temperature of the highlands is about 65 degrees Fahrenheit, about like that of South Carolina. The coldest month is February and the warmest August. Snow seldom falls, except in the high mountain regions, but the heat in the summer is never extreme except at mid-day in the lower sections of the land.

The winds of Palestine are indeed "His ministers" (Ps. 104). The prevailing winds are from the west and are very regular. Coming from the Mediterranean Sea, they strike the cool air of the highlands and bring rains in the winter. This steady wind is utilized by the farmer in threshing his grain. The winds from the north, south and east are neither frequent nor regular. The north wind is dry and cold (Job 37:9). The east and south wind coming from the desert is most unwelcome (Luke 12:55) because it brings sand and heat from the desert, causing discomfort and damage (Hosea 13:15). The terrors of this wind (sirocco) are often spoken of in the scriptures (Jer. 18:17; Ezek. 27:26; Ps. 48:2).

The rainfall is a most interesting phenomenon. In other lands, of similar latitude sunshine and rain alternate throughout the year, but not in Palestine. There is a season when there is rain, "the rainy season," and another when there is none, "the dry season." The rainy season begins about the last of October and continues until the last of March. Rain comes at varying intervals during this season. Soon after its beginning ploughing starts and crops are sown. The winter rains continue and then the rains of early spring mature the crops. When this rainy season is over absolutely no more rain falls until October comes again. This remarkable regularity of the seasons was an incentive to faith in God (Deut. 11:14). Occasionally, however, the regularity failed and a drought occurred (I Kings 17, Ruth 1). It is easy to see how vitally these climatic conditions would affect the life and habits of the people.

8. Variety of Physical Features.

While Palestine is a small country it has in it most of the physical features found in almost all the other countries of the world. Snow-clad mountains and sultry depressions, deserts and fertile plains, barren, rocky hillsides and green valleys, all can be found in this little land.

As a whole the country is more mountainous than is commonly supposed. The western highlands which stretch over the entire length of the land are real mountains and yet are less than forty miles from the sea. The eastern highlands are very similar. To the north are the beautiful Lebanon mountains, the highest of which is Mt. Hermon.

Jerusalem is built on a hill 2,500 feet high in the western highlands of Judea. Several prominent hills or "mounts" are frequently mentioned in connection with this city. The eastern hill of the city is Mt. Moriah, where some think Abraham took his son Isaac to offer as a sacrifice. Upon this mount the temple was later built. At the present time a Mohammedan mosque occupies the hill and faithful Moslems look for Mohammed to return to this hill. Mt. Olivet, 3,000 feet high, is most frequently mentioned in the Bible. It is directly east of the temple area, and is separated from the city proper by the valley of Kidron. The Garden of Gethsemane is on the lower part of the western slope of the mount as one ascends from the Kidron valley. It was from the mount of Olives, sometimes called the Mount of Ascension, that Jesus ascended at the close of his earthly career.

In Samaria, just north of Judea, are Mt. Gilboa where Saul and Jonathan met death, and Mt. Ebal and Mt. Gerizim (known as mounts of cursing and blessing) so famous in Old Testament history.

In Galilee the two well-known hills are the Hill of Nazareth, familiar to all students of the life of Jesus, and beautiful Mt. Tabor, prominent in Old Testament history, and sometimes (erroneously) identified as the place of the Transfiguration.

Palestine is famous for some of its plains. The largest of these is the plain of Esdraelon, one of the best known of any in history, since on this plain so many great events occurred. It is triangular in shape and lies between southern Galilee and northern Samaria, and between the Mediterranean Sea and the Jordan valley. It is the most fertile section of Palestine. Ancient roadways run through it, and some of the most decisive battles of Hebrew history were fought on it. Indeed many famous battles have been fought here since Biblical times.

The Plain of Gennesaret, situated northwest of the Lake of Galilee, is well watered and fertile. In Jesus' day it was literally a luxuriant garden. The plain of Jericho around the ancient city by that name is really in the Jordan valley. It is still fertile and is capable of producing good crops and fruits. The plain of Sharon in the center of the costal plains is famous for its fruits and flowers.

Between the various mountains and hills of Palestine there are a number of familiar valleys. While not as fertile and productive as we would find in the United States, they were regarded by Old Testament people as extremely fertile. For example the Psalmist describes these as follows:

> The hills are girded with joy,
> The pastures are clothed with flocks;
> The valleys also are covered over with corn;
> They shout for joy, they also sing. (Ps. 65:12-13.)

The best known of these are the valley of the Jordan, the valley of Jezreel, the valley of Hinnom and the valley of the Kidron.

9. Plant Life.

In modern Palestine there is but little woodland. In fact trees and shrubs have never been very abundant there. However, quite a number of trees, shrubs and flowers are mentioned in the Bible. Space will not permit any description of these, but we mention a few of these, such as the acacia, cedar, fig, juniper, myrtle, oak, olive, palm, sycamore, terebinth (turpentine tree) and thorn bush. In different parts of the land, flowers such as anemone, cyclamen, crocus, gladiolus, hyacinth, iris, oleander, orchid, poppy, and tulip are still to be found.

10. Animal Life.

There has always been a rather large variety of animal life in Palestine. In the waters of the Lake of Galilee and in the Mediterranean Sea there was an abundance of fish in Biblical times. We find frequent mention of fishing in the New Testament, since in those days it was an important industry. A large number of different birds still live in Palestine. It is said that probably one hundred different bird species are residents there and some two hundred other species are migrants. These include such as domestic hens and chickens, doves, pigeons, sparrows, swallows, eagles, herons, cranes, ravens, owls and others.

Land animals of many different kinds were there during Biblical times, and some of these are still to be found there. The beasts of burden were the camel, the ass, the ox and the horse. Sheep and goats were perhaps the most common of all. A number of others are mentioned such as lions, leopards, foxes, jackals and wolves.

11. Natural Divisions.

We shall now give further attention to a study of the physical features of the different sections of this interesting little country. Nature has divided Palestine into four distinct sections which run throughout the length of the land from north to south. Beginning at the western boundary, the Mediterranean Sea, and going eastward, these divisions are: (1) The Maritime Plains, a series of low, sandy and fertile plains extending along the shores of the Mediterranean. (2) The Western Highlands, a great backbone of mountains forming the chief part of Western Palestine. (3) The Jordan River Valley, the deep depression running through the heart of the land. (4) The Eastern Highlands, the hills and plains of Palestine east of the Jordan.

(1) *Maritime Plains* — The Maritime or Coastal Plains lie between the Sea on the west and the mountains of Galilee, Samaria and Judea on the east. At the northern end this territory is very narrow, in some places scarcely a mile wide. It widens out as one goes south until at the lower end it attains the width of some twenty-five or thirty miles. This strip of coastal land naturally divides itself into three sections. At the north is the plain of Acre and Tyre. Just below this, starting at Mt. Carmel is the beautiful and famous plain of Sharon. At the lower end is the larger and more productive plain of Philistia. This latter was the home of the Philistines, almost continuously the enemy of the Hebrews, for a thousand years.

We shall not speak of each of these divisions of the coastal plains separately since they are so much alike. These plains, especially in the southern part, are fertile lands, famous for their products. Sharon and Philistia were great fruit growing and grain producing lands. Apples, oranges, lemons, grapes, pomegranates, dates, melons, wheat, rye and barley grew in abundance. The wild flowers of Sharon are familiar to every student of the Bible (Song of Solomon 2:1). In the past few years one of the most phenomenal developments in all the history of Palestine has taken place around the cities of Haifa and Tel-Aviv, in this region. The population of these cities has been multiplied by ten while extensive orchards and farms are being developed in this historic plain. Philistia is the largest of these plains and is still a big producer of grain and grapes. This writer will never forget his first glimpse of this beautiful plain early in the morning, with its numerous flocks and beautiful vineyards and orchards.

Let us remember, however, that the Hebrew people did not conquer all this Maritime Plain. To the north was Phoneicia, always independent of the Hebrews, and to the south, Philistia, never subjugated. The coast has never had a good harbor but through the centuries a number of cities have flourished along this costal plain. Beginning at the north were Sidon, Tyre, Acre, Joppa, Caesarea, Lydda (Lud), Gaza, Ashkelon, Ashdod, Ekron and others.

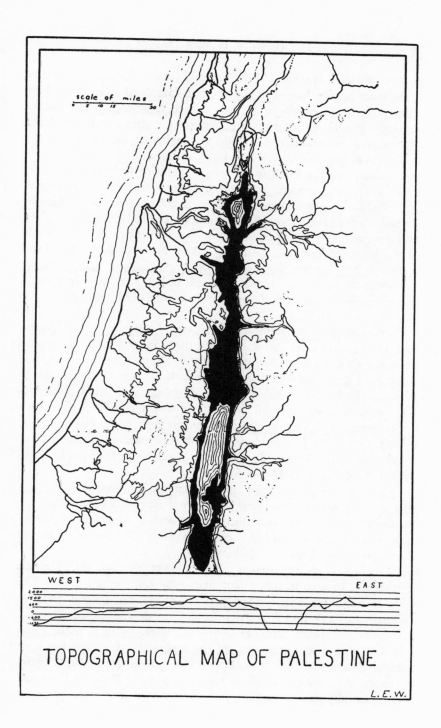

scale of miles
0 5 10 15   30

WEST   EAST

2000
1500
600
0
-400
-10..

TOPOGRAPHICAL MAP OF PALESTINE

(2) *Western Highlands* — The second natural division of Palestine is the main plateau known as the Western Highlands. This long, high ridge, varying in height from 1,000 feet to 2,500 feet, begins in the Lebanon mountains in the north and runs southward to the desert of Arabia. It is customary to divide this highland into three sections: a. Galilee, b. Samaria, c. Judah or Judea. Between Galilee on the north and Samaria on the south is the famous plain of Esdraelon, the only break in the long western plateau, which has already been mentioned.

a. Galilee is a mountainous country, beautiful but not productive. Its boundaries varied through the centuries, but its area may be given as approximately 1,500 square miles. It was settled by the brave people of the tribes of Issachar, Zebulun, Asher, Naphtali and later, Dan. Galilee is best known, however, as the region where Jesus grew up and spent the major part of his life. Some of her cities most frequently mentioned were Nazareth, Cana, Capernaum, Kedeth, Shunem, Nain, Bethsaida and Endor.

b. Samaria lies just south of Esdraelon and north of Judah. On the east is the Jordan river and on the west the plain of Sharon. Its area is approximately 1,500 square miles. It too, is mountainous, but has some good agricultural and pastoral lands. It has had a very important place in the history of the Hebrews. Abraham and other patriarchs lived in it. It was conquered by Joshua and occupied by the Israelites for centuries. It was the home of the ten northern tribes (Kingdom of Israel). Its historical importance is seen by the mention of such names as Mt. Ebal, Mt. Gerizim, Jacob's Well, Shechem, Bethel, Ai, Dothan, Shiloh, Megiddo, Jezreel and Samaria.

After the conquest of the city of Samaria by Assyria in 722 B.C. this territory became the home of a mixed race of people, called the Samaritans. They have maintained their existence here until the present time. Only a few remain but they still worship God according to the ancient customs of their forefathers.

c. Judah, or Judea, makes up the lower part of the Western Highlands. In area it, too, is approximately 1,500 square miles. The country has three rather distinct sections; (1) the Eastern hills or "wilderness," (2) the Western hills sloping down toward Philistia, called the Shephelah, and (3) Southern Judea. Judea is more rocky and barren than any other part of the highlands, though it has been cultivated and used as a makeshift for pasturage through many centuries. While not as fertile as the other parts of Western Palestine, it is historically most important. Jerusalem was, and is now, the center of life for this region as well as all Palestine. No other city has been so famous, no other one so often besieged and conquered, no other one so tenderly enshrined in the hearts of millions of men of many centuries. David captured it from the Jebusites about 1,000 B.C. and since then it has symbolized the life and activities of the Hebrew race and of the three great religions—Judaism, Christianity and Mohammedanism. Does not every traveler long to stand within the walls of this sacred city and in imagination reconstruct in part, at least, some of the momentous events enacted on this famous spot?

(3) *Jordan River Valley*—The most interesting and unique geographical feature of all the Holy Land is the Jordan River valley. There is nothing else just like it in all the world. This great ravine starts at the top of the Taurus mountains in the north and runs far into the desert south of Palestine, a distance of 550 miles. In the mountains it is as high as 3,000 feet above sea level while at the deepest part of the Dead sea it is nearly 2,600 feet below sea level. This gorge or rift varies in width from one to fourteen miles.

In Palestine proper there are three sections of this valley. We consider these in their order from north to south; a. The Lake of Galilee, b. The Jordan River itself, c. The Dead Sea.

a. The Lake of Galilee, called also the Sea of Gennesaret, Sea of Tiberias, and Sea of Chinnereth, is one of the most beautiful little bodies of water to be found anywhere. The mountains on the east and west tower high above its clear waters. The surface of the lake is 682 feet below the level of the sea and at one point it is about 600 feet deep. It is shaped like a pear or a harp. In general its width is about seven miles and its length nearly twelve miles. It is fed by several streams from the mountains of Galilee and the hills to the east, but its chief supply comes from the upper Jordan in the north. It is a beautiful and refreshing body of water. The ancient rabbis said: "Jehovah hath created seven seas, but the sea of Gennesaret is his delight."

During the three years of his ministry, Jesus spent much of his time on or around this lake. Several of his disciples made their living by fishing in its waters. In this beautiful region he performed many miracles and uttered some of his most profound teachings.

b. The Jordan valley from the lower part of the Lake of Galilee to the upper end of the Dead Sea is a deep depression. The Arabs called this rift the Ghor. It is sixty-five miles long. Through the heart of this valley the Jordan river flows. It runs a very crooked course and because of its numerous windings measures about 110 miles in length though a straight line from the Lake of Galilee to the Dead Sea is only sixty-five miles long. In this sixty-five miles the river falls about six hundred and ten feet. This rapid descent gives it the name of Jordan or "Descender." The river is not very wide, varying from one hundred to two hundred feet, except during the rainy season when it overflows its banks and covers the Zor, that lower section adjacent to and above its banks. These annual floods have strewn the valley with driftwood and covered it with mud. In ancient times there were no bridges across the Jordan, but ordinarily it was only from three to ten feet deep and could easily be forded. When General Allenby gained possession of Palestine in 1917 he had a bridge erected across the river opposite Jericho. This bridge bears his name and is in use today. The river can not be used for commercial purposes and the heat there in the summer (as high as 118 degrees) is so intense that but few people live in the valley.

c. The large body of water into which the Jordan empties is called the Dead Sea, though in Old Testament times it went under the name of the Salt Sea, Sea of Arabah and Sea of the Plain. It occupies the deepest part of the great rift. The surface of its waters is 1,292 feet below sea level and at one point the sea is about 1,300 feet deep, thus the great gorge is about one half mile below sea level. The sea is about fifty miles long and averages about ten miles in width. The remarkable thing about it is that it has no outlet. The only way for its waters to escape is by evaporation, and this extracted moisture forms an almost impenetrable haze which hangs over the sea constantly. But in the process of evaporation the chemical substances which abound in its waters are left behind. These waters are 25% solid matter and hence are so buoyant that one can scarcely sink in them. But they are poisonous to all life. In fact not a single living thing, plant or animal, is to be found here, hence its name, Dead Sea. In 1925 the British government published an estimate of the minerals in the Dead Sea waters. These included 2,000,000,000 tons of potassium chloride, 12,000,000,000 tons of sodium chloride (salt) and large amounts of calcium and magnesium chloride and magnesium bromide. In addition, a French scientist, Dr. Georges Claude, contends that the gold in the Dead Sea, if recovered, would be worth $50,000,000,000.

(4) *Eastern Highlands* — The fourth and last natural division of Palestine is the Eastern Highlands, now called Transjordania. Geo-graphically it is so much like the Western ridge that a discussion of

this is not necessary here. It was inhabited by various tribes or nations until its conquest by the tribes after the Exodus. The divisions of this territory changed frequently during Hebrew history. It is a great agricultural and pastoral country. Today this country is a part of Arabia and still yields enormous grain crops and produces hundreds of thousands of cattle, sheep and goats. Just before the time of Christ several large and prosperous cities of Greek and Roman people were situated here. This region was called the Decapolis. Extensive and elaborate ruins of these can still be seen in the region southeast of the Lake of Galilee. But the real home of the Hebrews was west of the Jordan and most of the events in their history took place in the Western highlands.

12. Cities of Palestine.

During the period of approximately 1500 years that the Hebrews occupied the land of Palestine they lived in cities and villages, as well as in the open country. Most of the cities of Palestine which they later occupied were built by the Canaanites or other peoples before them. During the process of conquest the Hebrews possessed the open places first and later subdued the cities which they rebuilt and enlarged. But they did build a few cities of their own such as Samaria and Jezreel.

13. Location of Cities.

In the selection of a site for a city there were two important considerations. (1) They had to be built on a hill as this afforded a natural means of defense from attack. The height of these hills varied. At Megiddo the hill was from fifty to ninety feet above the plain. Jerusalem stands on a hill some seventy-five to one hundred and fifty feet high with the result that it was so easily defended that it took the Babylonians theee years to conquer it (II Kings 17:5). (2) The other requisite was a good water supply. Every Palestinian city of importance had a good spring near it. Sometimes a city, Jericho, for example, would be built even in an open plain to insure a water supply.

14. General Plan.

The plan of these ancient cities was much like that of cities in the Orient today. Since walled cities were strongholds it was best not to have the center of the city too far from the walls, hence most of these cities were contracted into as small space as possible. These cities were never large. All of Canaanite Jericho was small enough to be placed in the Colosseum at Rome. Ancient Megiddo had an area not larger than eleven acres, while Jebusite Jerusalem did not exceed thirteen acres in area.

15. Walls.

The walls of the cities are interesting. In earliest times they were simple, usually only a few feet high, as at Gezer. As time passed and civilization developed, these walls later became thick, well-built structures with towers at regular intervals. The walls of Jerusalem afford a good illustration of this. At first these were built of simple stone, or even clay or brick. But later on they were made of cut, and even dressed stone. The study of the walls of these ancient cities reveals many interesting things and throws light upon the history of the people who made them and lived within them.

16. Gates.

The gates of ancient cities played an important role in the life of the people. In early times these were simple openings in the walls. Later on they were more elaborate. They were equipped with bronze or iron bars and bolts (Deut. 3:5; Neh. 3:6, etc.). Sometimes these gates had chambers overhead (II Sam. 18:24ff) where the city watchman would be stationed (Jer. 6:17). Sometimes as at Gezer, the gate consisted of a protruding tower into which one entered at the side and turned a right angle to enter the city. The passageway of this gate at Gezer was forty feet wide. Oftentimes, as at Beth-Shemesh, there were rooms on either side of the passageway through the tower. During part of their history the Jews had these gates closed on the Sabbath (Neh. 13:19). Near the gates were open places, used as centers of community life. Here contracts were made (Deut. 25:7; Ruth 4:1f) and judicial assemblies held (Amos 5:12; Isa. 29:21) and buying and selling took place (II Kings 7:1) and public announcements were made (Jer. 17:19). Here was the center of social intercourse and here strangers who had no home in the city passed the night (Judges 19:15).

17. Streets.

The streets of these cities were narrow and usually crooked. Even the "street called straight" (Acts 9:11) was not straight like the streets of a modern Western city. In early times these were not paved. Herod Agrippa II, who lived about the first Christian century, paved the streets of Jerusalem for the first time. The streets were unsanitary and foul smelling, as garbage was dumped into them without any regard for sanitation. The disposal of the garbage was left to the scavenger dogs (Ex. 22:31; Ps. 59:6). Even today in Jerusalem the traveler sees almost unbelievable evidences of filth and garbage. The famous street of David in Jerusalem is called today "the street of a thousand smells" and the designation is deserved. These streets were never lighted at night. It seems that the only provision made for their care was the service of a night watchman (Isa. 21:11, Ps. 127:1, etc.).

Along these narrow, winding streets were the shops of merchants. It seems that certain streets were used as bargain streets (I Kings 20:34, Eccl. 12:4, etc.). Here the merchants with reckless disregard of order, displayed their goods. Jeremiah (37:21) speaks of a baker's street, Nehemiah mentions a quarter used for goldsmiths and spice merchants, and of a fish gate. Later, Josephus speaks of quarters used by wool merchants. On certain streets in ancient Jerusalem one can purchase almost any article such as live stock, hay, meat (covered with flies), drugs, beads, laces, drinking water, soft drinks and so on.

The bazaar is an important feature of a modern Oriental city. It is a covered arcade with a row of narrow shops on either side. Every traveler visits these, and must learn to "bargain" with the merchant for his goods. Our Western custom of having a fixed price, from which there is no deviation, is unknown there. These merchants ask at first an exorbitant price, expecting the buyer to press for a lower price. The writer bought an article first priced at $8.00 for $1.00 and at that did not secure any exceptional bargain.

18. Some Biblical Cities.

During the course of Hebrew history in Palestine there were a number of cities of great importance. In the southern part of the land in the territory of Judah was *Hebron*. It was one of the oldest. The patriarchs stopped here and called it home for a long time. It was the seat of David's government while he was king of Judah alone. Today it is a city of about 10,000 population. The chief object of interest is the cave of Machpelah, the burial place of Abraham and some of his family. *Jericho* was a prominent city on the east side of the western highlands, not far from the Jordan river. It was the strategic city captured and destroyed by Joshua. Today it is a small village of only a few hundred population. *Jerusalem* was and is the most famous of all the cities of the Holy Land. We do not know just when is was founded. The Hebrews took it from the Jebusites in the days of David. He made it a great city. Throughout the years of

Hebrew history it was the center of life in their land. It is now a city of some 70,000 people. *Samaria* was built by King Omri to become the capital of the Kingdom of Israel (10 Northern tribes) about 880 B.C. It remained the center of life until it was taken by the Assyrians in 722 B.C. In New Testament times it was an important city, though there is nothing there now but the ruins of former days. *Caesarea* on the coast was built by Herod the Great just before the birth of Christ, hence it had no place in the life of Old Testament peoples. It was essentially a Roman city and was the home of Roman officials in New Testament days. *Nazareth,* a city of southern Galilee, likewise is unnoticed in Old Testament history. It is immortal as the boyhood home of Jesus. Today it is a little city of some 6000 people. *Capernaum* was on the northwest shore of the Lake of Galilee and was a thriving city in the days of Jesus. It was a military station of the Romans and the home of the tax collector. Jesus made this city his headquarters for his popular Galilean ministry. There is no city there now; even the exact site of the city is in dispute. But archaeologists have found there the ruins of one of the Jewish synagogues of New Testament times, probably the very one in which Jesus taught.

Let us say in conclusion that this little land was an ideal "training ground" for God's people. Here they were taught those truths which their race has given to all mankind. This otherwise insignificant country was the arena where were enacted the world's greatest events. As such it has had and will continue to have an abiding interest for the students of the Bible.

Chapter III

ARCHAEOLOGY AND THE BIBLE

1. Introduction. 2. Definition of Archaeology. 3. The Field of Archaeology. 4. How the Excavators Work. 5. History of Biblical Archaeology. 6. Work in Bible Lands. (1) In Egypt, (2) In Babylonia and Assyria, (3) In Elam and Persia, (4) In Palestine. 7. Some Significant Discoveries. 8. Some values of Biblical Archaeology. 9. Interpreting Results. 10. A brief Bibliography.

Archaeology and the Bible

1. Introduction.

There are many areas from which the student may now receive help in understanding the Bible. Archaeology, that science now well known even to the casual reader, is proving to be of exceptional importance in the study of the Old Testament. In the daily papers, in various kinds of magazines and in special books any person may read absorbing accounts of impressive discoveries made by archaeologists. The chance discovery of a significant coin, the uncovering of an ancient city or the opening of an old tomb may create a mild sensation and start a series of speculations as to the value or importance of this "find" rescued from the oblivion of centuries. These discoveries may pertain to some Biblical subject or they may be wholly secular in nature. At any rate, most of the reading populace of America knows about the work of the archaeologists.

2. Definition of Archaeology.

What then, is archaeology? One eminent excavator has called it "The Mirror of the Ages." Literally it means discussing or dealing with old things or antiquities. This definition, however, is hardly adequate, since history or some other subject might have the same general meaning. To be more specific we may say that archaeology is that science which deals with the discovery, evaluation and interpretation of materials or relics such as pottery, ornaments, cutlery, sculptures, implements of war, written documents on stone, clay tablets, papyrus and any other objects which belong to some period of the past which we are interested in studying. This science, now well developed, has one chief objective. Its main function is to give life to these remains, to place them in their proper setting so that the reader may understand the life of people in this particular period.

3. The Field of Archaeology.

Naturally we are concerned in this study with archaeological discoveries made in Biblical countries. However, it should be said that the field of archaeology is by no means limited to Biblical lands. For many years scholars who have no particular interest in the Bible have been doing extensive work in Greece and Italy and other non-Biblical regions and have made discoveries which have done much to throw light upon the civilizations of ancient Greece, Rome and other peoples. Their work is extensive and important but naturally can not be considered in this connection since our concern is with those discoveries which have contributed to a better understanding of the Bible itself.

The field of Biblical Archaeology is a big one. For more than a century scholars have been recovering vast treasures of the remains of civilizations of Biblical times. These discoveries have come from every Biblical country. They are to be found in many famous museums in various countries. Many volumes have been written to describe and evaluate these discoveries.

4. How the Excavators Work.

It will be of interest to the student to learn something of the actual procedures employed by archaeologists in doing their work, in order that he may better understand the vast scope of the field and appreciate some of the difficulties and problems of these scientists. This will be of assistance in realizing the value and significance of the contributions made by the archaeologists.

To begin with we should say that occasionally an important "find" is made by accident, and that occasionally a remarkable discovery will be made by one not actually engaged in specific archaeological research. A truant schoolboy found the mouth of an old tunnel under the walls of ancient Jerusalem, and obeying the impulse for adventure, went far into this conduit and accidentally discovered the famous Siloam Inscription, the oldest piece of writing in the Hebrew language in existence today. But in the great majority of cases important discoveries are the result of a carefully planned program of excavating. Excavating is now a science. It is big business involving money, scholarly directors, and large numbers of local laborers.

Most of the work is done by a foundation, or a corporation of people who are interested enough to provide large sums of money for this work. These corporations are usually connected with some large university, such as Harvard, Pennsylvania, Chicago and others, both in America and in other countries. Some of these located in the country where the excavating is to be done, as the American School of Oriental Research in Jerusalem. These groups foster the work which is done under the direction of one or more noted scholars who are authorities in the field where they are to work. These scholars must be not only trained specialists, but men who can plan wisely and handle efficiently the many details connected with this enterprise. In addition to all the detailed preparations necessary for their work they must secure the official permission of the government of the area where they expect to work. This is not always easy and usually involves delay and some disappointments. When permission has been granted the actual work of excavating must be done by local laborers.

To illustrate the procedure we may take the work done on a so-called "tell" or mound. The mounds, still to be found in most of the Bible lands, are often the site of an ancient city or community of people. In early days a settlement would be made on an elevated spot where a supply of water was available. This settlement might have lasted for a century or more, or it might have existed for only a short time until another group had come along, overpowered the original settlers, leveled their city and then proceeded to build their own upon the ruins. This settlement in turn would be over-run by another who would also build upon the remains of the former. Since ancient people built simple structures without digging down for a foundation, each community of settlers left a layer or stratum on this mound. In some cases eight or more strata have been found, as at Gezer, dating back as far as 1400 B.C.

The task of the excavator is to remove each layer or stratum, starting at the top, of course, which would represent the ruins of the latest occupants of the mound. These strata are usually well defined and the trained archaeologist has no great difficulty in determining where one stops and another begins. Thus in these mounds, "the silent sentinels of hoary ages," there are rich treasures of the past. "These are the dust heaps of the ages, the surviving witnesses to forgotten peoples and civilizations. Here are the sacred repositories of the millenia which hold the priceless evidences of progress when human culture was in the making. In these great mounds, accordingly, archaeology comes into the treasure houses of antiquity. Their story, whether regarded from the standpoint of the mounds themselves or from that of the mound builders, has all the elements of fascination and romance."*

The excavators, beginning at the top, proceed to remove all the debris and dirt a layer at a time. It is tedious and meticulous work, since each spadeful must be carefully sifted and every object examined.

*Adams, J. McKee: *Ancient Records and the Bible*, p. 24. The Broadman Press. Used by permission.

A tiny piece of pottery, a ring, or some other small object may have great value. Hence the laborers must be closely supervised and every object must be saved, cleaned and preserved for later classification and study. All objects of value are kept and in due time the ones of value find their place in some museum where they are kept for study or for public exhibition.

When the project has been completed these scholars devote themselves to the study and the interpretation of their "finds." These results, or the conclusions of these specialists, are then made available to the public. Usually the more significant ones will appear first as a feature article in the newspapers and magazines. Detailed studies are later printed in the "bulletins" of the foundation sponsoring the project. Still later the interpretation of these results, together with those of other projects will appear in book form. The list of books in the field of Biblical Archaeology is already large and is steadily growing.

5. History of Biblical Archaeology.

It will be well at this point to sketch briefly the interesting history of archaeological research in the leading Biblical countries. To begin with, it is a comparatively modern development, having evolved very largely within the past century. The ancient Greeks and Romans were not concerned with any scientific study of the past. It probably never occurred to them to dig into the ruins of past centuries. With the fall of the Roman Empire and the coming of the "Dark Ages" there was even less interest in such studies. In the Middle Ages the chief concern of the limited number of scholars was primarily in theology. A critical study of the Bible and its background probably never occurred to them. The Renaissance period was a time for the revival of interest in and study of the classical antiquities. But students in this period were not concerned with digging up the ruins of ancient cities. They devoted themselves to the study of the languages and literatures of the past. Any material remains of ancient peoples that may have been accidentally discovered were valuable only as interesting curiosities or adornments.

Early in English history there were a few men who were interested in such matters, but it was not earlier than the 18th century that scientific archaeology came into being. Methodical study of antiquities in foreign lands had its beginning with the foundation in 1732 of the Society of Dilettanti, a group of young men deeply interested in these studies. They sponsored the work of five scholars who went to the Aegean world to make a survey of the surviving remains of ancient Greek life. It was in the 18th century also that a start was made in excavating at Herculaneum, Pompeii and Palmyra.

The exploration of Bible lands had its real beginning under Napoleon. In 1798 he entered Egypt, taking with him something less than one hundred scholars to study the ancient monuments there. There they found the famous Rosetta Stone and many other interesting remains. This is regarded as the beginning of Biblical Archaeology as a modern science.

6. Work in Bible Lands.

Our brief survey of the history of Biblical archaeology can best be done by tracing the significant accomplishments in each of the four or five Biblical countries. We may take these in the following order: Egypt, Babylonia and Assyria, Elam and Persia, and then Palestine itself.

(1) In Egypt — As stated above, Napoleon was responsible for opening up the treasures of ancient Egypt for the world. His archaeologists published the results of their labors in seven large volumes between 1809-1822. This monumental work known as "Description de l'Egypte" was an amazing achievement.

Among the treasures discovered by these men was the Rosetta Stone, which contained an inscription written in three languages — Hieroglyphic Egyptian, Demotic and Greek. Scholars already familiar with Greek were able to find the key to the ancient Egyptian language hitherto undecipherable. This opened up the life of ancient Egypt, and led to the systematic exploration of Egypt by many European nations. Champollion, Rosellini, Perring and others found vast treasures of antiquities which they have described in several texts. In 1883 the British founded the Egypt Exploration Fund which furnished such leaders as Naville, Gardner and Petrie. In 1896 W. M. Flinders Petrie organized a group of English scholars which later took the name of the British School of Archaeology in Egypt.

France had her part in this enterprise through the labors of such men as Gautier, Jaquier de Morgan and others. Germany also entered the field with gratifying results. The outstanding American scholar in Egyptian archaeology was Dr. J. H. Breasted. He organized the Oriental Institute of the University of Chicago. Every Egyptologist knows something of the monumental work of this famous scholar.

Work has continued in Egypt as conditions permitted up to the present time. Ludwig Borchardt, G. A. Reisner, C. S. Fisher, H. E. Winlock and others have done notable work there.

In addition to the work of the excavator two other fields have yielded remarkable results in Egypt. Written historical documents such as the *Sinuhe Romance,* the travels of Wen-Amun to Phoenicia, the Pyramid Texts, the Coffin Texts, the Book of the Dead, and others have furnished valuable light on the life of ancient Egypt and also on early Hebrew life. A number of "literary texts" such as the one attributed to one Neferrohe, and the Admonitions of Ipuwer have also given much information on the religious life of the Egyptians.

The most famous of all recent discoveries in Egypt was that of the tomb of Pharaoh Tutankhamun (about 1350 B.C.) by Howard Carter in 1922.

(2) In Babylonia and Assyria — As early as the 12th century Benjamin of Tudela became interested in the ruins of Babylon and Nineveh. By the 18th century British travelers began bringing back to England reports of vast ruins seen by them in these lands. They were particularly interested in the wedge shaped writings which they found on some clay tablets.

The first real excavating in this area was done by the French government official, Botta, and his successor Place (1842-55) at Nineveh. Here were discovered the palace of the Assyrian king, Sargon. Between 1845-49 Layard found the palaces of Ashurnasipal, Shalmaneser, Sargon, and Sennacherib. Vast treasures of sculpture, reliefs and inscriptions were uncovered. Finding the key to the translation of these records was now the difficulty. This was made possible through the work of Rawlinson. Hinks, Norris, Smith and others deciphered these records and opened up all the treasures of these kingdoms to the students interested in these ancient peoples.

The enthusiasm aroused by these remarkable discoveries resulted in great activity on the part of scholars of several nations. In the museums of France, England and the United States are to be found some of the most amazing discoveries of all time. Almost every part of these ancient lands has been explored and excavated. The results have thrilled the scholars of the world.

The mass of materials from this area is so large that we can not even summarize them here. These include lists of kings, various kinds of chronicles, lists of year dates, building inscriptions, poems, historical romances and so on.

(3) Elam and Persia — As early as the 14th century travelers in ancient Persia were intrigued by the inscriptions which they found on the walls of the king's palace in the capital city of Persepolis. At last a German scholar, Grotefeud was able to detect the names Darius, Xerxes and Artaxerxes, ancient Persian kings, in these strange inscriptions. Sir Henry Rawlinson, a young British officer, about 1835 copied the famous inscription in three languages on rock at Behistun. Years of patient labor resulted in the deciphering of this and in the discovery of the key to the ancient Persian language.

About 1890 J. de Morgan, a Frenchman, excavated Susa (Biblical Shushan), the capital of ancient Elam. He uncovered unbelievable treasures, such as the record of this early civilization, and a number of Babylonian monuments taken by the Persians from ancient Babylonia, and the famous Code of Hammurabi. In this way the life of ancient Elam and Persia was opened to the public.

A very significant work was done by Ernest Herzfeld of the Oriental Institute of the University of Chicago (1931-35) in the systematic excavation of Persepolis. He uncovered a procession staircase of Darius Hystaspes, and a room nearby which contained several thousand clay tablets in Elamite language. He found also the palaces of Darius and Xerxes.

(4) In Palestine — Naturally the "Holy Land" itself is of primary interest to the student of Biblical archaeology since one would expect to find here the results that bear most directly on the Bible story. Because of this fact this little country has been extensively "worked" by archaeologists. Centuries before the Crusades, travelers visited the Holy Land, because of their interest in it as the scene of the great events of Biblical and Christian history. However, prior to the past one hundred years these pilgrims were concerned with objects that remained above the ground. Leading the procession of those who sought to identify sacred sites was the American scholar E. Robinson (1838-52). Renan and others continued his work. The British *Palestine Exploration Fund* was founded in 1865. The first work, led by C. Warren, was the excavating of the east hill of Jerusalem. Later, Conder and Kitchener made for them a survey of Western Palestine and in 1880 the Great Map of Palestine, a monumental work, was published. This map was accompanied by seven volumes of notes. A bit later Eastern Palestine was surveyed and the results published. Notable work in Southern Palestine was done by Clermont-Ganneau (1873-74).

By about 1890 the modern systematic excavations in Palestine were under way. These have continued (with occasional interruptions) up to the present time. Flinders Petrie began his work at Tell-el-Hesey (Biblical Simeon) in 1890. F. J. Bliss continued the work at Simeon and from 1894-97 worked in Jerusalem. Bliss and R. A. S. Macalister did much work on mounds near Jerusalem. The most valuable of these was Macalister's discoveries at ancient Gezer. Sellin opened up the mound of ancient Taanach, and later excavated Jericho. Schumacher had remarkable results at Megiddo. Garstang worked at Ashkelon and later at Jericho. By 1925 Macalister and Duncan began work on a pretentious scale in Jerusalem.

To deal adequately with the work of archaeologists in Palestine in the past fifty years would require at least one large volume. We shall have to be content with a bare listing of the most important of these enterprises.

Harvard University has done extensive excavating at ancient Samaria, The University of Pennsylvania at Bethshan, the Oriental Institute at Megiddo, Dr. W. F. Albright and J. L. Kelso at Bethel, Elihu Grant at Beth-shemesh, Sellin at Shechem, Kjaer at Shiloh, Petrie at various places in southwest Palestine, Mallon in eastern Palestine opposite Jericho, Starkey at Lachish, and French Dominicans at ancient Tirzah, are among the most significant in the past fifty years. Needless to say that almost continuous work has been carried on in and around Jerusalem and at Jericho. By far the most sensational of all "finds" has been the famous Dead Sea Scrolls in caves near the head of the Dead Sea in 1947 and following.

7. Some Significant Discoveries.

During the course of our studies we shall give brief consideration to some of the most valuable archaeological discoveries in the historical setting to which they belong. However, since this chapter is devoted entirely to archaeology we shall list at this point some of the most striking discoveries so the reader may have a brief acquaintance with them beforehand.

Creation Tablets — Several accounts of the creation, which bear striking resemblances to the Genesis account have been found in Babylonia.

The Fall of Man — The Adapa myth which resembles the story of the Fall of Man and a Babylonian story which tells of the expulsion of man from a garden have been recovered.

Flood Tablets — These Babylonian tablets were translated in 1872 by George Smith. While they are fragmentary they bear a very remarkable resemblance to the Biblical account given in Genesis 6-8.

Tell-el-Amarna Letters — These letters, discovered in 1887-88, were written on clay tablets in Babylonian cuneiform by prominent officials in Palestine to the Pharaohs of Egypt about 1300 B.C. Their value lies in the description of life in Palestine about the time of the Exodus. In these letters the word Habiri (probably Hebrews) occurs.

The Rosetta Stone — As we have already noted, this notable inscription written in three languages was discovered in Egypt during the expedition of Napoleon.

The Code of Hammurabi — In 1901-02 at ancient Susa, the French archoeologist de Morgan uncovered this famous mounment. It is about eight feet high and more than two feet through. It contains 247 laws (3600 lines) written in cuneiform and is the code of the great Babylonian King Hammurabi (Biblical Amraphel of Genesis 14:1) who lived about 1900 B.C., approximately the date of Abraham. These elaborate laws, covering all aspects of life, bear remarkable similarity to some of the laws of Moses. This monument is in the Louvre Museum in Paris.

The Moabite Stone — This stone, three and one half feet high, two feet wide and one foot thick, was found in ancient Moab in 1868. It was erected by Mesha, king of Moab, about 850 B.C. and refers to Mesha's achievement in throwing off the yoke of Israel, as given in II Kings 3. It is a striking corroboration of the Biblical account. This famous stone is also in the Louvre Museum in Paris.

Invasion of Shishak — On a wall in the temple of Karnak in Egypt was found a record by Shishak, Pharaoh of Egypt, telling of his campaign into Jerusalem in the reign of Rehoboam. It confirms the account of this invasion given in I Kings 14:25.

The Siloam Inscription — In 1880 a schoolboy accidentally found an underground passageway under the walls of ancient Jerusalem, and following this long conduit found on the stone walls some writing. He told his experience to the German scholar named Schick, who investigated and discovered this valuable inscription. This proved to be the record of the workmen who cut this remarkable tunnel 1700 feet long in solid rock under ancient Jerusalem around 700 B.C. (time of Hezekiah) to provide a supply of water in time of siege. This is the oldest known piece of Hebrew writing.

Excavations at Gezer — The discoveries made by Dr. R. A. S. Macalister at ancient Gezer have provided the most revealing and reliable information on the life of the peoples of Canaan as far back as 1400 B.C. He uncovered eight strata on the mound and was able to give invaluable light of the social, cultural, and religious life of the ancient Canaanites.

Inscriptions of Sargon II — A baked prism or cylinder containing the record of the expeditions of Sargon II of Assyria (722-705 B.C.) now in the British Museum tells of the conquest of Samaria by Sargon in 722 B.C. This account not only corroborates the statements in the Biblical record (II Kings 17) but furnishes further information not found in the Bible.

The Cylinder of Sennacherib — In the British Museum another very valuable inscription is to be found. This prism is a long one containing 487 lines. It records eight expeditions of Sennacherib, king of Assyria (705-681 B.C.). In this inscription is a passage which describes Sennacherib's siege of Jerusalem in the reign of Hezekiah. It is worthy of note that this pagan monarch did not mention the destruction of his army of 185,000 men nor his failure to conquer the city. This is only natural, however, since the purpose of these inscriptions was primarily to boast of the achievements of such rulers.

The Dead Sea Scrolls — In the spring of 1947 the first of a large number of ancient scrolls were found (accidentally) by some Bedouins in a small cave about seven miles south of Jericho. This discovery, when once understood, led to frantic and continous searching in other caves nearby. These first scrolls *The Isaiah Manuscript* and *The Habakkuk Commentary* and the *Manual of Discipline* were translated and immediately gripped the imagination of the world. Other remarkable "finds" coming rather constantly from these caves near the Dead Sea have proved to be tremendously valuable. In all, nearly 100 manuscripts of Old Testament books have been recovered. These included several manuscripts of Isaiah, the five books of Moses, the Psalter, the Minor Prophets, Ecclesiastes and parts of Daniel. Of course, the value of these discoveries is inestimable. Up to this time the oldest known manuscripts of the Old Testament went back to about 900 A.D. Scholars were amazed at the closeness of these scrolls (dated approximately 100-200 A.D.) to the text of our Old Testament.

No one can tell what other scrolls may yet be found in this area. Nor do we know the full significance of what has been found until these have been carefully studied and translated. We may be sure, however, that these scrolls constitute one of the most valuable discoveries in the history of Biblical Archaeology.

8. The Values of Biblical Archaeology.

By this time the reader will have come to see something of the help which Archaeology offers in the study of the Bible. Dr. Roy Lee Honeycutt, Jr., Professor of Old Testament in Midwestern Baptist Theological Seminary, summarizes for his students the general contribution of archaeological discoveries to understanding the Bible under two headings:

1. Biblical people lived in the Near East many centuries ago. Until recent times scholars knew but little of the life of these people. Now we can see how these people lived and thought as revealed in the literature of the Egyptian, Sumerian, Assyrian, Babylonian and Syrian nations. We can reconstruct the cultural life of these neighbors of Israel. Only in recent years have scholars been able to reconstruct the chronology of ancient peoples of the Near East. This has also aided greatly in establishing the chronology of Israel.

2. Israel was a nation among other national groups in the ancient Near East. Their contact with these other peoples was more vital than we once imagined. The literature of Egypt and Mesopotamian countries contains many striking parallels to that of Israel. The Law Codes of the Sumerians, Assyrians, Babylonians and Hittites give us an excellent view of the legal and governmental life of these nations. These codes, especially that of Hammurabi, throw light on the laws of Moses. The historicity of the patriarchs has been established by the famous Mari Tablets and the Nuzi Texts. Practices and customs of living as found in these writings are amazingly similar to those recorded of Abraham and other patriarchs. In these documents and inscriptions there are quite a number of historical records which speak of actual contacts of various kinds with the people of Israel. The primary sites uncovered in Palestine furnish very substantial help in understanding the customs of living and the religious practices of the Israelites.

These are but a few of the areas where archaeology assists the student in gaining a better appreciation of the Bible, but they are representative.

9. Interpreting Results.

In our enthusiasm over the striking results of archaeological research in the understanding of the Bible the temptation is to expect too much of it and to make extravagant and unjustified claims or "proofs" based on these discoveries. We should remember that the primary purpose of these scientists is not to prove or to disprove anything, but rather to get the facts. Many of their discoveries have strengthened the faith of Christian people in the validity of the Biblical record. Many others have had no bearing on the authenticity of this record. We must exercise great caution in asserting too positively what archaeology does or does not "prove."

In closing let us say that this new science has contributed greatly to our understanding of the Bible. One of its chief contributions has been to rescue much of the Bible from the far-off, imaginary, "fairyland" atmosphere which unfortunately surrounds it for so many students. Through the discoveries of these scholars we can see Abraham, Moses, David and others as real men who lived in a real world. We are able now to reconstruct with fair accuracy the details of their life, see them in their real setting and understand better the character they exhibited and the work which they did. To establish these Biblical figures as historical characters and to gain an intelligent understanding of the life of their day is a worthy accomplishment.

Archaeological research will continue. Even more remarkable discoveries may be made. Biblical scholars will await with eagerness the results of the work of the excavators and will welcome whatever help they may furnish us in our quest of a better understanding of the Bible.

In this brief discussion of archaeology it has been possible only to introduce this field of study. A full treatment of even the most significant matters in this important field lies outside the scope of these studies. Fortunately, however, there are available many excellent books on Biblical Archaeology which can be used by the student for obtaining information which will be most illuminating. These books, containing hundreds of attractive illustrations, are prepared especially for students in Old Testament courses. Carefully selected assignments in one or more of these books should be mastered by the student in addition to the regular textbook assignments. A well planned schedule of these "outside" readings will be a rewarding experience for the student of the Old Testament.

10. A Selected Bibliography.

For the benefit of students who are interested in learning more about this fascinating field we are giving herewith a brief list of some of the best books for study as recommended by Dr. William H. Morton,

Professor of Biblical Archaeology at Midwestern Baptist Theological Seminary.

Albright, W. F., *Archaeology and the Religion of Israel*, Baltimore: Johns Hopkins Press, 1956.

Albright, W. F., *The Archaeology of Palestine*, Baltimore: Penguin, 1960.

Burrows, Millar, *What Mean These Stones?*, New York: Meridian, 1960.

Cross, Frank, *The Ancient Library of Qumran*, New York: Doubleday, 1958.

Finegan, Jack, *Light From the Ancient Past*, 2nd Edition Revised. New Jersey: Princeton University Press, 1946.

Frankfort, H., et al., *The Intellectual Adventure of Ancient Man*, Chicago: University of Chicago Press, 1946. *Before Philosophy*, Baltimore: Penguin, 1954.

Harding, G. L., *The Antiquities of Jordan*, New York: Crowell, 1959.

Kenyon, K. M., *Archaeology in the Holy Land*, London: Ernest Benn, 1960.

Kramer, S. N., *From the Tablets of Sumer*, Indian Hills, Colorado: Falcon Wing's Press, 1956.

Pritchard, J. B., *The Ancient Near East*, Princeton, New Jersey: Princeton University Press, 1958.

Wright, G. E., *Biblical Archaeology*, Philadelphia: Westminster, 1957.

Wright, G. E. and Filson, F. V., *The Westminster Historical Atlas to the Bible*, Philadelphia: Westminister, 1956.

Chapter IV

THE HEBREWS AS A NATION

Section I — Periods of Hebrew History.

1. Introduction. 2. Period of Beginnings. 3. Hebrew Patriarchs. 4. Egyptian Slavery and Deliverance. 5. Conquest and Organization. 6. Hebrew Monarchy. 7. Captivity and Restoration. 8. Interbiblical Period. 9. New Testament Period. 10. Jews Since New Testament Times.

Section II — Neighbors of the Hebrews.

1. Introduction. 2. Chaldeans. 3. Egyptians. 4. Neighbors in Palestine. 5. Syrians. 6. Assyrians. 7. Babylonians. 8. Persians. 9. Greeks. 10. Romans.

CHAPTER IV
The Hebrews as a Nation

Section I—PERIODS OF HEBREW HISTORY.

1. Introduction.

Before entering upon the study of the details of Old Testament history it will be profitable for the student to get a kind of "bird's eye" view of the main periods of their history and to learn something of the several important nations or peoples who were their neighbors during this time of approximately twenty centuries. It is always well in the beginning to have a sort of preview of the field one is entering. It saves confusion of mind and gives definiteness to the task.

The history contained in the Old Testament is easily arranged into some six or seven periods or divisions. While there is some difference of opinion among scholars as to the exact dates in some cases, as for example the Exodus, all the authorities in this field are practically agreed as to the general periods of Old Testament history. For our purposes it seems well to define these divisions or periods as follows: The period of beginnings, the patriarchs, Egyptian slavery and delivery, conquest and organization, the Hebrew kingdom, the captivity and the restoration, the interbiblical period. For the sake of completeness, though it is not included in the scope of this work, we add a word about the New Testament period and the Jews since the first Christian century.

2. Period of Beginnings.

The first eleven chapters of Genesis cover the period from the time of creation to the time of Abraham. This period is concerned with beginnings. The Genesis account tells of the creation of the world and is climaxed by the creation of man and the institution of the home and the Sabbath. Then follows the story of the Temptation and Fall of man, with its consequent punishment. This is followed by the story of Cain's slaying of Abel, and the birth of Seth. The account of the wickedness of the race, the building of the Ark, and the Flood is then related. The accounts of the new start after Noah, the building of the Tower of Babel and the confusion of tongues are then given.

3. Hebrew Patriarchs.

The second period begins with Abraham, 1900-1800 B.C. and goes to the time of Moses 1350-1250 B.C. This history is recorded in Genesis

12-50. The contents of this period may be summarized as follows: The
Call of Abraham and the record of some of his accomplishments, the
experiences of his son Isaac, the stirring stories of Jacob and his twelve
sons, the heroic struggles and achievements of Joseph in Egypt, and
finally, the account of the coming of the sons of Jacob (Israel) to
Egypt and their experiences there up to the death of Joseph.

4. Egyptian Slavery and Deliverance.

This period begins with the work of Moses and goes to the time
of the conquest of Palestine by the children of Israel. There is some
difference of opinion as to the time of Moses' work. While the exact
date has not been finally determined there seems just now to be a
turning to the date of approximately 1300 B.C. Be that as it may, this
period in the history of the Hebrews is full of interesting and important
history. These events are recorded in the books of Exodus, Leviticus,
Numbers and Deuteronomy. Moses is the chief figure in this era. He
was born and reared in Egypt, adopted by the daughter of Pharaoh
and trained in the best Egyptain learning and culture. He fled to the
land of Midian and there, after a residence of some forty years, was
called to be the deliverer of the Hebrews from Egyptain slavery. He
organized the Hebrews and led them forth from Egypt to Palestine
through a period of some forty years. They were led first to Sinai
where they received the Law. From there they went to Kadesh-
Barnea about eighteen months after their departure from Pharaoh's
land. Upon their failure to exercise faith and enter the "Land of
Promise" they were forced to wander for nearly forty years. Moses
led them through many trying experiences to the land of Moab east
of the Jordan, where he relinquished his leadership, commissioned
Joshua to be his successor and then bade farewell to his people before
his mysterious death in the silent hills of Moab.

5. Conquest and Organization in Canaan.

The period begins with Joshua's work as leader in crossing the
Jordan river to capture Jericho and includes his further conquests.
After the so-called conquest of the land of their fathers (Abraham,
Isaac and Jacob) Palestine was divided among the twelve tribes.
Joshua finished his labors and the people were left without an out-
standing leader. The period that follows is called the period of the
Judges and was a time of apostasy, decline and failure. It was the
"Dark Ages" of Hebrew history. These Judges, who really were only

military deliverers, were not great national figures. The last and the greatest of these was Samuel who bridged over the chasm between the period of the Judges and the establishment of the Kingdom (1100 B.C.).

6. Hebrew Kingdom.

This period is the most glorious one, from a material point of view, in all Hebrew history. It began about 1100 B.C. and closed in 587 B.C. Samuel anointed Saul as the first king who started auspiciously, but ended his career in disaster. His accomplishments were not outstanding. His reign of forty years left the Hebrew people in a weak state, harassed by their enemies, and discouraged. David assumed leadership then and was one of the greatest of all the kings of the Jews. He reigned for seven and a half years at Hebron in southern Palestine and then became king over all twelve tribes. He captured the ancient city of the Jebusites (Jerusalem) and made it the capital of his kingdom. He rapidly organized his forces, and in brilliant military movements soon subdued his enemies and gave his nation a magnificent start. He died as an old man, after forty years' reign, and was succeeded by his son Solomon. Solomon inherited this strong kingdom and then inaugurated his great building program including fortresses, his palaces, and the temple of Jehovah in Jerusalem. Solomon's reign marked the climax of the golden age of Israel's history. The splendor and the fame of his reign were the pride of the Hebrews and the envy of the world. But he ended his career, after forty years' reign, almost as a failure. The seed of rebellion had been sown as a result of Solomon's lavish expenditure of money and the consequent imposition of very heavy taxes, and immediately after his death this rebellion broke out. His son Rehoboam succeeded him and then the ten northern tribes revolted and established the kingdom of Israel which existed for about 250 years as a rival to the southern kingdom, Judah. The northern tribes finally established a capital at Samaria. In 722 B.C. Samaria fell, after a siege of several years, and the best people of these ten tribes were taken into Assyria as captives. With this event the record of the ten tribes came to an end. Judah, the southern kingdom, continued to exist as a small but mostly independent nation after the fall of Samaria until 587 B.C. when their beloved city was finally captured and destroyed. Then most of the Hebrews were taken into captivity in the land of Babylonia near the ancient city of Ur, the original home of Abraham their forefather. Thus the kingdom of the Hebrews came to an end.

7. *Captivity and Restoration.*

The next period, 587-400 B.C., closes the record in the Old Testament. This includes the Captivity and the Restoration. These captive Hebrews remained in Babylonian exile, not as slaves but as colonists, for about seventy years. Three distinct groups made the long journey back to the old homeland of Palestine after the famous decree of Cyrus the Great, king of the Persians and sovereign of the Jews. Under the leadership of Nehemiah the walls of ancient Jerusalem were rebuilt, and Zerubbabel was successful in rebuilding the temple. Ezra was the great reformer and teacher of the Jews in this restored kingdom. It was only a small kingdom, subject to the king of Persia, but it was distinctly spiritual in nature. About 400 B.C. the Old Testament closes with the Hebrews back in Palestine, but not as an independent kingdom.

8. *Interbiblical Period.*

The seventh period of Hebrew history (400-5 B.C.) is not recorded in our Bible. It is called the "Interbiblical Period," and was an era full of changes and developments. The Persian control of the Jews lasted until 332 B.C. when, under Alexander the Great, the Hebrews, together with most of the world of that time, were conquered by the Greeks. This was a critical time for the Jews, involving much suffering and change. It lasted until 167 B.C. when these persecuted Jews, under the leadership of Judas Maccabeus rose up, won their independence and established their own kingdom. This period of independence came to an end in 63 B.C. when the Roman army under Pompey swept into Palestine and conquered their little country. Roman rule lasted until after the death of Christ and terminated with the destruction of Jerusalem by Titus in 70 A.D.

9. *New Testament Period.*

The next period of Biblical history is the New Testament period (5 B.C.-100 A.D.). The Jews were under the Roman rule. In Palestine, now but a small province in the great Roman empire, Christ was born and reared. He began his ministry about 26 A.D. and after three brief years, was crucified. But his death did not end his work. He rose from the grave and instructed his disciples as to their work. After his Ascension they were empowered by the Holy Spirit for their work of establishing a spiritual kingdom of which there would be no end. The book of Acts relates some of the facts of the growth, development and spread of Christianity. Through the labors of Paul and others the religion of Jesus was given to peoples outside of Palestine. When the New Testament period closed about 100 A.D. the church was established in most of the Mediterranean world.

10. The Jews Since New Testament Times.

A word about the subsequent history of the Jewish people should be given here. In 70 A.D. Titus, the Roman general, quelled a rebellion of the Jews in Jerusalem by destroying the city and killing most of the Jews in it. In this final destructive move of the Romans the Jews were completely subjugated. They were scattered abroad into other countries to join their brethren who had been dispersed in former centuries. From the second century until 1948, when the little nation Israeli came into being they had no national home. They have been found in nearly all countries since then and today they are to be found in all parts of the civilized world. But they are largely a people without a country. In spite of almost inconceivable persecutions and sufferings they have continued to exist. There are over 15,000,000 of them in the world today.

Section II — NEIGHBORS OF THE HEBREWS.

1. Introduction.

During the centuries of their history as a nation the Hebrew people had many neighbors. While it is true that they were taught to regard themselves as a select people with a special mission from God, nevertheless they were affected by the life of contemporary nations. In our discussion of these nations with their influence upon the Hebrews we shall treat them in the order in which they come in the historical record.

2. Chaldeans.

Abraham, the "father of the faithful" was a citizen of Ur of the Chaldees at the time of his call. While the history of these people has not been completely reconstructed we know that it dates as far back as 4500 B.C. However we do not know much about them until the period just prior to Abraham. In this period there was a highly developed civilization in Chaldea. The site of ancient Ur has been uncovered and the remains found here show it as a great center of commercial, cultural and religious life. The greatest king was Hammurabi (1900-1800 B.C.). His remarkable code of laws has been discovered. This code of 247 laws dealing with the greatest variety of human activities throws a flood of light on the life of that great country. Abraham, as a citizen, would be familiar with all phases of the life of this nation, and thus would be a prominent, educated, wealthy man selected by God for a distinct mission.

From Ur of the Chaldees, Abraham journeyed to Canaan. Not a great deal is known of conditions in Canaan prior to its conquest by Joshua about 1300 B.C. But a few facts are significant. In a sense there was a vital relation between Canaan and Chaldea. Trade relations were kept alive, and it seems as if they used the same general form of language. And yet life in Canaan was of a pastoral nature, without the evidence of great commercial and cultural activities. As a wealthy chieftain Abraham moved with dignity and influence among the less highly developed peoples of Canaan.

3. Egyptians.

Abraham had some contact with Egypt. He and his wife Sarah, found refuge there in the time of famine. However, it was not until the time of Joseph and his brethren and their descendants that Egypt came into prominence in the Bible story. The Biblical records give a number of instances showing vital contact between the Hebrews and the Egyptians. In Genesis and Exodus we have the account of the coming of the sons of Jacob to Egypt, their life of slavery there and their deliverance by Moses.

Undoubtedly these long years spent in Egypt profoundly influenced the life of the Hebrews. Around 950 B.C. during the reign of Rehoboam, Sheshonk (Shishak) invaded Judea and pillaged the temple (I Kings 14:25). Tirhakah of Egypt took the part of Hezekiah in his struggle against Sennacherib the great Assyrian king about 701 B.C. (II Kings 19:9f). Pharaoh-Necho of Egypt marched through Palestine to fight Assyria and at Megiddo, Josiah, attempting to stop him, was killed (II Chron. 35:21-23). Pharaoh-Hophra sent his army to aid Zedekiah against the Babylonians (Jer. 37:5, 7, 11). With the destruction of Jerusalem by the Babylonians in 587 B.C. many of the Jews fled to Egypt and among these was the prophet Jeremiah. Tradition says that here Jeremiah was killed by his own people. Certain it is that from this time on many Jews lived in Egypt. When Alexander the Great conquered the world and founded his great city in Egypt (named Alexandria) there were many thousands of Jews there. Under the reign of Herod the Great in Palestine, Jesus as an infant was taken to Egypt by his mother and Joseph to escape the decree issued by Herod (Matt. 2:13-15).

The Egyptians had a religious system of their own. It was partly animistic and partly mythological. The worship of spirits was its leading feature. The doctrine of immortality was prominent. They held that the counterpart of each individual would survive with him after death so long as the body remained incorrupt. Hence they developed the art and practice of embalming the dead. Their religious system called for temples, priests, and a regular ritual of worship. Evidently religion occupied a prominent place in their life and yet this religion somehow seems never to have exercised any great influence on any other nation or people.

The Hebrews, coming as they did from the little land of Canaan to live in this great Egyptian civilization, naturally would be affected by it. This was especially true in the case of Joseph, who rose to such heights of influence there, and Moses who "was instructed in all the wisdom of the Egyptians" (Acts 7:22).

4. Neighbors in Palestine.

For approximately one half of their 2000 years of history, as recorded in the Bible, the Hebrews lived in the little country of Palestine. During this time they were surrounded by various tribes or races of people, both inside the narrow limits of their land and just outside its borders.

When the Hebrews came into Palestine about 1300-1250 b.c. the land was inhabited by a rather large number of independent groups such as the Philistines, Phoenicians, Gibeonites, Gergashites, Midianites, Hittites, Jebusites, Canaanites and so on. It is impossible to speak of all these and since they were much alike we shall discuss only two or three of them.

The *Philistines* lived in southwest Palestine in a fertile stretch of land extending along the coast of the Mediterranean Sea from Joppa to the borders of Egypt. They were non-Semitic in origin and came from Crete and the islands of the Aegean Sea. They organized themselves around their five chief cities (Ashdod, Ashkelon, Ekron, Gaza, and Gath). These circuits were ruled over by five lords (Judges 3:3; Josh. 13:13, etc.) apparently independent of each other. They sometimes stood together and fought against a common enemy as one group. They had a religion which was Semitic in character with soothsayers (Isa. 2:6) and priests and diviners (I Samuel 6:2) and temples (Judges 16:26).

It was inevitable that they must soon come into conflict with the Hebrews. Indeed, there were frequent wars between the Philistines and the Hebrews up until the time of the Babylonian captivity.

The *Phoenician* people lived in northwest Palestine. Their territory was a narrow strip of coast land extending from the Orontes river on the north to Mt. Carmel in Palestine. We do not know a great deal about their origin. Their language was a Semitic tongue a little different from the Hebrew. We first meet the Phoenicians in the time of David and Solomon. They were an independent people with an extensive merchant marine and were skilled artisans, whose chief city was Tyre. Their location made it necessary for them to rely upon seafaring enterprises for a livelihood. They were skilled shipbuilders and had commercial transactions with every nation within reach. On the land they had regularly established trade routes used in exporting and importing goods. When Solomon extended his trade relations with distant nations the Phoenicians were employed to man his ships. When Jonah fled from the face of the Lord he sailed on a Phoenician vessel. They were especially famous for their purple dye, known over the entire Mediterranean world.

Their religious life centered around the worship of some fifty or more divinities. The most important of these gods were Adonis or Tammuz (Ezek. 8:14), Molech, Melkarth, Ashtoreth, or Astarte (mentioned often in the Old Testament), Tanith, and Baal. Baal seems to have been the most prominent. They built their temples and altars on high places and worshiped their gods with great ceremony which permitted and encouraged sensuality.

The Old Testament mentions a number of contacts of the Hebrews with these people. A treaty was made with them for mutual gain (II Sam. 5:11f). King Hiram furnished some of the material for Solomon's temple (I Kings 5). Ahab, king of Israel, married Jezebel, daughter of Eth-baal, King of Sidon (I Kings 16:31). In the early stages of his fight on Baal worship Elijah was sent to Zarephath in Phoenicia where he remained for awhile (I Kings 17:9f).

The *Canaanites,* a vigorous people, were the leading race in Palestine at the time of the Hebrew conquest. They were well acquainted with Babylonian culture before the Hebrews came into the land. They were at times subject to the Egyptians and at times independent. But apparently they had no centralized government. Thus they offered no organized resistance to the invading Israelites and yet they were never completely conquered or exterminated by the Hebrews. A policy of compromise was adopted by the invading Hebrews and in a real sense they were vitally affected by the demoralizing practices of the Canaanites. They were essentially an agricultural people and seem to have had a certain degree of culture, though their life appears to have been crude and barbarous. Instead of raising these Canaanites up to their standards of religious life and worship the Hebrews sank to the low levels of the worship of the Canaanites. The excavations of Macalister at Gezer have thrown a flood of light on the religious life and practices of these people.

Let us now look briefly at the life of some of the immediate neighbors of the Hebrews, that is those who lived just along the borders of her land. We shall speak of three of these.

The *Ammonites* occupied the territory between the Jordan river and the desert of Arabia. They were a nomadic people and had but few cities. They were fierce fighters and marauders, making frequent incursions into neighboring lands. Jeremiah (41:6-7) speaks of their cruelty to their foes. Jephthah is a good illustration of their crude manner of living (Judges 11:1-34). They were the descendants of Benami, the son of Lot by his younger daughter (Gen. 19:38). Frequent struggles took place between them and the Israelites (II Sam. 12:30; II Chron. 27:5). They were bitterly denounced by the prophets (Amos 1:13; Jer. 49:1; Ezek. 25:2ff; etc.). During the Restoration period they were hostile to Nehemiah (Neh. 2:10). The tribe was governed by a king who usually had a poorly organized government. They were gross idolaters.

The *Moabites* occupied the region directly east of the Dead Sea. Here they maintained existence as a distinct people for over a thousand years. They had numerous cities and large flocks of sheep and goats. Their fertile lands produced immense supplies of grain. They descended from Lot (Gen. 19:37; Deut. 2:9-18), and thus were distantly related to the Hebrews. To the land of Moab went Elimelech of Bethlehem to escape the famine in Judah. Ruth, the daughter-in-law of Elimelech and Naomi, was a Moabitess (Ruth 1-4). David later subdued them (II Sam. 8:2), but during the time of Rehoboam they regained their independence and kept it until the time of Omri when they were subdued and forced to pay an enormous tribute. Under their king, Mesha, they later rebelled, overthrew the power of Israel and became free again. Their account of this victory is recorded on the famous Moabite stone, one of the most interesting pieces of archaeological evidence in existence. Rivalry between the Moabites and the people

of Judah seems to have remained constant from this time till the fall
of Jerusalem in 587 B.C. After the fall of Jerusalem the Moabites
gradually passed out of existence so far as any Biblical records go.

The *Edomites* lived in the region southeast of Palestine. The land
is sometimes called Seir, though usually Edom. The name is derived
from the color of the red sandstone hills of the region. Just prior to
New Testament times it came to be known as Idumea.

The Edomite people sprang from Esau, the brother of Jacob, hence
they were regarded as kinsmen of the Hebrews. They refused to
allow the Israelites on their way to Canaan to pass through their
territory (Num. 20:18-21). The next mention of them in the Old
Testament is when Saul defeated them (I Sam. 8:13-14). During the
reign of Jehoshaphat they failed in their attempt to invade Judah
(II Chron. 20:22). When Nebuchadnezzar, king of Babylon, made
his successful attack on Jerusalem they assisted him. For this they
were bitterly denounced by the prophets (Isa. 34:5-8; 63:1-4; Jer. 49:17).
Later on they settled in southern Palestine and seemed to have
prospered. During the time of the Maccabees (167 B.C.) they were
subdued and forced to submit to Jewish practices and laws. They were
finally incorporated with the Jewish nation.

They too, were idolaters in worship (II Chron. 25:14-15, 20). They
seem to have adopted from their predecessors the habit of living in
caves. Even now the whole region abounds in caves and grottoes
hewn in the soft sandstone. Discoveries at Petra have revealed some
of the most interesting temples and tombs.

5. *Syrians.*

To the north of Palestine lay the historic country of the Syrians,
whose boundaries varied from time to time. We may think of it as
about three hundred miles in length from north to south and from fifty
to one hundred and fifty miles in width. The first occupants of this
land seem to have been the Hittites, Jebusites and Ammonites. Later on
the people living here were of mixed blood. Damascus was their chief
city, the city with the longest continuous history of any in the world.
During the time of David (1050 B.C.) the Hebrews came into contact
with them (II Sam. 8:2, 4, 13). From that time until Syria was attached
to Assyria by the fall of Damascus (732 B.C.) there were constant
contacts between Syria and the Israelites, most of which were hostile.
These people later became part of the Babylonian empire then passed
to the Persians, and still later, to the Greeks under Alexander the Great.

Finally they were vanquished by the Romans in 64 B.C. We know but little of their cultural and religious life as separate people since these changed with the varying fortunes of their nation.

6. Assyrians.

The Assyrians occupied the upper part of the rich valley between the Tigris and Euphrates rivers. Nineveh was their most famous city.

Their history goes far back into antiquity. In early history they were dependents of ancient Babylonia. When the old Babylonian empire collapsed they soon came to be an important world power. Under Tiglath-Pileser or Pul (II Kings 15:19) about 745 B.C. and his successors, they nearly succeeded in conquering most of southwest Asia. The ten northern tribes were conquered and taken into exile by them. Only by a miracle were the people of Judah saved. In 612 B.C. Nineveh, their cruel and infamous capital, was conquered by the Babylonians and their national life ended.

As a people they were barbaric and cruel. Against their national pride and savage warfare the Hebrew prophets often thundered. Their religion was coarse and sensual. They had a number of gods, the chief of which was Asshur, who was first and foremost a war god, hence their emphasis on warfare. Undoubtedly the Hebrews were affected by their religion. At least Ahaz, king of Judah, was guilty of subscribing to some of their religious practices (II Kings 16:11; 23:11).

7. Babylonians.

The territory of Babylonia was the fertile land lying between and beside the lower Tigris and Euphrates rivers. In this fertile country fine cities flourished. In these cities were beautiful gardens and magnificent temples and palaces. Great commercial enterprises with people of distant countries were established. Their culture was extremely advanced. They developed in full a system of weights and measures. They led in making weapons and in creating various types of pottery. They made extensive studies of the sun and stars and developed a science of mathematics. They had a written language and literature and used the famous cuneiform system.

The Hebrew people were affected by these people in many ways through a long period of time. Trade routes from Egypt to Babylon passed through Canaan. In later centuries in the struggles between the nations for supremacy in southwest Asia the Hebrew people came in contact with Babylonia. During the reign of Nebuchadnezzar when he was endeavoring to conquer all the lands of the Mediterranean, the little Hebrew kingdom of Judah, after stout resistance, was finally subdued in 587 B.C. The best of the Hebrew people were taken away into this land for the long, bitter exile. During the seventy years of exile Babylonia rapidly declined and in the year of 538 B.C. Cyrus the Great conquered them and thus the Babylonian empire came to an end.

The religion of the Babylonians was polytheistic. They built magnificent temples and developed elaborate rituals in their worship. But this was crude and sensual. Against the defects and demoralizing nature of this worship the teachers of Israel constantly warned the Hebrew people.

8. Persians.

Persia as a nation exerted an influence on the Hebrews for about two centuries. As stated above, Cyrus, king of Persia, conquered Babylon in 538 B.C. Thus he became the king of the Jews. The Hebrew people lived under Persian rule from this time until the conquest of Alexander the Great in 332 B.C. Some of the exiles returned to Palestine, though most of them remained in the land of their captivity. Those who returned were given a degree of freedom by Persia, though they were still Persian subjects. The Persian people were brave and impetuous, witty and passionate, but withal, generous toward others. They were polygamous and were extremely fond of the pleasures of the table. Their religion was a dualistic system, probably devised or perfected by Zoroaster (600 B.C.). This form of religion had but little effect upon the religion of the Hebrews, especially those who went back to the homeland.

9. Greeks.

Chronologically speaking, the Greek people were the next nation with which the Jews had to deal. This new contact was most important and far-reaching. The Greeks were the first Europeans really to influence the Jews.

The Greeks were introduced to the East through the conquests of Alexander the Great. In a few brief years the Persians were routed, driven back and conquered by this vigorous race of people. In an incredibly short time Hellenism or Greek culture was forced upon this part of the Orient.

The Greek philosophy of life differed in almost every point from that of the Oriental, especially the Jew. When this new way of thinking engulfed their nation they faced a crisis. The conservative element at once regarded all this as idolatrous and as such was to be opposed even unto death. It challenged the law of Moses; it threatened the survival of all the teachings of their fathers. Out of this conservative group probably came the development of the Pharisaic party, the patriots of the Inter-Biblical period. On the other hand certain Jews saw good features in Hellenism and came to look upon it with favor. From this group probably came the beginnings of the Sadducaic party of New Testament times.

In a marvelous way the Greek race contributed to the process of preparing the world for the coming of Christ. They gave the world an intellectual and cultural background, an openness of mind, a cosmopolitan viewpoint, a universal language, without which, humanly speaking, the work of Jesus and his apostles could not have been done.

10. Romans.

The beginnings of Roman history go back to the eighth or seventh century before Christ, but in the century before the birth of Jesus the Roman came to be master of the Mediterranean world. This mastery was extended over Palestine, and thus over the Jews, in 63 B.C. under Pompey. Rome continued to exercise her control over the Jews as long as they remained a nation. Palestine was a province of the Roman Empire. The Romans were harsh and uncompromising in their dealings with the Jews. The Jews were stubborn and resentful of this. For the most part the Romans did not like the Jews and in turn were hated by the Jewish people. Uprisings were frequent but were put down in blood. There was much dissatisfaction and distress.

And yet Rome furnished the background and provided the situation for the world-wide propagation of the gospel of Christ. The Roman world was a unified world, held together by force. Life and property were safe. Intercourse was easy and frequent, and a universal language was spoken. Under such conditions — and only under these — was it possible for the Gospel to be given to the world. Thus Rome unknowingly joined with the other neighbors in making a contribution to the world-wide mission of the Hebrews.

Chapter V

PERIOD OF BEGINNINGS

From the Creation to Abraham
GENESIS 1-12

Section I — Introductory Matters.

1. Extent of This Period. 2. Nature of Bible History. 3. The Period of Beginnings.

Section II — The Creation, the Temptation and the Fall of Man.

1. Importance of This Account. 2. Not a Scientific Account. 3. Form of the Story. 4. Some Unanswerable Questions. 5. Order of Creation. 6. Creation of Man. 7. Dignity and Superiority of Man. 8. First Home. 9. Dignity of Work. 10. Sabbath. 11. Temptation. 12. Sin. 13. Punishment. 14. Elements of Hope.

Section III — From the Fall to Abraham.

1. Extent of This Period. 2. Sons of Adam and Eve. 3. New Beginning with Seth. 4. Longevity of the Patriarchs. 5. Career of Noah. 6. Tower of Babel. 7. Commercial and Cultural Life. 8. Archaeological Items.

CHAPTER V

The Period of Beginnings

Section I — INTRODUCTORY MATTERS.

1. The Extent of This Period.

There are seven periods of Old Testament history. The first of these is known as the Period of Beginnings. It starts with the creation of the world and extends to the time of Abraham 1900-1800 B.C. The records of this period include the accounts of the creation of all things; the first family; the Temptation and Fall of man; the experiences of Cain, Abel and Seth; the work of Noah; and the tower of Babel.

2. The Nature of Bible History.

In these studies we are assuming that the history found in the Old Testament is genuine history. The Old Testament contains narratives, essays, addresses, proverbs and poetry. These writings furnish information on the lives of great leaders, on the political, social, economic and religious life of the Hebrew people, and of surrounding nations also. Particularly in the book of Genesis we have much historical material which is found nowhere else. Without these revealing accounts we would know practically nothing of the early history of mankind. When we study these books of the Old Testament we are dealing with authentic historical documents of great significance.

The Old Testament, while throwing light upon the history of other early races, is particularly concerned with the history of the Hebrew people. It is devoted to the giving of leading facts in their life as a nation, beginning with their origin and continuing to the period just preceding the birth of Christ. The facts related in these Old Testament books constitute the only record of the Hebrew people as a nation.

In dealing with the Old Testament as history we shall find that it differs from ordinary history. The writers are not particularly concerned with the usual facts of history such as military, political, economic and social forces. They are not attempting to present a chronological account, giving in detail a record of their achievements in these areas. These matters appear to be incidental. The chief concern of the writers in the Old Testament is the religious life of Old Testament peoples. They are interested in the progress of man's effort to comprehend God and the ever-enlarging revelation of God to men. This emphasis on religion is discernible in every part of the Old Testament. For example, the writer of II Samuel 8:1-11 tells in a few sentences of David's conquest of seven surrounding nations. while the same writer uses several chapters to tell of David's great sin and its disastrous consequences for David and the nation. The student may find numerous other illustrations of this principle.

3. Period of Beginnings.

This first period of Old Testament history is appropriately called the time of beginnings. It is the beginning of the physical universe, of the human race, of sin and its consequences, of God's plan of redemption, of the family and of the Sabbath. The very name Genesis means beginning. This book is divided into two general sections: (1) Chapters 1-11, which contains the accounts of the creation, the temptation and the fall of man, the flood, and the tower of Babel. These chapters serve as an introduction not only to the Bible and Hebrew history, but also to the history of the human race. (2) Chapters 12-50 which begins the story of Abraham and his descendants, is chiefly concerned with the history of the Hebrew people.

SECTION II — THE CREATION, THE TEMPTATION AND THE FALL (Genesis 1-3).

1. Importance of These Early Chapters.

It would be difficult to overstate the importance of these first chapters of Genesis. For the past century the scientific method has steadily increased in favor until now it practically overshadows all others and all but dominates our thought. During this past century the first three chapters of Genesis have been critically examined and studied to a degree not true of any other document ever written. Some scholars have sought to discredit these accounts by showing that they are inconsistent with the views held by modern scientists. Other scholars have approached them with the sincere purpose of discovering the truth, with the desire to gain a better understanding of their content. Millions of people have read and reread these classic accounts with a growing appreciation of their value and importance. These chapters are important because they are the only orderly, consistent and valid account we have of the beginnings of our world. We should recognize the fact that without these we should not have a basis of philosophy or theology. Practically every great theological doctrine can be traced directly back to the Genesis account of the creation, the Temptation and the Fall of man.

2. Not a Scientific Account.

The crucial question in the minds of many students is, Are the teachings of Genesis 1-3 consistent with the findings of modern science? To begin with, we should recognize the fact that the writer of these chapters was not concerned with science as we understand it. He knew nothing of our scientific approach or method, and hence was not concerned with it. He certainly was not attempting to produce a detailed account which centuries later might be said to be correct or incorrect judged by the scientific method. It is both improper and unfair to take statements made by this writer centuries ago, put them over against scientific views now held, and attempt to determine whether the Genesis account is true or false. In this connection it should be said that no real scientist will claim that he now knows the whole truth. The conclusions of the scientists are constantly changing. A textbook in any of the material sciences which is up to date now will be out of date ten years hence. The writer of these accounts was concerned not with the scientific but with the religious emphasis. He was interested in God's part in the creation of the universe. In this first chapter of Genesis the expression "and God" is found thirty times. Indeed almost every sentence in the chapter is a statement of what God did or said. The writer does not specify the method or process used in the creation of the world. To him the important fact is that the eternal God is the sole creator. Matter is not eternal, God alone is eternal. God is not confined to the universe; He is *over* all and *in* all.

3. Form of the Story.

As a literary production Genesis 1-3 is a classic. The form in which is it presented is important. "For consciseness, concreteness, picturesqueness and beauty, and for naturalness of method the story of creation is not excelled in all literature. In six brief, beautiful paragraphs it shows how God, as a creative Spirit, acting through successive periods, prepared the world for the residence of man and put him in it. The record then returns to the story of the creation of man, with whom God is especially concerned, and gives more in detail the facts concerning his creation, condition, duties and blessings, along with the danger to which he was exposed.

"The first chapter has the rhythm of a great poem with the same refrain at the close of each stanza (verses 5, 8, 13, 19, 23, 31). It describes an orderly progress of creation according to the will and word of God, and, in beautiful language, shows how the whole universe finds its explanation in God. It is especially a poem about God and His works. The four great verses of the chapter are verses 1, 27, 28, and 31. They describe, or declare, the creative power and work of God, man's likeness to God, his place in the created universe and the perfection of God's work. Those are put at the very beginning of the narrative and furnish a good start for all religious thinking."*

This first chapter is really a magnificent religious poem declaring God to be the creator of all things.

4. Unanswerable Questions.

In the study of these chapters many interesting questions will arise for the thoughtful student. When did the creation take place? What process was used in creating the universe and man? Were these "days" periods of twenty-four hours as today, or were they longer periods? Did Satan appear in person? Where was the Garden of Eden? Why did the tempter appear to Eve rather than to Adam? All such questions are interesting, but are not essential to an understanding of the events. It is impossible to answer some of these. The answers to others are matters of opinion.

5. Order of Creation.

The Genesis account of the creation is concise and orderly. Six creative "days" are given specifying what was created each day. (1) Light was created and divided from darkness. (2) The firmament or atmosphere surrounding the earth was made. (3) Water and land were separated and the earth was covered with vegetation. (4) The sun, moon, and stars were made to give light upon the earth. (5) Marine life, and winged fowl were created. (6) Land animals, and man were created.

While the author of this account was not concerned with scientific precision, it is remarkable how his account corresponds in general to the modern scientific view. Lower forms of life were created first. The order is progressive reaching its climax in the creation of man.

*Tidwell, J. B.: *The Bible Period by Period*, page 20. Baptist Sunday School Board. Used by permission.

6. *Creation of Man.*

It is to be noted that in all instances, except in the creation of man, God simply spoke and these other things came into being. But with man it was different. "And God said, Let us make man in our image, after our likeness; and let them have dominion over the fish of the sea, and over the fowl of the air, and over the cattle, and over all the earth." (Gen. 1:26) "And the Lord God formed man of the dust of the ground and breathed into his nostrils the breath of life; and man became a living soul." (Gen. 2:7.)

7. *Dignity and Superiority of Man.*

Man was created last and is superior to all other creatures. He was made a living soul, created in God's image. Man's likeness to God is not in his physical being (limbs, eyes, ears, etc.) for "God is a spirit." Man is like God in intellectual, moral and spiritual qualities. Made after God's likeness man is endowed above all other creatures. He alone has intelligence. He is to keep company with God, to have fellowship with Him. He is to "multiply and replenish the earth" and to subdue it. He is to "have dominion over all other creatures." To man is entrusted the great responsibility of working with God as his intelligent agent in his eternal purposes for man and the world.

8. *The First Home.*

To the first man Eve was given as a "help-meet," or companion. They were to be husband and wife on a basis of equality. This was the first home and was based on the institution of marriage. Monogamy was unquestionably the ideal, even though in later times men departed from this ideal and practiced polygamy. Husband and wife were to meet the needs of each other. In this institution God has provided the ideal plan for the propagation of the race. The coming of children was desired and expected. Husband and wife were to provide the home, the ideal situation for the nurture and training of children. The home was thus the first institution of society; first in time and in importance.

9. *Dignity of Work.*

Adam and Eve were given a home, or a "garden" in which to live. Adam was commanded by Jehovah "to dress it and to keep it." Thus work was ordained in the providence of God and is not to be regarded as punishment sent by God upon man for his disobedience. God provided work for man before the Temptation and the Fall, because it is indispensable to life and is essential to the happiness of men. It is not a curse but a blessing. Without work people could not live and without it men would be miserable and useless. All really happy and useful people have learned the thrill and the satisfaction of achievement by hard work.

10. Sabbath.

In this story of the creation we have the beginning of another important institution, the Sabbath day. "And on the seventh day God finished his work which he had made; and he rested on the seventh day from all his work which he had made. And God blessed the seventh day and hallowed it." (Gen. 2:2-3.) In later times God specifically commanded men to rest on the seventh day. (Exodus 20:8-22.) There are good reasons for the observance of the Sabbath day. It should be done, not because it is an arbitrary command of God without reason, but because it is a basic and fundamental law of life. Man is so constituted that he needs one day out of seven for rest, for the recovery of his physical powers to their normal standard. Scientific experiments made in recent years have demonstrated the truth of this statement. Man needs one day out of seven also for worship, for fellowship with God, and for the development of his spiritual life.

11. Temptation.

The record of the Temptation and the Fall of man is one of the most significant and important ever written. The eternal interests of all mankind are involved in this experience. Again many surface questions arise which are comparatively unimportant. To begin with, we must recognize the presence and authority of an evil power. This evil one had one vicious motive, namely to overthrow the work of God and to cause man to doubt the character and the goodness of God. If the tempter can succeed in causing man to question the integrity and love of God he can achieve his purpose. It is to be noted that the appeal of Satan is based on three desires, which ordinarily are perfectly legitimate — the desire for the beautiful, for food, and for knowledge. The plea of the evil one is based on untruth. His argument was along this line: God is not fair to you. He has given you much, but not enough. You are not permitted to eat of the "fruit of the tree of the knowledge of good and evil," because if you eat of this you will know as much as he, and he does not want this to happen because you then will be his equal. This argument was subtle and fatal. Eve tasted and ate; she then did the natural and expected thing, namely, to involve Adam in this experience. With the acquiescence of Eve and Adam Satan had accomplished his purpose. Sin had entered the lives of the first human beings.

12. Sin.

Up to the time of this experience man was in a state of innocence, but his transgression brought a change in his whole nature, in his relation to God and in his condition. Man now appears to have been conscious of his guilt, for he sought unsuccessfully to escape God. The old relationship had been broken. Sin had been committed. Then too, when faced by his sin he, like all men since his time, sought to place the responsibility for his action on some one else. Adam's defense was "The woman whom thou gavest to be with me, she gave me of the tree, and I did eat." Eve likewise, tried to excuse herself saying, "The serpent beguiled me, and I did eat."

13. Punishment.

Naturally Adam and Eve must be punished for their transgression. The brief statement of the penalties for their sins were: the serpent was to crawl on its belly and eat the dust of the earth, Eve was forced to occupy a place of subordination to man and of great suffering, Adam was condemned to a life of toil and suffering.

While a full discussion of the consequences of the Fall upon the human race does not lie within the scope of this book we may say that the condition and the destiny of all mankind were involved in this tragic occurrence. This doctrine has been taught by the Christian church through all the centuries of its history. Paul held that the sin of the "First Adam" which affected all men, could be atoned for only by the death of the "Second Adam."

Naturally, every thoughtful student raises the question: Why should man be tempted? Naturally also there are various answers to this question. There have always been those who declare that this was unfair to man, holding that it was a trap set by God for him. But such was not the case. There was a necessary reason for the temptation. Man was made in the image of God with the priceless privilege of exercising his choice. If man was to be free, and not an automaton, he must have an opportunity for the exercise of the faculty of choice. His choice must bring with it the usual consequences. If he chose wisely and did not sin certain consequences would ensue. If he chose wrongly he must likewise take the consequences. But to be free he must have the opportunity of making a choice. This necessity reflects not the selfish jealousy of God, but his goodness and his desire for man, who is his creature.

14. Elements of Hope.

Despite the tragic failure of man in this great crisis, with its consequences of pain and punishment, the door of hope was not closed. Man was not forsaken by God, who still loved him despite the sin he had committed. There is a glorious promise of victory to the seed of the woman. (Gen. 3:15.) The struggle between the two opposing forces will be long and hard, but victory will ultimately come through one who was a man and yet infinitely more than man.

Section III — FROM THE FALL TO ABRAHAM.

1. Extent of This Period.

The account of events included in this section is to be found in Genesis 4-11. Geographically the setting is probably in the valley between the Tigris and Euphrates rivers. When the period began is not known since we have no hint of the time of the expulsion from Eden. The period closes some time prior to 1800 B.C. which is the approximate date of Abraham, the great character with whom the next period begins.

2. Sons of Adam and Eve.

We are told that Cain and Abel, the first sons mentioned in the record, were born to Adam and Eve after their expulsion from Eden. We have but few facts about them. In some respects they were probably as much alike as two brothers usually are. In other respects they were radically different. Cain was jealous and wicked in spirit, while Abel seems to have been generous and reverent. Cain was an agriculturist, Abel a shepherd.

The story of Cain's slaying his brother Abel, is a familiar one. Abel's sacrifice to God, made in a spirit of true worship, was acceptable, while that of Cain was not acceptable because it was made in the wrong spirit. Insane with jealously, Cain slew his brother, thus becoming the first murderer known in history.

For this murder God punished Cain by banishing him from his home land. Cain, overwhelmed by the enormity of his punishment, complained that it was greater than he could bear. Whereupon God extended mercy and protection to him. Cain went to the land of Nod, found a wife and established a race which came to be known for its great energy, enterprise and inventions, but also for polygamy, violence, and murder.

3. New Beginning With Seth.

After the death of Abel and the banishment of Cain, another son, Seth, was born to Adam and Eve. Through this son the chosen people of God were to come. From this line came the spiritual leaders of Israel. One descendant was Enoch who "walked with God, and he was not, because God took him." Another was Noah, the preacher of righteousness who built the ark and perpetuated the race.

4. Longevity of the Patriarchs.

Every reader of these accounts is immediately impressed with the extended age of these early characters. Naturally the student will ask what is the explanation of this. How was it possible for one to live several hundred years? Did Methusaleh actually attain the age of 969 years? Various scholars have suggested some possible explanations of this interesting problem. (1) Some hold that the name used, Lamech for example, refers in these cases not to an individual but to a family or a tribe. (2) Others feel that the word "year" as used here did not mean a period of twelve months as with us, but referred to the lunar month. Thus Methusaleh's age 969 years should be divided by thirteen, which would give his real age. (3) Still other scholars insist that in this early period man's body was stronger and that it was expected that he should live longer; a shorter span of life was the result of dissipation and sin. These explanations may or may not be of value, but at any rate they are interesting.

5. Career of Noah.

The wickedness of this early civilization was great. "The earth was full of violence." (Gen. 6:11.) "And Jehovah saw that the wickedness of man was great in the earth, and that every imagination of the thoughts of his heart was only evil continually. And it repented Jehovah that he had made man on the earth and it grieved him at his heart." (Gen. 6:5-6.)

Noah, a teacher of righteousness, was to be the agent of God in his dealings with this wicked civilization. Noah alone was a good and faithful man among all these wicked people. All his efforts in calling men to repent were in vain. Sterner measures were necessary so God announced to Noah his purpose to destroy the world by a great flood.

He commanded him to build an ark by which he and his wife, his three sons and their wives and all the different species of animal life, would be spared. When they were safe inside, the door of the ark was closed by God himself and then came the floods of water from heaven above and from the fountains of the deep. For forty days and nights the flood continued until the earth was covered. The Bible account does not give any details of the terrible struggle of the people outside the ark in this dreadful disaster. One must use imagination to gain any conception of the horrible experiences caused by the flood, when the waters reached the top of the mountains and every living creature except those in the ark died.

For long months the ark floated on the waters covering the land. At last it was grounded on Mt. Ararat. After another period of waiting while the waters assuaged Noah sent forth a raven and a dove to determine the state of the flood waters. When the waters had receded his first act was to offer to the Lord worthy sacrifices of "every clean beast and of every clean fowl" saved by the ark. God then promised Noah that never again should the earth be destroyed by flood waters. The rainbow was given to him and his family as a pledge of this promise. A notable covenant was then made between God and his servant Noah. Thus the human race made a new start. This time it should have improved; they should have learned to "abhor that which is evil, and to cleave to that which is good." But again the results were disappointing. Sin and wickedness were not yet conquered. Even Noah himself was guilty of drunkenness, and his younger son committed grievous sins.

Scholars today differ widely on the question of the origin of various races. While such studies have their value it may be that unanimity of opinion can not be reached. History reveals the fact that the lot of certain races has been exceedingly unfortunate. Among Christians everywhere today, however, there is a growing concern that all races be given the rights and privileges to which they are entitled.

6. Tower of Babel.

The story of the Tower of Babel is an interesting one, but still has elements of mystery in it. For example, scholars do not agree as to the reason for the building of this tower. However, in Genesis 11:4 the writer seems to indicate that its purpose was to make a great name for men and to keep them from being dispersed over the earth. To keep the command of God "to multiply, and replenish the earth, and subdue it" required arduous work, living in far distant areas, enduring the hardships of the pioneer. It was far easier and more desirable to live amid the benefits of civilization. This sin offended God and must be punished. Their proud structure was never completed, for God confused their hitherto common speech and scattered them abroad, to begin nations in different parts of the earth.

7. Commercial and Cultural Life.

We have no detailed record of the beginnings of civilization, but we know that there were two great empires of antiquity, Babylonia and Egypt. Which of these was the earlier we can not tell. For many centuries before Abraham these two empires flourished, one on the banks of the Euphrates, and the other in the valley of the Nile. Archaeologists are certain that their discoveries in these areas go back as far as 4000 B.C. Babylonian civilization seems to have reached its climax in the reign of Hammurabi, some nineteen hundred years before Christ.

The earliest records introduce Egypt to us as a full grown empire. When and how it originated and developed we do not know. The pyramids and other Egyptian monuments reveal the amazing faculty of early Egyptians for erecting stone structures and buildings. What tools and devices were used by the Egyptians as early as 3000 B.C. in cutting and placing huge stones with such precision in these pyramids? Certainly they knew much of mathematics and astronomy and other sciences. They had a well developed system of culture and learning. They had a well organized government which dated back centuries before the time of Abraham.

In these early empires sculptors, masons, miners, potters, jewelers and other workmen were well advanced in their art. They seemed to have been organized into unions or guilds! Great commercial enterprises flourished, with merchants and bankers doing business on an international basis. Goods were transported over sea and land. The Phoenicians on the northeast shore of the Mediterranean as early as 3000 B.C. were sending their ships westward out of the Mediterranean into the Atlantic along the shores of Africa, and probably as far distant as the British Isles. In recent years archaeologists have been so impressed by the great similarity of discoveries in Central America with ancient Egyptian life that some are of the opinion that Egyptian ships may have crossed the Atlantic and left on the western hemisphere some of the evidences of their great culture many centuries before the Christian era. Certainly the peoples of the Biblical world were advanced in cultural and commercial life before Abraham came on the scene.

While we do not know the origin of writing we do know there were great libraries with dictionaries and other writings extensively used. These were written in cuneiform, the Babylonian script, which was practically a universal language, thus making a unity of language and culture for this early period.

8. Archaeological Items.

There are a number of pertinent archaeological items belonging to this period of beginnings in Bible history.

The Mesopotamian documents dealing with the creation and the flood were brought to light by Rawlinson and others 1852-1854. They were found at Ashurbanipal and were in cuneiform script. Altogether we now have some five or six accounts dealing with the creation and the flood: (1) The Semitic-Babylonian version of the Epic of Creation made up of seven tablets. (2) The Sippar Tablet in two languages. (3) The Gilgamesh Epic consisting of 12 tablets. (4) The Nippur Tablet discovered by the University of Pennsylvania. (5) A number of smaller tablets found at various places.

The discovery and translation of these tablets produced a sensation among Bible students. There are certainly very obvious similarities between the Biblical accounts of the creation and the flood and these tablets. Naturally we can not enter here any discussion of this involved problem. Suffice it to say that these discoveries are extremely significant. "The relations existing between the tablets and the Bible narratives indicate ancestral connections, or points of contact which can not be brushed aside or explained away as of no consequence."*

So far archaeologists have found no document resembling the account of the Tower of Babel, though the Ziggurats of ancient Babylon are most suggestive. A pyramidical temple discovered in old Mexico is strikingly similar to the description of the ancient Tower of Babel.

There are quite a number of traditions of the Fall of man. Four fragments of the Adapa myth dealing with this have been found. In these there are certain similarities with the Bible account as for example,

*Adams, J. McKee: *Ancient Records and the Bible*, p. 64. The Broadman Press. Used by permission.

Adam and Eve are tempted "to become like God knowing good and evil." However, there are very radical dissimilarities. Whatever may be the early connection between these Adapa tablets and the Genesis account the record of these tablets is striking and provocative.

Chapter VI

THE HEBREW PATRIARCHS

(GENESIS 12-50)

Section I — Introduction.

1. Survey of the Period. 2. Beginning of the Hebrew Race. 3. God's Purpose for the Hebrews. 4. Civilization of This Period. 5. Life Among the Hebrews. 6. Ur of the Chaldees.

Section II — Abraham and Isaac.

1. Early Life of Abraham. 2. Call and Covenant. 3. Journeys of Abraham. 4. At Shechem. 5. At Bethel. 6. Down to Egypt. 7. Back to Bethel. 8. At Home in Hebron. 9. Rescuing Lot. 10. Covenant Renewed. 11. Hagar and Ishmael. 12. Destruction of Sodom and Gomorrah. 13. Birth of Isaac. 14. Sarah and Keturah. 15. Isaac and Rebekah. 16. Character of Abraham. 17. Sons of Isaac. 18. Character of Isaac. 19. Other Descendants of Abraham.

Section III — The Career of Jacob.

1. Prominence of Jacob. 2. Character of Jacob. 3. Birthright and the Father's Blessing. 4. Fleeing from Home. 5. From Bethel to Haran. 6. Jacob's Family. 7. Return to Canaan. 8. Reconciliation With Esau. 9. From "Jacob" to "Israel." 10. Back to Bethel. 11. The End of a True Romance. 12. At Home Again. 13. Later Experiences of Jacob.

Section IV — The Career of Joseph.

1. An Inspiring Career. 2. His Early Life. 3. Sold Into Slavery. 4. Slave and Prisoner in Egypt. 5. Dreams of Plenty and Famine. 6. "Second Only to Pharoah." 7. The Brothers' First Visit to Egypt. 8. Their Second Visit to Egypt. 9. Living in Egypt. 10. Death of Jacob and Joseph. 11. Social and Religious Life of the Patriarchs. 12. Archaeological Items.

CHAPTER VI

The Hebrew Patriarchs

(GENESIS 12-50)

SECTION I — INTRODUCTION.

1. Survey of the Period.

The period which we are now to study begins with the call of Abraham and closes with the death of Joseph in Egypt. Geographically nearly all the ancient Biblical countries are involved. Beginning in Chaldea on the Persian gulf the records take us through the Mesopotamian valley, Haran, Syria, Palestine and Egypt. Prior to this period we could not be specific as to dates or geographical locations. In this period we can be sure of the approximate date of Abraham and we are on sure ground geographically. We consider these records as actual history since we are dealing with characters who are real and with events and localities which are generally recognized as authentic.

2. Beginning of the Hebrew Race.

For many years competent scholars have held that with Abraham we have the real beginning of the Hebrew people as a race. Abraham was selected for this purpose and certainly this idea dominates the covenant relationship between Jehovah and him. In both the Old Testament and the New this idea is emphasized. The Hebrew people themselves always looked upon Abraham as founder and father. Thus we are to deal with one of the outstanding characters in history as we enter upon the study of this period. In every respect he was a great man. With him a new era in history was inaugurated.

3. God's Purpose for the Hebrews.

In calling Abraham to be the head of a new race God had a specific purpose. This chosen race was to be his peculiar people. They were elected to be the chief medium in his program of revealing himself to mankind. His blessings upon the race and the dealings with them had religious significance, "In thee shall all the nations of the earth be blessed." What a high and holy mission for any people! Greece has made her intellectual and cultural contribution, Rome has given her law and idea of government to the world, and other nations have left their respective contributions to the enlightenment and welfare of humanity, but no nation has made as high and as noble a contribution as the Hebrew people.

4. The Civilization of This Period.

We have abundant sources for the study of the life of this period. From the study of these sources one is impressed by the advanced stage of culture, learning and progress in the ancient Babylonian empire, whose influence dominated the countries of the "Fertile Crescent." A common language was used in the whole area, making communications between different peoples easy and frequent. Extensive trade enterprises were conducted on land. Some years ago a tablet was discovered on which was recorded a contract between two men for the renting of a wagon. The owner who lived in Babylonia at the time of Abraham specified in his contract that the renter of the wagon was not to drive it to the sea (Mediterranean). The Phoenecians and others sent their ships to far distant ports in the Mediterranean world. Irrigation by canals was used to insure good crops in the fertile land between the Tigris and Euphrates rivers. Workmen were skilled in the manufacture of metals, ornaments and fabrics.

There were great libraries filled with volumes some of which have been translated. Astronomy, mathematics, and other sciences were taught. Elaborate buildings testified to the knowledge and skill of architects and workmen. The banking and legal professions were well developed and orderly government was maintained. The solar year had been calculated and time was divided as we now have it in the 60 unit system of rotation (sixty seconds to the minute, sixty minutes to the hour). The Code of Hammurabi, c 1900-1750 B.C., of which we shall speak later, gives a revealing insight into the highly developed civic, business and social life of these people.

It is to be remembered, therefore, that Abraham lived in an advanced civilization, though it was deficient in moral and spiritual qualities. This gives a new meaning to the whole career of this remarkable man, and of the unusual mission committed to him by God.

5. Life Among the Hebrews.

At this point it will be well to look briefly at the chief features of the life of the Hebrew people in this period. They were a nomadic people, living in tents and moving frequently, having at the time no settled home, but looking forward to the time when they could be at home in the "Land of Promise." They were shepherds and farmers, and they seem to have been acquainted with some of the arts. Western people need to be reminded that nomadic life was not like that of the modern "gypsy," but that it was an honored and highly respected life.

Abraham and his descendants were not wandering tramps nor marauders, but were wealthy, distinguished citizens. They touched the foremost civilizations of the time. They had great flocks and herds, money, jewels and expensive robes. They displayed the finest traits of Oriental culture such as hospitality and generosity and courtesy. Abraham was a dignified chieftain and apparently was accepted by his contemporaries as a distinguished adviser and citizen.

Their government was simple, being patriarchal in nature. The central idea was the high position of authority held by the father or head of the tribe. His authority extended to every area of life. In the family he was the chief leader. To him the wife and all the children looked for guidance and judgment in all cases. He was head of the house. Even after their marriage his children were subject to him as long as he lived. In case of his death the eldest son assumed leadership of the family. However, his authority seems to have been a benevolent one, not autocratic nor tyrannical. The chief was also the leader in all phases of life among his tribe. He was a military leader. He served as priest in religious matters. In civil affairs he was the judge whose decision usually was final. In the Orient today this idea still prevails to a remarkable extent.

6. Ur of the Chaldees.

Abraham's original home was Ur of the Chaldees. This city on the Euphrates River near the Persian Gulf was one of the most important in early history. Extensive excavations have been made there, the most valuable by Woolley. These ruins cover several square miles and from these some very remarkable "finds" were made. These include royal palaces, tombs, cuneiform inscriptions, a ziggurat, and a temple of Nebuchadnezzar. Down beneath the several layers or strata of ruins excavators found a deep deposit of silt which indicated that at one time the area was under water and human occupation had been interrupted. Some scholars hold that this is evidence of the Flood, though others feel that this may not be conclusive evidence. Archaeologists were deeply impressed by the discovery of the tomb of Queen Shub-ad who had not been buried alone. With her were ten women, probably her servants, who had been slain and buried with her so as to serve her in the next world. Outside this tomb were the skeletons of five men who were probably placed there as guards to prevent any intruders from disturbing the queen and her attendants. The large temple of the moon-god was uncovered. Deposits of jewelry and

ornate carvings and a frieze of human and animal figures dating back
to 3000 B.C. were found. Along with these were many other treasures
which bear testimony to the remarkable civilization which flourished
here prior to the days of Abraham. The more recent discoveries at
Mari, an ancient Mesopotamian city north of Ur, give substantial
proof of the advanced cultural and civic life at the time of Abraham.

SECTION II — ABRAHAM AND ISAAC (Genesis 12-24).

1. Early Life of Abraham.

The great character in these narratives is introduced to us by the
name of Abram (high father) which was later changed to Abraham
(father of a multitude). His wife was first known as Sarai and later
as Sarah. The story begins with a man named Terah who lived near
Ur with his three sons, Abram, Nahor and Haran. Haran died
prematurely.

Abraham, a shepherd like his father, apparently was wealthy since
he was owner of large flocks and herds and a company of servants.
We would assume that it was a family belonging to the higher ranks.
The immediate family included Abraham, his wife Sarah, and a
nephew Lot (son of Haran). His father Terah and his family together
with Abraham, Sarah and Lot left the vicinty of Ur to move northward
to the city of Haran. This was a long journey of some five hundred or
more miles, but was accomplished with apparent satisfaction. From
now on the city of Haran was regarded as the family home. It was
situated on a small river which ran southward some sixty miles to join
the Euphrates. The city was already well established on an important
trade route. For centuries it remained a great commercial center which
figured prominently in the experiences of these ancient nations; in fact
its history continued to the 13th century after Christ. It, like Ur, was
the center of the worship of the moon god Sin. Some years after the
settlement of his family here Terah died. Nahor, son of Terah,
continued to live in Haran, but Abraham was not to remain in this
city. His great venture of faith committed to him by God, was to
take him to far distant points among strange peoples.

2. Call and Covenant of Abraham.

According to the word of Stephen in his great defense, it was before
his coming to Haran that Abraham received his call. (Acts 7:2-4.)
This being true his stay in Haran was meant to be only temporary.
From there he would journey "unto the land that I will show thee."

The call which came to Abraham was an event of great significance, "the most important religious event since the fall of man — a new starting point for a genuine religion." The scope and the implications of this call are worthy of note. "Now Jehovah said unto Abram, Get thee out of thy country, and from thy kindred, and from thy father's house, unto the land that I will show thee: and I will make of thee a great nation, and I will bless thee, and make thy name great; and be thou a blessing; and I will bless them that bless thee, and him that curseth thee will I curse: and in thee shall all of the families of the earth be blessed." (Genesis 12:1-3.) This is both a command and promise. The promise extended into the long centuries ahead. He was to be the founder of a new race, the father of a new faith which presages a close and intimate relation with God. This new people was to receive special revelations from God and to pass them on to others. "This covenant (between God and Abraham) contained four promises: (1) A great nation, fulfilled in the Hebrew people. (2) A great name, fulfilled in that Hebrews and Christians and Mohammedans all call him their religious father. (3) A land, fulfilled in the possession of Canaan by the Hebrews. (4) A blessing to all nations. This, through the preaching of the gospel, is still in the process of fulfillment."*

Some time after the death of his father Terah, in Haran, Abraham prepared to obey the great command. Consider for a moment the courage and the faith necessary for such an undertaking. To his family and friends such a venture would be termed visionary, impractical and foolish. Did they ridicule him and perhaps sneer at him? We should remember that travel was limited in those days. They had no modern highways, no road maps, no experienced traveler upon whom to rely for directions and suggestions. To make even a brief journey in familiar territory was a big undertaking. In our day when so many people are "world travelers" we are inclined to underestimate Abraham's vision and courage. We should understand also that he had great possessions, hundreds of camels, thousands of sheep, goats and oxen, many servants with their implements, furniture and tents. A tremendous amount of planning and labor would be necessary, especially since they were to pass through long reaches of barren desert country. Abraham must have had great faith in God! By this faith he proved himself worthy of founding this new race.

*Tidwell, J. B.: *The Bible Period by Period,* p. 66. Baptist Sunday School Board. Used by permission.

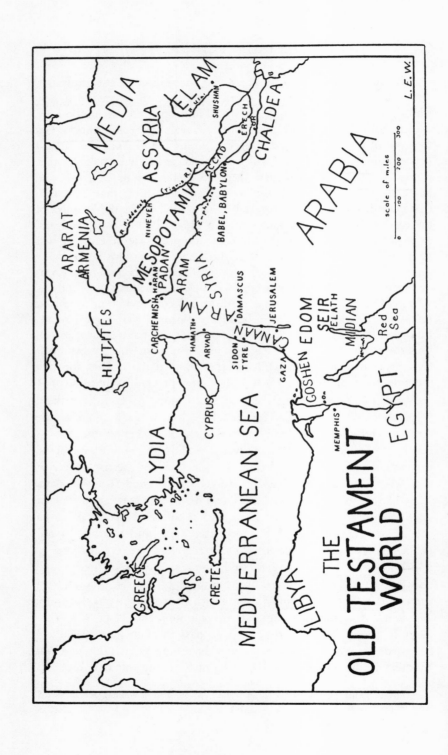

THE
OLD TESTAMENT
WORLD

MEDIA

ELAM

ASSYRIA

CHALDEA

ARARAT
ARMENIA

MESOPOTAMIA
PADAN

HITTITES

ARAM

SYRIA

ARABIA

LYDIA

GREECE

CRETE

CYPRUS

MEDITERRANEAN SEA

LIBYA

EGYPT

MEMPHIS•

GOSHEN EDOM
SEIR
ELATH

MIDIAN

Red
Sea

GAZA

JERUSALEM

CANAAN

DAMASCUS

SIDON•
TYRE•

ARVAD•

HAMATH•

CARCHEMISH•
HARAN•

NINEVEH

R. HIDDEKEL (TIGRIS R.)

R. EUPHRATES

ACCAD

BABEL, BABYLON•

ERECH

UR

SHUSHAN•

R. ULAI

L.E.W.

scale of miles

0   100   200   300

3. The Journeys of Abraham.

It will be helpful to the student to get a brief outline or summary of his journeys before relating the details of these experiences. From Ur of the Chaldees he moved to Haran. Journeying southward he entered Canaan making his first stop at Shechem. He then moved a few miles farther south to Bethel. From this point he traversed southern Canaan and entered the land of Egypt where he and Sarah lived for some time. Leaving the land of the Nile he re-entered Canaan and returned to Bethel. After a stay at this point he moved again to Hebron in southern Palestine which he considered home for the rest of his life.

4. At Shechem.

We should keep in mind the fact that Abraham did not have a "blue print" of his future travels. He was to go by faith to "a land which I will show thee." "He went forth not knowing whither he went." His travels took him to the very center of Canaan before he made his first stop. It was at Shechem in the plain of Moreh, where he felt impelled to pitch his tents. In this favored spot dominated by the two famous peaks (Mt. Ebal and Mt. Gerizim) later to figure prominently in Bible history, was a green valley with good pasturage and fresh water. Here Abraham built an altar unto Jehovah who appeared to him with the promise that he would give this land unto him. "The Canaanite was then in the land," and perhaps for this reason Abraham was led to move on.

5. At Bethel.

Twenty miles south of Shechem was Bethel to which Abraham now moved. On the plain just east of the village he pitched his tent. Here again he built his altar to Jehovah and worshiped him.

6. Down to Egypt.

Breaking camp at Bethel, he continued to move southward. As he came into this territory he found a famine ravishing the land making food scarce and pasturage insufficient. To the fertile Nile valley he and his company now repaired. This experience of going to a strange and different country in quest of food was a still further test of his faith. How would he, a nomad coming from a hostile land, be received in the highly developed civilization of this rich land? He must have had anxieties about this since the record tells of an expedient agreed upon by him and Sarah. This scheme, revealing the weakness of Abraham (even the greatest servants of God have their weak points), is told with complete frankness which gives validity to the account. Fearing that his own life would be endangered if the Pharaoh of Egypt knew that Sarah, a beautiful woman, was his wife, he persuaded Sarah to pose as his sister (in fact she was his half-sister). She agreed to the proposal and was taken to the royal harem, whereupon Jehovah sent plagues upon Pharaoh. Pharaoh after discovering the truth, in great fear ordered Abraham and Sarah immediately to leave the land after making rich gifts to them. An old papyrus, "Story of Two Brothers," gives an account of one of the Pharaohs bringing into his court by force the beautiful wife of another man and then slaying her husband. The generous treatment of Abraham and Sarah in this instance is unusual, probably an act of Jehovah!

7. Back to Bethel.

When commanded by Pharaoh to depart from his land Abraham obeyed at once. Remembering the favorable prospects back at Bethel, his second stop in Canaan, he now made his way thither where for some time he made his home. His flocks and herds, like those of his nephew Lot now multiplied so rapidly that a crisis arose. There was not sufficient pasture and water for all. Strife had developed between the rival herdsmen and serious trouble seemed imminent. In this crisis Abraham displayed great magnanimity of soul. Calling Lot to his tent he reminded him that they were brethren and there should be no strife between them. He then made the generous proposal that Lot look over all the land about them and take his choice. It was best to separate. Lot agreed to the proposal and after his survey of the territory chose to go down into the fertile valley of the Jordan where there was an abundance of pasture and water. He took the best, but in going to his new home he invited the tragedy which later came to him and his family as a sympathizer in the wicked life of the people of Sodom and Gomorrah. How magnanimous was Abraham! All this territory was his. He could have commanded Lot to go anywhere. But instead in the interest of peace he allowed Lot to make his choice. His generous love for Lot is later exhibited in his daring rescue of him after he was captured and taken far to the north by hostile kings.

After Lot's withdrawal to settle in his new home, Jehovah again appeared to Abraham to renew the covenant with him, to promise all of this goodly land to him and his descendants.

8. At Home in Hebron.

Abraham now made his last move when he returned to southern Canaan to establish his home at Hebron. While he later traveled from here to other points, he went only on temporary journeys, leaving his family at Hebron. This ancient city located at the head of a valley on an elevated plain was famous for good pastures and fine vineyards. The city has had a long history, figuring prominently in the Old Testament records. Here Abraham had many notable experiences, including the visitations of Jehovah under the famous oaks of Mamre. In Hebron Abraham bought a burial place for himself and his family, the historic cave of Machpelah, where he, Sarah, Isaac, Jacob, and others of his family were buried. The modern tourist can see only the barred entrance to this cave. Perhaps later the tomb may be opened so that we may see the actual spot where the remains of these famous people were laid to rest.

9. Rescuing Lot.

Sometime after Lot chose the valley of the Jordan as his home, calamity came upon him and others in the region. Chedorlaomer with his allies came from Mesopotamia and in a sudden attack defeated the kings of Sodom and Gomorrah and took captive a large number of people with their possessions. Lot was among those captured. Upon hearing this Abraham took three hundred and eighteen servants with arms, hurried to the Jordan valley and, moving northward up the valley, pursued the company until he overtook them in the region of Dan. Here he defeated Chedorlaomer, then followed the company as far as Damascus, rescuing Lot and his possessions. In view of all the circumstances this exploit reveals Abraham as an able warrior. Still later he was instrumental in rescuing Lot from death in the disaster that destroyed these two wicked cities.

Upon his return from Damascus Abraham was met by a man named Melchizedek, king of Salem, and priest of the most high God. There is much about this strange figure that is still a mystery. He blessed Abraham and seems to have been familiar with the high mission of Abraham as the founder of a new race.

10. The Covenant Renewed.

Shortly afterward Jehovah appeared again to Abraham renewing the covenant and promising specifically that he should have a son of his own blood. Abraham and Sarah, though married for many years, were still without an heir. What a disappointment this must have been to both. What must have been the thoughts of Abraham in view of God's promise that he would be the father of a race and yet the years passed without a son of his own? He must continue to hope and to have faith in God. Now in his vision he was assured that his seed should be as the sands of the sea and the stars of the heavens in number. He accepted this in faith. "Abraham believed God and it was accounted to him for righteousness."

11. Hagar and Ishmael.

Even after God had spoken to Abraham a period of time passed and yet there seemed to be no sign of the fulfillment of the promise of a son. Sarah suggested to her husband that he now take as his wife Hagar, one of her handmaids, since in the promise to him it had not been specified that Sarah was to be the mother. Abraham accepted the proposal and in due time Hagar bore him a son whom she called Ishmael (whom God hears). Ill feeling between Sarah and Hagar soon developed and ultimately Hagar and her son were forced to leave the home.

Other years passed bringing Abraham to the age of ninety-nine years when once more God appeared to him and assured him that now the time had come for the fulfillment of the promise. Sarah was to be the mother of his son, but he himself and all male descendants hereafter should submit to the rite of circumcision. His name was changed from Abram (exalted father) to Abraham (father of a multitude). At first Sarah doubted, and even laughed at what appeared so utterly impossible. This son was to be called Isaac (laughter).

12. Destruction of Sodom and Gomorrah.

The sacred writer at this point gives a lengthy account of the terrible destruction of the two wicked cities in the Jordan valley. Without giving all the details we should note the earnest plea made by Abraham that the city should be spared; that not even ten righteous men could be found; that Lot was warned to gather his family together and flee the city before all were destroyed; that they could not be persuaded to leave, and that Lot and his wife and two daughters were saved only by being dragged from the city; that Lot's wife lingered and disobeyed the command not to look back, was killed and became a mound of salt; that Lot's daughters in order to save themselves from the shame of childlessness made their father drunk and became the mothers of two sons, Moab and Ben-Ammi, by their own father.

These cities were utterly wiped out when "the Lord rained upon Sodom and Gomorrah brimstone and fire from heaven." Just how this disaster occurred is a matter of speculation. Many scholars believe that in this volcanic region which is laden with various chemicals, a thunderstorm broke and severe lightning ignited the city and caused it to burn in fierce heat.

13. The Birth of Isaac.

We turn from this picture of tragedy to view a happier scene. At last God's promise was fulfilled. Sarah conceived and bore to Abraham a son who was named Isaac. Was ever a son more welcome or did a father ever have greater pride in his boy? In due time the boy was weaned, the event was celebrated by a feast, and when Ishmael mocked Isaac, Sarah now demanded the unconditional expulsion of Hagar and her boy. They were banished to dwell in the desert where Ishmael grew up later becoming renowned in the use of the bow. He later married an Egyptian and to them were born twelve sons and one daughter. These sons of Ishmael became the ancestors of the Arabs "their hand against every man and every man's hand against them."

In the meantime Isaac grew into boyhood and was naturally the idol of his parents. The greatest trial and test of Abraham's faith was now to come. He was commanded by Jehovah to take this boy, his only son upon whom so much depended, and to offer him in sacrifice. Though he was not able to understand this awful command, nevertheless Abraham met the test. Nowhere is there to be found a more touching story than this account of the aged father's struggle between obedience to God and love for his son. Every sentence throbs with deep emotion (read Hebrews 11:17-19). The great man of God proved his faith, his beloved son was spared and immediately thereafter God renewed his covenant promises to him.

14. Sarah and Keturah.

Amid the familiar scenes around Hebron, Sarah, the aged companion of Abraham, came to the end of her days. In the cave of Machpelah, where he himself was later to be placed, Abraham laid to rest the body of Sarah. Some years later, after the marriage of Isaac to Rebekah, Abraham was married to Keturah who bore him six sons.

15. Isaac and Rebekah.

The story of the betrothal and marriage of Isaac and Rebekah is told in detail in a long chapter (Gen. 24). The student interested in ancient Oriental life will study carefully this beautiful and illuminating story. According to Oriental custom the parents took the initiative and made the arrangements for the marriage of their sons and daughters. Abraham insisted that the wife of Isaac should come, not from the wicked Canaanites, but from his own people back at Paddan-Aram. The devoted servant (Eliezer) who was entrusted with the responsibility of discovering the girl found Rebekah, the daughter of Bethuel, the nephew of Abraham, who agreed to go back to Canaan with him to become the wife of Isaac. "And Isaac brought her (Rebekah) into his mother Sarah's tent, and took Rebekah, and she became his wife; and he loved her; and Isaac was comforted after his mother's death." To Isaac and Rebekah were born twin sons, Esau and Jacob.

16. Character of Abraham.

At the ripe old age of 175 years the grand old man of faith came to the end of his days. His body was placed beside that of Sarah in the family burial place, the cave of Machpelah, by his sons Isaac and Ishmael.

To speak adequately of the character and the contribution of Abraham would require more space than is available in this study. In evaluating this man one is tempted to use superlatives. However, the simple fact is, that here was one of the really great men of history. Some marvel that such a man could live in this time of history. He was great in character and in achievements. His character was not perfect as we have already seen, but his good qualities so far overshadow his weakness that it is comparatively unimportant. Essentially he was a man of peace; he could and did fight when it was necessary, but he was a peacemaker. He was generous and unselfish in spirit. His courage is revealed in many trying experiences. He was loyal to the truth and to his family. He was a good business man whose prosperity was known abroad. His good judgment and his wise counsel frequently served his family and friends. He was a man of integrity. Most striking of all his noble traits was his religious faith. He was "fervent in spirit, serving the Lord." His superb faith in God met every test. His interest in others is illustrated by his frevent intercession for the wicked people in Sodom and Gomorrah. The service and worship of

God were always first in his life. We can not imagine a man more fitted to fulfill the duties and to sustain the honors that devolved on the father of a nation.

The achievements of Abraham are most remarkable. Through experiences of war and peace, adversity and prosperity he led his family and founded a nation. He achieved in material things, but in religious character he is pre-eminent. Three great faiths of mankind — the Jews, Christians and Mohammedans — embracing almost half the human race, look upon him as their spiritual father. Indeed, through him all the nations of the earth have been blessed.

"Regarded from the standpoint of his unparalleled spiritual mission, the Patriarch stands as the most pivotal and strategic man in the course of world history, greater than Egyptian pharaohs, Babylonian or Assyrian monarchs, Alexander the Great, or any other. It is not incidental nor accidental that the three appellations applied to him were never spoken of any other man, viz., Abraham, the Friend of God; Abraham, the Father of the Hebrew people; and Abraham, the Father of all believers. It is not incidental nor accidental that from this man comes the most rigid conception of monotheism the world has ever known, nor that the only monotheistic peoples yet to appear in the world course, namely, Hebrews, Mohammedans, and Christians, trace their lineage, either through flesh or faith, to Father Abraham."*

17. The Sons of Isaac.

Esau and Jacob, the twin children born by Rebekah to Isaac, early revealed disappointing traits of character. Esau (unguarded, profane) seems never to have had a serious mind and never manifested any appreciation of the family heritage and destiny so cherished by Abraham. He was harmless, but without purpose or ambition. He did not have in him the makings of a man. Jacob (supplanter) was notoriously tricky and unscrupulous, with great ambitions for himself. He could without hesitation stoop to deceive his own brother and even his blind old father. Many students are disturbed by what on the surface appears to be the approval of God upon Jacob with all his deceptions. Was God unfair to Esau when he selected Jacob above him? It may be helpful to remember that even God can not do much with a man who has no serious purpose, no appreciation of higher values, no ambition for himself. But God can take a man

*Adams, J. McKee: *Ancient Records and the Bible,* pp. 187-188. The Broadman Press. Used by permission.

like Jacob with worthy ambitions but who admittedly is inclined to deception in his actions, and change his character so as to use him for a great purpose. In other words, a man with questionable ethics but a worthy objective potentially is worth more than a harmless man who has no ambition.

18. The Character of Isaac.

The record of Isaac's life is comparatively brief and is undramatic. His was a quiet life characterized by his love of peace and his devotion to God. But he was a man of strength and is not to be dismissed as an inconsequential character who made no real contribution. He had to live in the unhappy position between a father whose greatness overshadowed all other men of the time, and a son, Jacob, whose career was so dramatic and colorful.

19. Other Descendants of Abraham.

As we bring to a close our study of Abraham and Isaac it will be well to look briefly at the various descendants of Abraham apart from Isaac. As previously stated, Ishmael settled in the desert of Arabia. It appears that the family of Ishmael mingled with the families of Abraham's six sons by Keturah. Most of these people continued to live in the deserts, though some became settled agriculturists and merchants. From these descendants came the Arab people, who for many centuries have occupied these desert wastes. The descendants of Esau occupied the picturesque country south of the Dead Sea known as Edom. These Edomites were bitter enemies of the Hebrews and in succeeding centuries are frequently mentioned in connection with the Jews.

The sons of Lot's daughters, the Moabites and the Ammonites, settled east of the Dead Sea and the Jordan River. They too, had frequent contact (usually hostile) with the descendants of Isaac.

Section III — THE CAREER OF JACOB (Genesis 24-36).

1. Prominence of Jacob.

Jacob occupies a large place in the history of the Hebrew people. His activities, particularly during the latter half of his life as a prince of God, overshadow all other men of the time. His sons became the heads of the twelve tribes of the nation, and thus are kept continuously before the Hebrew people in their history.

Jacob (supplanter), in a memorable experience during the night on the river Jabbok, as he moved back to his old homeland, became

Israel (prince of God). This change in names is significant. Prior to this he was chiefly characterized by clever, treacherous dealings. From now on he was the prince of God.

2. Character of Jacob.

The early years of Jacob's life are remembered mainly for his two acts of treachery; purchasing Esau's birthright and deceiving his blind father to steal Esau's blessing. These two incidents are familiar to every student. We should not excuse Jacob for these two deeds, nor approve his ethics. However, it may be well to remember two or three facts. Esau cared nothing for these privileges which Jacob wanted. Jacob had great ambition (not to be condemned) and real appreciation of these things which had meant so much to Abraham and Isaac. Rebekah, Jacob's mother, encouraged him in his unethical designs. It should be remembered also that Jacob later suffered the consequences of his deeds.

3. The Birthright and the Father's Blessing.

According to Hebrew law the first-born should always possess the birthright, which involved a double portion of the property. It carried with it also the privilege of leadership in the family and tribe. Thus Jacob had good reasons for wanting the birthright which belonged to Esau because, even though he and Jacob were twins, Esau was the first-born. Among the Hebrews, as with other Oriental people, great importance was attached to the ceremony in which the father formally gave his "blessing" to his children. It carried the authority of a will, and involved, especially in religious matters, a sort of prophecy or foretelling of their place in the future. The father's pronouncement of greatness for the future naturally would be coveted by young Jacob.

4. Fleeing from Home.

In these stories we get a glimpse of a divided family. Rebekah was passionately devoted to Jacob, always taking his part and encouraging, if not actually engineering, his ambitious designs. Isaac, while not aggressive, was inclined to favor Esau. Thus, when Jacob had carried out his design against Esau, who in his anger became a threat to Jacob, Rebekah assisted Jacob in his plans to escape, and circulated a previously arranged tale that he was going away to secure a wife.

Jacob fled from the fury of his brother, and naturally would turn northward to seek the home of his mother's kinspeople. His first day's travel brought him to Bethel, a well known stopping place, where his grandfather Abraham had previously lived. At this point the homesick, lonely Jacob spent a memorable night. Here Jehovah, the God of his fathers, spoke to him. Jacob made his solemn vow to Jehovah promising in return for Jehovah's favor his faithful service and one tenth of his possessions. He enjoyed the blessings of Jehovah, but became so absorbed in other things that he later forgot his sacred vows to God.

5. From Bethel to Haran.

Leaving Bethel he journeyed northward to Haran, the old home of his mother Rebekah and her family. Though he did not know it at the time he was to spend twenty eventful years in this area. Shortly after his arrival he met Rachel, the daughter of Laban who was the brother of Rebekah. Jacob fell in love with her at first sight. "And Jacob kissed Rachel, and lifted up his voice, and wept." This is the beginning of a romance which lasted through the years and was terminated only with the untimely death of his beloved Rachel years later on his return to his ancestral home at Hebron.

6. Jacob's Family.

The writer of Genesis gives in considerable detail the experiences of Jacob with Laban, the brother of Rebekah, his mother. Jacob, who was a shrewd bargainer, had no particular difficulty in dealing with easy-going Esau, but in Laban he met a worthy foe. Laban's treachery is first exhibited in his deception of Jacob at the time of his marriage. By the terms of their agreement Jacob was to work for seven years for Rachel. "And Jacob served seven years for Rachel; and they seemed unto him but a few days, for the love he had to her." In good faith Jacob kept his part of the contract. The time for the wedding came. The ceremony was at night and the bride was heavily veiled. Only after the ceremony did Jacob discover that Laban had deceived him by substituting Leah, the older sister, for Rachel. When Jacob hotly protested his father-in-law calmly stated that it was not customary "in our place to give the younger before the first-born." Jacob loved Rachel but was informed by her father that he could have her only by working seven more years. He had no alternative but to accept the terms of Laban. However, he understood now the character of the man with whom he was to deal. In his subsequent dealings with Laban he was able not only to take care of himself, but to become prosperous. In the meantime his family was growing.

Leah, Rachel and two concubines bore children to him. The writer of Genesis mentions twelve sons and one daughter.

7. Return to Canaan.

The years at Paddan-Aram passed swiftly, if not too happily for Jacob. He never intended to live here permanently so the vision of God with the command to return to Canaan was welcomed. But in carrying out the command he faced two difficulties. Laban, for obvious reasons, did not want him to leave. Then too, he was fearful of his meeting with Esau back at home. After one unsuccessful attempt he was at last able to escape with his family, his flocks and herds. This journey home would be difficult enough without the problem of meeting Esau. But Jacob, resourceful and determined, made his way homeward.

8. Reconciliation With Esau.

Esau and his descendants were settled in the land of Edom, directly south of Hebron and the Dead Sea. Jacob could have settled in central Canaan without having to meet Esau, but he was now determined to clear up the old difference with his brother, and to live in peace. As he followed the old route southward in Palestine east of the Jordan he came to the little river Jabbok which emptied into the Jordan river one hundred miles north of Mt. Seir, Esau's home. From here he sent messengers requesting a reconciliation with Esau. His emissaries returned with the announcement that Esau was coming with four hundred men to meet him. Deeply disturbed, Jacob prepared for the worst. To his great surprise, however, Esau came not to war, but with peaceable intent. Jacob presented costly gifts to his brother and the two were reconciled. Esau returned to his own home, leaving Jacob to follow his course homeward without interference.

9. From "Jacob" to "Israel."

On the banks of the Jabbok while anxiously awaiting his meeting with Esau, Jacob had a very stirring experience. He spent a whole night in prayer, struggling with an angel. Whatever difficulties we may have in explaining the details of this strange experience, certain important facts are clear. God spoke to Jacob, made a covenant with him and changed his name from Jacob (supplanter) to Israel (prince of God). From this time Jacob was a changed man. The weaknesses in character up to now so prominent in his career, began to disappear.

Henceforth life was characterized by a deep devotion to the work of God. He was now a man with a mission. His strong gifts were to be used no longer for unworthy and selfish purposes, but for God. He was at last a prince of God walking in the ways of Abraham.

10. Back to Bethel.

After his experiences east of the Jordan, Jacob moved westward across the river and settled for a while at the old city of Shechem. While here his two sons, Levi and Simeon, were involved in difficulties with the Canaanites which made it necessary for them to move. Directed by God he brought his family to Bethel where as a fugitive he had previously made his vow to Jehovah. No doubt he had failed to keep this vow in his years at Haran. At any rate he now renewed the vow and Jehovah, the God of his fathers, spoke to him words of great promise concerning his place in the program of the Hebrew people. "And God said unto him, I am God Almighty; be fruitful and multiply; a nation and a company of nations shall be of thee, and kings shall come out of thy loins; and the land which I gave unto Abraham and Isaac, to thee will I give it, and to thy seed after thee will I give it." (Gen. 35:11-12.) After this experience he built an altar and worshiped there calling the place Bethel (house of God).

11. The End of a True Romance.

Leaving Bethel he proceeded southward with his family and possessions. A short distance south of the place where Jerusalem now stands, a great loss came to him. Here his beloved Rachel gave birth to his last child who was given the name Benjamin, but Jacob's joy was soon mingled with sorrow, for in this experience Rachel died. From the time of their first meeting years before Jacob had loved her with a genuine devotion. Her death now left him bereft and deeply grieved. Naturally he wanted to place her body in the ancient burial place at Hebron, but due to circumstances this could not be done. So he laid her to rest in a plot hard by the road-way just north of Bethlehem and set a pillar above her grave to mark the spot. The traveler on the road from Jerusalem to Bethlehem today sees this place marked now by "the Tomb of Rachel."

12. At Home Again.

Jacob was destined to experience more trouble because of his sons who were reckless and undisciplined. Even before he finally reached Hebron their behavior brought fresh problems and embarrassment to him. At last he came to Hebron whence he had fled years ago. With what emotions he must have hurried to his father, now enfeebled by old age! Did this old man and his son talk over the deceptive deeds of the ambitious young man in other years? Did Isaac now realize that even though Jacob's methods had been foul and false, God had brought about the proper outcome after all? Be that as it may, Isaac's time was fast running out. Before long Isaac "gave up the ghost, and died, and was gathered unto his people, old and full of days" (one hundred and eighty years). He was tenderly laid away by his sons Jacob and Esau.

13. Later Experiences of Jacob.

While the career of Jacob extends for some years over into the career of Joseph, which we shall relate more fully in the next section, it may be well to summarize these later experiences at this point. Hebron was to be his home in Palestine. His ten older sons wandered from place to place pasturing their flocks. Joseph, next to the youngest son, was sold by them to be taken as a slave to Egypt, though they deceived their father by pretending that his favorite son was destroyed by wild beasts. It was only years afterwards that these sons, going down to Egypt for grain at the time of famine, discovered that Joseph was alive and was next to Pharaoh as ruler in Egypt. They brought with them, not only this welcome news to Jacob, but the invitation of Joseph for his father, with all his sons and their families, to come to Egypt to live during the years of the famine. The old patriarch thus went down to Egypt, met his long-lost son, and lived in comfort the remainder of his life. Just before he died his sons gathered about his bedside for their father's blessing. When he had exacted from them the promise to bury his body not in Egypt but in the cave of Machpelah at Hebron, with that of his father, "he yielded up the ghost and was gathered unto his people."

SECTION IV — THE CAREER OF JOSEPH (Genesis 37-50).

1. An Inspiring Career.

There is no more admirable or attractive man in all of the Old Testament than Joseph. He possessed so many desirable qualities — generosity, high ideals, unselfishness, clean living, a forgiving spirit — that one is inspired by even the most casual study of his life. From the standpoint of literature alone, the story of Joseph ranks as one of the greatest narratives ever written. This classic story will never cease to be a favorite, especially with young people.

2. His Early Life.

Joseph was the first-born son of Jacob and Rachel, Benjamin the last. For some reason Joseph seems to have been the favorite son of his father. Perhaps the fact that he was the son of Rachel may have contributed to this. It may have been because the wild, reckless dispositions of his elder brothers were in such contrast to his gentle, responsive attitude toward his father. Or did Jacob surmise this early that this lovable boy of his was destined to great things under Jehovah his God? Joseph had two remarkable dreams, the meaning of which was unmistakable, and he (perhaps thoughtlessly) related these to his elder brethren. This, together with the undisguised favoritism their father had already exhibited toward Joseph, aroused the anger and jealously of his brothers to the point of danger.

3. Sold Into Slavery.

The ten older brothers, like all shepherds, must find pasturage for their flocks. Beginning early in the season in the south around Hebron they worked northward. After an absence from home of several weeks Jacob naturally was anxious for news of them. Accordingly he sent Joseph, bedecked in the handsome coat he had given him, to get a report from his sons. The lad journeyed north for some miles and finally overtook them at Dothan near Shechem. They saw him at a distance, and in jealousy and anger decided at first to slay him. Reuben dissuaded them from this evil deed, but in the temporary absence of Reuben later they decided upon another plan which was suggested by the approach of some Midianite merchants on the way to Egypt. They could sell Joseph as a slave to these merchants. When this transaction was completed they took his coat, rent it, dipped it in the blood of a kid and then took it to Jacob with the declaration that they had found this coat by accident. Their father would naturally assume that his son had been slain by wild beasts. This heartless deception of their father reveals the cruel and unprincipled nature of these elder sons of Jacob.

4. Slave and Prisoner in Egypt.

When Joseph reached Egypt he was sold as a slave to Potiphar, an officer of the Pharaoh. Joseph accepted the situation, behaved wisely, and soon was in such high favor with his master that he was placed in the highest position of the household. Then came Joseph's great temptation. Potiphar's wife became infatuated with him and used every means to induce Joseph to commit adultery with her.

In his refusal Joseph exhibited great strength of character. "How then can I do this great wickedness and sin against God?" She then charged him with the very crime which he had refused to commit. Naturally a slave would have no chance before Potiphar when accused by his own wife. On evidence which was wholly circumstantial Joseph was convicted and placed in prison. In this experience also the Lord was with Joseph so that he soon rose to a place of authority over all the other prisoners. Among the prisoners were the chief cup-bearer and the chief baker of Pharaoh. Each of these had a dream which Joseph interpreted. The butler was to be restored to Pharaoh's favor in three days, but the baker was to die. Joseph's prediction was realized, but the butler, being released, straightway forgot his promise to intercede for Joseph.

5. *Dreams of Plenty and Famine.*

Joseph remained in prison for two more years. Then Pharaoh himself had two dreams which none of his wise men could interpret. In this connection the butler remembered Joseph who had interpreted his dream and favored him. At his suggestion Joseph was summoned and appeared before the Pharaoh. Upon hearing these dreams Joseph announced the meaning of them as coming from Jehovah his God. The seven fat kine and seven good ears denoted seven years of abundant crops which were to be followed by seven years of famine as denoted by the lean kine and poor ears. He advised Pharaoh to appoint a food commissioner to store up supplies in the years of plenty against the years of famine which were to follow.

6. *"Second Only to Pharaoh."*

To his great surprise Joseph was appointed by Pharaoh to assume responsibility for the program which he had just recommended. He was dressed in royal robes and was given an Egyptian name, Zaphenath-Paneah (revealer of secrets) and an Egyptian maid, Asenath, was given to him as his wife. To Joseph and his wife, two sons, Ephraim and Manasseh, were born. At thirty years of age this young Hebrew who was sold as a slave, occupied the most prominent position in the rich and famous land of Egypt. Joseph, with amazing executive gifts, began his work and as the land produced abundant harvests in these favored years he stored up grain for the lean years to come. Then came the famine when all the land suffered and people from surrounding countries came to Joseph for supplies. His position was "second only to Pharaoh"; his service comparable to that of any man of his time.

7. The Brothers' First Visit to Egypt.

The effects of the famine were not confined to Egypt. In Canaan the pastures withered, cattle died, and men were hungry. Jacob and his sons, like all others, were in need of food. So the ten older brothers came down to Egypt to buy grain. When they came into the presence of Joseph they did not recognize him, probably thinking that the hard life of a slave had long since killed him. But he recognized them, though he did not reveal himself. He tested them by rough treatment, accused them of being spies, and agreed to sell them corn only on the condition that their brother Simeon should be kept as a hostage until they should bring the youngest brother, Benjamin, to take his place. Reluctantly they agreed to these terms. After departing they were surprised and puzzled to find that each man's money had been placed in his sack of corn. Upon their return they told Jacob of their experiences, and the conditions on which they might go down again for grain. However, the aged father vowed that Benjamin should never leave him.

8. Their Second Visit to Egypt.

As time passed and the famine continued the family of Jacob was again forced to find food. Egypt offered the only hope. Judah then persuaded Jacob to let Benjamin go with him, vowing that he would assume full responsibility for him. Furnished now with double money and an extra gift, the brothers returned to Egypt taking their youngest brother with them. They were received courteously by court attendants, Simeon was restored to them and they were told that they were to dine that day with Joseph himself. When Joseph came at noon and saw Benjamin he was so overcome with emotion that he retired for a while to weep alone. The brothers ate with Joseph without recognizing him.

Next morning, having completed their purchase of grain they started their journey home. When only a short distance from the court they were overtaken by the servant of Joseph who charged that one of them had stolen his master's silver cup. They denied the charge but when their sacks were searched they were dismayed to find it in Benjamin's sack, where unknown to them it had been placed at the order of Joseph. Returning to Joseph they protested their innocence, but Joseph declared that Benjamin must remain in Egypt.

The intercessory plea of Judah, explaining the grief this loss would bring their aged father, and offering himself for his youngest brother's release, is one of the most eloquent and touching speeches in literature.

When Judah had finished, Joseph, unable to keep his secret longer, made himself known to them. This moving scene should be read in full in order to appreciate its beauty. At last Joseph told them to return to Canaan, tell Jacob all that had occurred and then to bring him and all his family to Egypt to live. One can imagine the feelings of these brothers, now forgiven and genuinely humbled, as they hurried home to tell their story to their father. Joseph provided them with wagons for the return to Egypt and sent rich gifts to his father.

9. Living in Egypt.

Jacob, overjoyed with the news of his son Joseph whose death he had mourned through the years, quickly decided to go to Egypt to see his son. At Beersheba on the way down God appeared to him, promised his blessings upon him in the transfer to Egypt and renewed his promise to him as to the destiny of his sons, and assured him that in due time his family should be brought back to their homeland of Canaan.

The account of Joseph's meeting his father, then introducing him to the Pharaoh and arranging for their living in Egypt reveals the noblest qualities in the life of one of the finest characters in the Old Testament.

10. The Death of Jacob and Joseph.

At the invitation of Joseph and by permission of the Pharaoh the families of Jacob were settled in the fertile territory in eastern Egypt, known as the "land of Goshen." Since they were shepherds they were to keep the regal herds. Thus they were happily occupied and were treated with courtesy and respect. At the age of one hundred and forty-seven years Israel, the aged prince of God, came to the end of his days. His sons, in keeping their promise, took his body after it was embalmed back to Canaan for burial in the cave of Machpelah beside that of his father. The death of their father brought no change in the status of the Israelites in Egypt. Joseph quieted their fears with the assurance of his good will and the Egyptians did not molest them. At the age of one hundred and ten years Joseph called his brothers about his bed, reminded them that in due time they were to return to Canaan, then having secured their promise to take his body back to the homeland with them, he quietly passed away. His body was embalmed, placed in a casket, and was kept until the time when they should go back to the land of their fathers. We close this period with the descendants of Jacob residing in Egypt, having been there approximately seventy years when Joseph died.

11. Social and Religious Life of the Patriarchs.

In closing our study of these patriarchs it will be well to look briefly at some aspects of their daily living. To begin with, they were not a crude, uncultured group, as is often supposed. Their life was flavored with certain refinements, hospitality, courteous entertainment, and an appreciation of finer things. To be sure nomadic life prevailed, but this does not assume barbarous customs. They were wealthy, having, in addition to their great flocks and herds, an abundance of jewerly (rings, bracelets, necklaces, earrings, jewels set in silver and gold), and precious metals which they used as money. There is also frequent mention of fine raiment.

The religious life of the patriarchs seems to have been very simple. They erected altars, made their sacrifices, and probably made offerings of the tithe to Jehovah. Prayer, simple but genuine, was offered in times of special need, and no doubt was a part of the daily life of devout men like Abraham. Their attitude toward God was one of genuine reverence and real faith. They gave evidence of the quality of their faith by the great respect that was always accorded the rights and the interests of other people. In a word, their religious life was without the elaborate forms later developed, but was humble and sincere.

12. Light From Archaeology.

Archaeologists have discovered many things which pertain to this period of Bible history. A few of the striking results of these discoveries may now be summarized briefly.

The man Abraham has been rescued from the vague, indefinite area of myth so that he can now be considered a real historical character. Let the statements of two competent archaeologists suffice as proof: "The extraordinary accuracy of the narratives of the Patriarchs, when tested by our rapidly accumulating material, is no longer surprising. . . . It is difficult to see anything remarkable in the conclusion which has been forced upon us by recent archaeological discoveries, that the saga of the Patriarchs is essentially historical."*

*Albright, F. W.: *Archaeology of Palestine and the Bible, 3rd Edition*, pp. 144-145.

"The Old Testament evidences supported by the independent testimony of secular literature, justifies us in holding that there was such a person, that he was an Aramean or Amorite, the founder and head of a clan that later developed into the Hebrew nation, that he lived originally at Ur in Mesopotamia, that he and his people moved thence into northern Syria, and subsequently into Palestine, and that he lived in about the twentieth century before Christ."*

The fact that the name Abraham has been found on cuneiform tablets which are dated at this period strengthens the contention that he was an actual person. It is very significant that the word *Habiru,* found in tablets in southern Babylonia, designating Aramean nomads of Abraham's time, is now accepted by reputable scholars as the same as the word Hebrew. This substantiates the view that Abraham was the father of the Hebrew nation.

The Biblical accounts of the sojourns of Abraham, Jacob, and Joseph into Egypt are not now considered unjustifiable "inventions," in view of the facts which are available. The Tell-el-Amarna tablets indicate that this was the time of the "empire age" of Egypt when the land of Canaan was a part of the empire, and travel between Canaan and Egypt was not only possible but was actual. Semitic traders are pictured on Egyptian monuments of this age, and the translations of old documents state that Bedouin travelers were allowed to pass freely over the border between the two countries.

Egyptian inscriptions tell of serious famines and of Egyptian assistance to people in such times. The Tell-el-Amarna letters tell of the rise of great power in Egypt of a man called "Dudu" (David) dating around the 14th century before Christ. His career is strikingly similar to that of Joseph in Egypt.

Not all the difficulties belonging to this period have been cleared up, but valuable help has come from the work of archaeologists dealing with life in Bible lands of this period.

*Woolley, Sir Leonard: *Abraham,* p. 50.

Chapter VII

DELIVERED FROM BONDAGE

Exodus, Leviticus, Numbers, Deuteronomy

Section I — Introduction.
1. Summary of This Period. 2. Chronology of the Period. 3. Egyptian Life and Culture.

Section II — Slavery and Deliverance (Exodus 1-14).
1. The Hebrews in Egypt. 2. Increase of the Israelites. 3. Their Changed Status. 4. Other Attempts to Suppress. 5. Birth of Moses. 6. His Boyhood and Education. 7. Crisis and Choice. 8. Life in Midian. 9. The Burning Bush. 10. The Great Task. 11. Resistance of Pharaoh. 12. Ten Plagues. 13. Passover. 14. Crossing the Red Sea. 15. Route of the Exodus. 16. Significance of the Exodus. 17. What Israel Learned in Egypt. 18. Archaeological Items.

Section III — At Mt. Sinai (Exodus 15-40).
1. A Study in Leadership. 2. Fresh Mercies Daily. 3. In the Wilderness of Sin. 4. The Suggestion of Jethro. 5. Around Mt. Sinai. 6. How the Law Was Communicated. 7. Law of Moses. 8. Ten Commandments. 9. Golden Calf. 10. The Tabernacle. 11. Code of Hammurabi.

Section IV — Wanderings in the Wilderness (Numbers 10-20).
1. Leaving Mt. Sinai. 2. Encamped at Kadesh-Barnea. 3. Breakdown of Faith. 4. Tragedy of the Forty Years. 5. Rebellion of Korah. 6. Mistake of Moses and Aaron. 7. Death of Aaron. 8. Fiery Serpents.

Section V — Advancing Toward the Promised Land (Numbers 21-36; Deuteronomy 28-34).
1. In the Territory of Sihon. 2. Kingdom of Og. 3. Among the Moabites. 4. Balak and Balaam. 5. Defeating Midian. 6. Settling East of the Jordan. 7. Selection of Joshua. 8. Farewell of Moses. 9. Death of Moses. 10. An Appraisal of Moses.

Delivered From Bondage

Section I — INTRODUCTION.

1. Summary of This Period.

In point of time involved this period covers several hundred years, from the time of Joseph's death to about 1250 b.c. The question of chronology here is a debatable one about which we shall speak later in the chapter. Geographically, the territory or countries concerned are Egypt, the wilderness area between Egypt and Palestine including the regions of Mt. Sinai, Edom, Moab, and eastern Palestine. The chief events to be considered are: the status of the Hebrews in Egypt after Joseph, the birth and preparation of Moses, deliverance from Egyptian bondage, the Exodus including the experiences at Mt. Sinai, the failure at Kadesh-Barnea, the forty years of wandering, the advance toward Canaan through Moab and eastern Palestine, the death of Moses and preparations for the conquest under Joshua.

The Biblical account of these events is given in four books, Exodus, Leviticus, Numbers and Deuteronomy. Exodus (going out) is so named because it is chiefly concerned with the departure of the Hebrews from Egypt. It contains forty chapters and begins with the story of the oppression of the Hebrews in Egypt and closes with the story of the tabernacle at Mt. Sinai. Leviticus, containing twenty-seven chapters, is the Levitical book which is concerned with the worship of the Hebrews (priesthood, offerings, and various laws). Numbers, thirty-six chapters, is composed of narratives, giving vivid experiences in the wilderness, legal matters and statistics. Deuteronomy (second law giving) containing thirty-four chapters, while largely devoted to the laws governing the Hebrew people, has important historical accounts of the experiences of the Hebrews journeying toward Canaan.

2. The Chronology of the Period.

For a long time the chronology involved in the events of this period has been a problem about which scholars have differed widely. It is difficult to fix the date of Jacob's moving his sons and their families to live in Egypt. It is equally difficult to speak with certainty about the date of the Exodus. To this writer the heart of the problem seems to be in determining the time for this historic departure from Egypt. In general there are two periods or centuries which are held by

different students as the time for this event. There are many who
insist that it was about 1250 B.C. and that the great Rameses II was
the Pharaoh of the Oppression. The other school holds that the proper
date was about two centuries earlier, namely 1450-1400 B.C. To present
adequately the involved arguments for each of these dates would
require far more space than is available in this study. In recent years the
later date (1250 B.C.) seems to have gained a majority of adherents.
Those who take this position are willing to concede that there are
strong arguments for the other date, and that there are some difficulties
involved in accepting a date as late as 1250 B.C.

3. Egyptian Life and Culture.

It will be profitable to the student at this point to get a glimpse
of the civilization and the cultural life in the Egyptain empire of this
period. In recent years we have been able to understand how far
advanced Egyptian life was. It was radically different from the nomadic
life of Semitic peoples like the Hebrews. The several hundred years
residence of the Israelites in Egypt must have affected them in many
ways.

In contrast with the pastoral life of Semitic peoples the basis of
Egyptian life was a settled one, mostly on small farms. However,
there were cities in which merchandising and other enterprises were
carried on. No doubt most of the people were poor and lived in small
homes or huts. Because of the mild climate they were able to cook,
eat and even sleep outdoors. However there were rich families who
occupied large homes built of brick, elaborately planned and furnished.
There were many slaves who cultivated the fields and served in the
homes of the wealthy. The lot of the slave there, as elsewhere, seems
to have been very hard. We are told that in the building of the famous
pyramid of Cheops, seen by every traveler in Egypt, approximately
100,000 slaves were employed for twenty years and that unknown
thousands of them were killed by overwork and abuse.

The mild climate, together with the rich soil deposited by the
regular overflow of the Nile river, made it possible to produce
abundant harvests of various crops including a good variety of fruits.
Wheat, barley, cucumbers, leek, melons, onions, beans, sesame and
lupin were grown in abundance. The rich pasture lands would support
large herds of cattle, sheep and goats. Milk, cheese, many kinds of
fish and different fruits were also available for food. Flowers of many
kinds were to be seen everywhere.

An ancient papyrus roll tells something of the plentiful and varied delights available to the citizens of ancient Egypt. "Its fields are full of good things, and life passes in constant plenty and abundance. Its canals are rich in fish; its lakes swarm with birds; its meadows are green with vegetables; there is no end of the lentils; melons with a taste like honey grow in the irrigated fields. Its barns are full of wheat and durra, and reach as high as heaven. Onions and sesame are in the enclosures, and the apple-tree (?) blooms. The vine and the almond-tree and the fig-tree grow in its gardens. Sweet is their wine for the inhabitants of Keim. They mix it with honey. The red fish is in the lotus canal, the Borian fish in the ponds; many kinds of Bori fish, besides carp and pike, in the land of Pu-harotha; fat fish and Khiptipennu fish are in the pools of the inundation; the Hanax fish in the full month of the Nile, near the city of the conqueror (Tanis)."*

In the arts and sciences they were well ahead of other peoples of their day. Their acquaintance with mathematics and physics is revealed in the construction of the pyramids and temples built by them. They had great libraries in which were the works of their scholars. There were schools where the young men of the upper classes were taught. One of the papyri speaks of the detailed instruction given these youth who were to be in government service. Reading, writing, spelling, grammar, arithmetic, geometry, bookkeeping, law and sacred literature were all in the curriculum. In Acts 7:22 Stephen speaks of Moses as being "learned in all the wisdom of the Egyptians." They were religious people and worshiped many different gods. They had their temples with many priests who were well educated and had a preferred place in society. They worshiped different animals, but the chief of these was the sacred bull Opis. This bull was kept in a magnificent temple and was worshiped by all the people. The Hebrew people evidently were impressed by this custom since during the Exodus when they decided to make a god which they could see they made the golden calf.

Section II — SLAVERY AND DELIVERANCE (Exodus 1-14).

1. The Hebrews in Egypt.

The Hebrew people were located in the fertile region of Goshen in the land of Egypt. Joseph died at one hundred and ten years of

*Blaikie: *A Manual of Bible History, Revised 1940*, p. 67. Thomas Nelson and Sons. Used by permission.

age, some seventy years after his father and his brethren settled in the land. There is a wide difference of opinion as to how long they remained in Egypt before the Exodus, and also as to how many "souls" there were when they made their departure from the land of Goshen. One matter however, about which there is no question, is the change in their condition between the death of Joseph and the beginning of the Exodus.

2. Increase of the Israelites.

Whatever may have been the total number of Israelites in Egypt in the days of Jacob, that number soon began to multiply. In Exodus 1:7 we read: "And the children of Israel were fruitful, and increased abundantly, and multiplied, and waxed exceeding mighty, and the land was filled with them." In this brief statement we have five expressions to indicate their rapid increase in numbers. In Exodus 12:37 we have the statement that at the time of their departure from Egypt they numbered six hundred thousand men, beside children. Was such an increase in numbers possible during their stay in Egypt? Many scholars hold that it was possible because of two or three considerations. They were an Oriental people who had the religious conviction that they should "multiply and replenish the earth"; they lived in a warm climate; and they would have to double their number only every twenty-five years in order to attain this number. Whatever view one may take of the actual number we may be assured that the number was "very great," they were regarded as a real threat to the government, and the Egyptians were determined to reduce their number.

3. Their Changed Status.

"There arose a new king over Egypt that knew not Joseph." As long as Joseph their kinsman, who occupied such a prominent place in governmental affairs, was alive they were in a favored position. They had homes, provisions and employment and were cordially accepted. As time passed, however, conditions changed. The new ruler inaugurated a new policy toward them. They came to be regarded as foreigners, and because of the very rapid increase in their number they were feared as a potential threat to the security of the government. The Pharaoh, now determined to reduce them to slavery, set cruel taskmasters over them and forced them to do the hardest kind of public work, that of making bricks. Under these conditions the sons of Jacob were no longer a free people, welcome guests in another land, but were slaves whose lot was one of oppression and suffering.

4. Other Attempts to Suppress.

Despite the cruel treatment inflicted upon them in this unbearably hard service the Hebrews continued to multiply. At length, when more severe measures were necessary, the order was officially given that all midwives serving at the birth of Hebrew children should kill the male babies but spare the females. The midwives refused to carry out these orders and the Hebrew boys were spared. Finally the Pharaoh issued the desparate command to all his people: "Every son that is born ye shall cast into the river." There is no way of knowing how many Hebrew boys were destroyed under this order. We know of one who was not destroyed.

5. Birth of Moses.

In this setting we are introduced to the life and work of the most important man in Old Testament history. Some secular historians rank this man Moses, as one of the greatest men in all history. Some one has estimated that one seventh of the Old Testament story is devoted to the work of this remarkable character. He was a statesman, lawgiver, historian, emancipator, poet and prophet.

Moses was the son of Amram and Jochebed, of the tribe of Levi. He had an older sister named Miriam and an older brother named Aaron. He was born at the time when Pharaoh's order for the death of all male Hebrew babies was being enforced. For the first three months his mother concealed him at home, but later was forced to find a hiding place elsewhere. Taking a little papyrus boat (basket) and making it water tight, Jochebed placed the boy in it and hid it among the reeds in the shallow waters of the Nile while Miriam stayed on shore to watch. A daughter of Pharaoh came to the river and discovered the ark. She opened it to find the boy whose frightened cries stirred her heart and caused her to announce her intention of adopting this beautiful child as her own. Miriam's suggestion that she get a Hebrew woman to nurse this baby enabled Moses' own mother to take charge of her boy. In this way God provided for the nurture and training of the one who was destined to perform such a magnificent task in history.

6. Boyhood and Education.

The record in Exodus is silent concerning the boyhood of Moses. In Acts (7:22) Stephen says that "He was learned in all the wisdom of Egypt." The writer of Hebrews (11:25) declares that he might have enjoyed all the pleasures of Egypt. It is not too much to imagine that as the adopted son of Pharaoh's daughter, he would be given the benefits of the best training available to the royal family and that he might have had a place in the fortunes of the royal family. We can be certain that his own mother in the intimacy of her relation with her son would tell him many a story of his forefathers (Abraham, Isaac, Jacob and Joseph) and would acquaint him with their plans for the Hebrew people as God's chosen race. It was the kind of story to grip his imagination, strengthen his loyalty to his own people and stir hopes and dreams in his heart. God was preparing a man for great achievements in the years to come.

7. Crisis and Choice.

The career of Moses naturally falls into three periods of forty years each. The first of these was the years of training and preparation in Egypt. The second period was spent in the land of Midian, and was a time of unconscious preparation. The third was the period of actual accomplishment of his task. When he was forty years old the crisis came unexpectedly. He saw an Egyptian beating one of his fellow-men. In righteous anger he slew the oppressor and hid his body in the sand. He had already made up his mind. Henceforth he was to cast his lot with his unfortunate people whatever the cost, having chosen "rather to suffer ill treatment with the people of God than to enjoy the pleasures of sin for a season: accounting the reproach of Christ greater riches than the treasures of Egypt: for he looked unto the recompense of reward." (Heb. 11:25-26). He probably expected that his brethren would accept him as their deliverer and support him, but an incident the next day convinced him that this was not the case. Hence to save his life, he fled to the wilderness of Midian.

8. Life in Midian.

The region to which he fled was the peninsula of Sinai, a desolate, barren area between two gulfs. Apparently he crossed this triangular peninsula to the eastern side around the Gulf of Akabah where the Midianites, the descendants of Abraham and Keturah, lived. Here he found employment guarding the herds of Jethro, the priest of Midian. He later married the daughter of Jethro, who bore him two sons. Here for forty years Moses lived the quiet life of a shepherd. He would have time for meditation on the things taught by his mother and for digesting the learning of Egypt. He would learn also the ways of the desert tribes and the source of food and water and, what was more important, would become acquainted with the topography of the land through which he was to lead the Hebrew people in the long, weary years of their wanderings between Egypt and Canaan. The hand of God can easily be seen in this period of the life of Moses.

9. The Burning Bush.

The years in the wilderness of Midian were brought to an end by a memorable experience near Mt. Horeb. While tending the flock Moses saw a bush burning with fire, but was puzzled to discover that is was not being consumed. Drawing nearer to learn the cause of this mystery he heard the voice of God speaking to him: "Moses, Moses . . . draw not hither; put off thy shoes from off thy feet, for the place whereon thou standest is holy ground." God then identified himself as the God of Abraham, Isaac and Jacob, told Moses that he had heard the cries of his people in bondage, that he was to deliver them, and that he, Moses was to be the leader in this great undertaking. Awed by the enormity of the task and feeling unworthy, he offered several reasons why he could not undertake this gigantic task. God answered each of these objections and at length Moses consented to undertake it. Special re-enforcements and encouragement were given him. "I will be with thee." He should have special signs to prove this authority. Finally Aaron, his older brother who was eloquent in speech, should go with him, and Moses himself was assured by the words of the Almighty: "I will teach thee what thou shalt say." A new epoch has opened. One of the monumental undertakings in history is about to begin.

10. The Great Task.

Was Moses fully aware of the obstacles and difficulties he must meet in his new undertaking? Certainly he knew some of them, but mercifully not all of them. One of the greatest obstacles was that of persuading the people themselves that they could and ought to do this. They had lost consciousness of their mission as a race. For long years they had been slaves, and their confidence in themselves had been destroyed by these years of servitude. They were defeated and demoralized. Moses was to build up their morale, persuade them that they could and must leave Egypt. Then too, he must get the consent of Pharaoh for their departure. One may wonder why Pharaoh would not readily consent to their leaving Egypt when for years he had sought to reduce their number. We should remember that they were still slaves, and that these hundreds of thousands of serfs were a big economic asset to the Pharaoh. To be sure he did not want them to be numerous enough to rebel successfully against him, but he would not willingly surrender this vast number who were working for him as slaves without any cost. After Moses had succeeded in overcoming these two difficulties, his real work was still ahead. To organize and plan all the details connected with the moving of this vast multitude of men, women and children with all their possessions, to provide for all their needs as they moved through a desert country infested with hostile tribes, was a task that might make any man shudder.

11. Resistance of Pharaoh.

Moses and Aaron, after establishing their leadership among their own brethren, now appeared before the Pharaoh to get his consent for their people to leave Egypt. Pharaoh defiantly refused to grant this and ordered his taskmasters to increase the already severe requirements made of these slaves. They must not only make the same number of brick hitherto required of them when the straw was furnished for the bricks, but in addition must provide their own straw. To overcome the resistance of this monarch God is to send ten plagues to the people of Egypt. The behaviour of Pharaoh in these crises is an interesting study. With the coming of each plague he gives his consent for the Hebrews to depart, but when the plague is stayed he changes his mind until a more severe pestilence is sent.

12. Ten Plagues.

The detailed account of these ten plagues with their results is too long to attempt to repeat here, but it is well to note that each succeeding plague became more severe than the former until the climax was reached in the death of the first-born in all the land. The order of these is as follows: (1) Water turned to blood, (2) Frogs, (3) Lice, (4) Flies, (5) Murrain, (6) Boils, (7) Hail, (8) Locusts, (9) Darkness, (10) Death of the first-born.

Every student will naturally ask the question, Were these plagues natural occurrences, which have taken place at other times in the valley of the Nile? Some scholars will answer that they are, and that there need not be any miracle here. It is true that at other times such plagues as lice and flies have been visited upon the land. However, in view of the increasing severity of these, and the timing of them (at the command of Moses), and the fact that the Hebrews were not subjected to them, it seems that the only satisfactory explanation of them is on the basis of the miraculous.

It should be remembered also that God had other purposes in mind by the use of these plagues. In this way the power of the God of the Hebrew people would be manifested. These plagues served also to frustrate the false ideas of the worship of the Egyptians. For example, the murrain (disease of the cattle) would expose the weakness of their worship of the sacred bull since this bull was expected to protect and save the cattle of the land. These miracles were a means by which Jehovah, the God of the Israelites, could show to all his power and superiority over the gods of the Egyptians.

13. The Passover.

The ordinance of the Passover, the first national religious feast of the Hebrews, was celebrated before the coming of the last plague, the death of the first-born in Egypt. Each Israelite family killed a lamb, partook of its flesh and then sprinkled its blood upon the door-posts of their home. The death angel was to *pass-over* the homes where this blood was spread. Thus the first-born children of the Israelites were spared while in all other homes the first-born children were stricken. This tragic event spread consternation over all the land and the Israelites were driven forth from the land. As they left they took with them jewels and other gifts which were "asked" (not "borrowed") of the Egyptians. The great movement was now under way. Their prayers had been answered and the days of bondage were over. Many hard experiences which were not anticipated were ahead, but at least they were now free and were on their way to the "Promised Land." From this time forth they were to observe annually this feast of the Passover. The slain lamb is a beautiful symbol of Christ.

14. Crossing of Red Sea.

Once on the march the Israelites proceeded from Rameses southward to Succoth on the first day. The next day they reached Etham. At this point the Lord gave direction to them by a pillar of cloud during the day and a pillar of fire by night. They were led, not around the north end of the Red Sea, but were commanded to make camp at Pi-hahiroth with the Red Sea in front of them. At this point they heard the forces of Pharaoh coming after them. To relieve their anxiety God caused the pillar of cloud and of fire to move from in front of them to a position behind them so as to hide them from the Egyptian army. In this crisis, with hills on either side, the sea in front and the Egyptians behind them, Moses prayed to God and received the command to go forward — in the face of the Red Sea. A strong east wind blew up during the night and caused the waters before them to divide and open up a passageway for them. The hosts of Israelites crossed during the darkness of night screened from their foes by the pillar of cloud. When all had safely crossed, the Egyptians, eager to overtake them, rushed into the passageway in pursuit of them. The wheels of their chariots came off, delay and confusion resulted and then the waters of the sea came back together to drown all the army of Egypt. Thus the Israelites were delivered from bondage and death. They recognized this as the deliverance of God and with great rejoicing Moses expressed their gratitude in a song of victory which he had composed for this purpose. (Exodus 15:1-18.)

15. Route of the Exodus.

The shortest route from the land of Goshen to Canaan would have been in the northeasterly direction along the coast of the Mediterranean. This familiar route was usually followed by travelers, and students naturally ask why these Israelites did not take this route. There were at least two good reasons why they did not. In the first place it would have led them directly into the territory of the Amalekites, a savage, fierce-fighting tribe of warriors. To lead the host of inexperienced Israelites, together with their wives and children, into this region would have meant nothing less than slaughter. A more important reason for following another course was the fact that God was to provide a specific course of preparation for their mission as a nation. They are not to go immediately to the Promised Land, but are to have a period of special instruction. They are to be led to the impressive setting of Mt. Sinai where the Law is to be given them and they are to be instructed in the details of this Law by which every phase of their living was to be regulated. This memorable experience at Mt. Sinai will be considered later in the chapter.

16. Significance of the Exodus.

The departure from Egypt completed in the crossing of the Red Sea is an event of great significance. In a real sense this marks the beginning of the Hebrew nation. They are now no longer a tribe of brethren with but little morale and limited vision, concerned chiefly with maintaining an existence. They are now a great multitude of people, a new nation conscious of some mission from God, embarking on the first stages of their course as a nation. Soon they are to learn

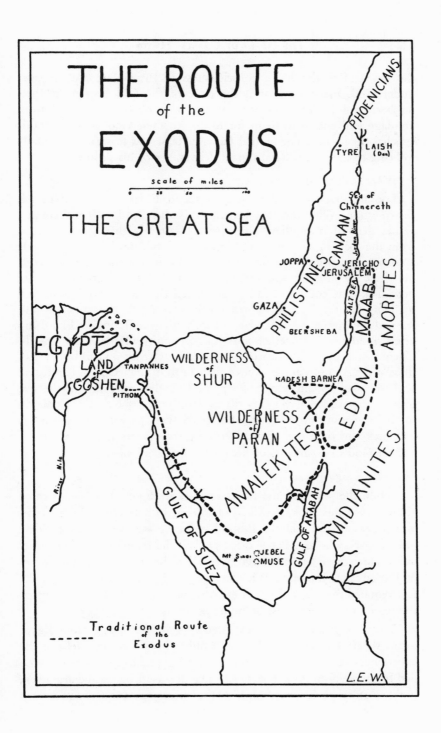

the law and to develop a consciousness of their place and purpose under God. From now until the close of the Old Testament their teachers and leaders will recount the miraculous deliverance from bondage and appeal to them for loyalty to their God because of this epochal experience. The annual Passover feast was to serve continually to bring to their mind God's great deliverance of his people.

17. What Israel Learned in Egypt.

Looking back over these long years in Egypt one is led to ask the question: What did they learn in this alien land? Were there any values derived from these hard years? Certainly they learned much from the social, governmental, business and cultural life of the people among whom they were forced to live. Their own life was nomadic, but here in this prosperous land, where settled agricultural life prevailed, they could not fail to get much that was desirable. Forced to "hang together" under oppression they were united as a people and learned the first lessons of loyalty to each other. Suffering and hardship often mold people together and produce unity of ideals and deeds. Then too, they would learn some religious truths. Could they not discern the strength and power of their faith in their God as contrasted with the shallow and empty forms of Egyptian religion? In the test of fire as oppressed slaves they discovered the real substance of religion in their relationship to God who heard their prayers, redeemed his promises and delivered them. Certainly these years in Egypt were a part of God's preparation of his people for their mission.

18. Archaeological Items.

While the work of the archaeologists in Egypt has been treated elsewhere in this book, it will be of interest to note two or three items which bear directly on the Biblical narrative we are studying. Some years ago Naville and Petrie discovered in the region of Goshen store-cities which have been declared by some to be the ancient storehouses of Pithom and Rameses. Whether the proof is conclusive or not the fact remains that these discoveries corroborate in general the view that the region of Goshen was the home of the Israelites in Egypt.

A unique parallel to the experience of Moses fleeing from Egypt to the desert (Asia) is the Tale of Sinuhe. This document tells of the experiences of a man named Sinuhe (an Egyptian of high rank) who fled from Egypt to Asia in 1970 B.C. The details of his escape are given, but the story of his hardships in the desert toward Canaan are of interest to every student of the life of Moses. It gives further proof of the frequent communications between the Egyptian people and the inhabitants of Palestine.

SECTION III — AT MT. SINAI (Exodus 15-40).

1. A Study in Leadership.

Having escaped from Egypt to enter the wilderness the problems of Moses were not over. In fact his real troubles were just beginning. The problem or organization and direction was a stupendous one. To administer the affairs of this vast multitude of people who were inexperienced in travel and unaccustomed to thinking for themselves required great skill and diplomacy. To guide them on the route, to deal with native tribes (sometimes involving war), to secure food and water, and to mediate differences among themselves were some of Moses' responsibilities. These were difficult enough had he been able to count on the united and hearty support of the Israelites themselves. Unfortunately, however, they caused some of his gravest difficulties. Again and again we are told of their complaining at hardships. They even charged Moses with the responsibility of getting them into these difficulties. Several times during the wilderness wanderings they openly rebelled against him. They even declared publicly their regret at having left Egypt and expressed the desire to be back there where they might eat the leek, garlic, onions, and melons of Goshen. At Mt. Sinai where they received the Law from God in the temporary absence of Moses, they erected and worshiped an idol in open violation of God's command. Moses as their authorized leader must deal with all these difficulties. The patience, tact, good judgment and unselfish spirit which Moses exhibited in dealing with this complaining and rebellious multitude is one of the most amazing exhibitions of great leadership in all history. Did any man ever attempt a greater task than Moses?

2. Fresh Mercies Daily.

God did not forsake Moses nor his people. To be sure they did meet difficulties frequently, but always they were directed by God and their needs were supplied. They were led by the pillar of cloud and fire. They were given manna and quail for their food. In their battles with hostile tribes they were led to victory. Miracles were very frequently employed to provide the necessities for their experiences in the wilderness. God kept his promises and led them in the way.

3. In the Wilderness of Sin.

The route to be followed by the Israelites was not the short direct way to Canaan. They were to go far down to Mt. Sinai to receive their law, and from thence move northward toward the Promised Land. Leaving the Red Sea they journeyed three days to reach a well called Marah, because its waters were bitter. These waters were miraculously sweetened for their use. They stopped next at Elim from which place they entered the Wilderness of Sin, which was a sandy plain extending along the east shore of the Red Sea. Here God provided manna and quail for food. Next they came to Rephidim (places of rest) where Moses struck the rock to produce water. At this point the Amalekites, a tribe of the Edomites, savagely attacked them, but through God's intervention they were defeated.

4. The Suggestion of Jethro.

In this general vicinity Jethro, the priest of Midian, whose daughter Moses had married, met Moses and brought to him Zipporah, his wife and his two sons. Naturally Moses would relate his experiences to Jethro, whom he had known intimately during his stay in the wilderness. Upon hearing of Moses' difficulties Jethro made a very practical and wise suggestion to him. He should appoint, "rulers of thousands, rulers of hundreds, rulers of fifties, and rulers of tens." (Exodus 18:25.) The substance of this wise suggestion was that Moses himself should not attempt to handle every minor detail, but should perfect an organization of helpers ranging from the lowest up to the highest. These subordinates should handle all matters except those of real importance which Moses himself should administer. This wise counsel was followed and resulted in genuine relief to Moses.

5. Around Mt. Sinai.

From this place they moved toward Mt. Sinai. In these majestic and awe-inspiring mountains there are a number of hills or peaks which may have been the scene of the giving of the Law to Moses. Each of several mounts has its advocates as the proper place for this great event. The arguments for these are involved and for our purposes here are not essential. Suffice it to say that somewhere in these mountains which rise up out of the surrounding plains and present such an austere and impressive appearance, God delivered the Law to the people. The setting for this great drama was selected for a purpose. Amid these towering peaks accompanied by the roar of thunder, God spoke to his people.

6. *How the Law Was Communicated.*

Before the delivery of the Law in the mount the people were prepared by special commandment. For three days they purified themselves and then led by Moses they came to the lower part of the mount where they were to remain. Under no condition were they allowed even to touch it. The Lord descended in a flame of fire and proclaimed in loud tones the Ten Commandments to all the people. The frightened people fled and then insisted that Moses alone talk with God. Accordingly Moses went into the mountain alone and God gave to him the detailed "Law of Moses." The decalogue was given to him on tablets of stone which were later to be entrusted to leaders of the Israelites. During this time instructions were given to Moses for the construction of the Tabernacle and the Ark or sacred chest.

7. *Law of Moses.*

It is customary to divide the long and detailed laws given to Moses into three general divisions. (1) The Moral Law which is briefly stated in the Ten Commandments. (2) The Ceremonial Law containing all the details of worship, such as sacrifices, the priesthood, holy seasons, and many other such matters. Every phase of the religious life of this new nation whose unique mission was a religious one, was provided for in these detailed instructions. (3) The Judicial part had to do with civil law involving such matters as property, administering justice, court procedures, punishing criminals and so on. This too, involved a very large number of details.

The giving of this Law of Moses marks not only the most important event in the history of the Hebrew people, but one of the most important in all history. It would be impossible to estimate the importance of this Law in human history. To the Israelites it was of the utmost significance. For them it was the absolute word of God forever to be observed.

For our present purposes it will be impractical to consider the ceremonial and judicial aspects of this Law. It should be said in passing, however, that the study of these two divisions would be a profitable experience. For example, one will be greatly impressed in studying the details of their judicial regulations to find that many laws which we think are "modern" were incorporated in this great deliverance more than three thousand years ago.

The Moral Law, or the Ten Commandments, should be considered in this connection since these are applicable to all people at all times.

8. *The Ten Commandments.*

These are so important that it will be well to re-state them in this text, even though many students may have memorized them in childhood.

(1) Thou shalt have no other gods before me.

(2) Thou shalt not make unto thee a graven image . . .

(3) Thou shalt not take the name of Jehovah thy God in vain . . .

(4) Remember the sabbath day, to keep it holy . . .

(5) Honor thy father and thy mother . . .

(6) Thou shalt not kill.

(7) Thou shalt not commit adultery.

(8) Thou shalt not steal.

(9) Thou shalt not bear false witness against thy neighbor.

(10) Thou shalt not covet . . .

Each of these commandments deals with man's relationship to God or to men. These are God's moral laws defining our duty. They are timeless and unchanging. All through the Bible they are emphasized as the heart of Man's obligations. They are a part of the laws of people in every land. No civilized nation could exist without these laws as a basis of its life. They are essential in life today because they are eternal truth.

9. *Golden Calf.*

In receiving the law at Sinai Moses was in the mount away from the people for forty days. In his absence the people did an almost unbelievable thing. Not knowing what had happened to Moses they decided that they should move from this mountain. It may be, as some have suggested, that they desired to return to Egypt. At any rate they desired to have "gods to go before them," and made their appeal to Aaron, the brother of Moses, who unfortunately yielded to their pleas. The Israelites brought their ear-rings and other pieces of gold jewelry from which Aaron molded a god in the form of a calf (sacred animal in Egypt). In a three day festival the people offered sacrifices before the golden calf preparatory to taking their leave. This deed shows how deeply the Hebrews had been affected by idolatry in Egypt. To commit such an act at any time would have been a gross sin, but to be guilty of idolatry at the very place where the commandment against idols had been given, and in so short time after receiving this commandment, made their sin doubly grievous.

God directed Moses to go down to the people at this juncture. When he saw the sin of his people he was filled with indignation. Seizing the calf he burned it with fire and scattered the ashes in water which he forced the people to drink. He then called upon the faithful people to slay these offenders. Three thousand were killed because of their sin. God, in his anger at their sin threatened to destroy all the people, but because of Moses fervent intercession for them, forgave them. The intercessory prayer of Moses for his people on this occasion reveals a greatness seldom found in men. Moses then returned to the mount where God gave to him the last of the laws for Israel.

10. The Tabernacle.

The Israelites remained at Sinai something more than a year. During this time they were occupied chiefly in learning the many details of the law which was to be followed by them ever afterwards. In this interval one of the most important developments was the building of the Tabernacle, the chief purpose of which was to represent God as dwelling in the midst of his people. Bezaleel and Aholiab were in charge of its construction but the people made free-will offerings of the necessary materials. Gold, silver, brass, goatskins and ramskins, linen and other fine materials were used.

The Tabernacle itself stood in the center of a rectangular space enclosed by a substantial tent wall, about one hundred and fifty feet long and seventy-five feet wide. The entrance was from the east. The Tabernacle proper was about forty-five feet long and fifteen feet wide. It was divided into two parts. On the east or front was the Holy Place and the west end was the Holy of Holies. The Holy Place was fifteen feet wide, fifteen feet high, and thirty feet long. This room contained the Golden Lamp or Candlesticks, the Table of Shewbread, and the Altar of Incense. The Holy of Holies, a perfect cube fifteen feet in dimension, was separated from the Holy Place by a beautiful and expensive veil. This room was kept in perfect darkness and was entered only once a year on the day of Atonement by the High Priest himself to make atonement for the sins of the people. This room represented the presence of God. It contained nothing but the Ark of the Covenant, a chest made of finest acacia wood overlaid inside and out with fine gold. The chest contained the Tables of Stone (Ten Commandments).

The Tabernacle with all its furnishings was to be taken with the Israelites in the journey to their home land. After reaching Canaan it was to be re-erected and used for the conducting of their worship.

It is worthy of note that the general plan of its construction was the pattern for the erection of Solomon's magnificent temple in Jerusalem, and was copied by both Zerubbabel and Herod the Great when they rebuilt the temple.

11. Code of Hammurabi.

This famous code of some three hundred laws enacted by Hammurabi, c. 1900-1750 B.C., was discovered in Susa in 1901. There is a striking similarity between many of these laws and those given to Moses c. 1300 B.C. Some students have been disturbed by this, feeling that Moses may have been dependent on this earlier code for many of the laws incorporated in his legislation. For this reason it may be well to call attention to two or three facts. In the first place Moses made no claim to originality in his code of laws. It is only natural that men in the course of hundreds of years would make laws against theft, murder and other such crimes. To say that the value of Moses' laws depends on whether or not he was the first one to formulate them is to take an untenable position. It should be pointed out that the entire Mosaic code is flavored by a spiritual idea that is utterly lacking in that of Hammurabi. "A comparison of the Code of Hammurabi as a whole with the Pentateuchal laws as a whole, while it reveals certain simularities, convinces the student that the laws of the Old Testament are in no essential way dependent upon the Babylonian law. Such resemblances as there are arose, it seems clear, from a similarity of antecedents and of general intellectual outlook: the striking differences show that there was no borrowing . . . There is a difference also in the content of the two codes. The Pentateuch contains many ritual regulations and purely religious laws, while the code of Hammurabi is purely civil. . . . In all that pertains to religious insight the Pentateuch is far in advance of Hammurabi's laws."*

SECTION IV — WANDERINGS IN THE WILDERNESS
(Numbers 10-20).

1. Leaving Mt. Sinai.

In the vicinity of Mt. Sinai the Israelites had spent about one year. It was a memorable year, one in which the foundations of their life as a nation had been slowly laid. Neither they nor their children could

---

*Barton, George A.: *Archaeology and the Bible, 7th Edition 1937*, p. 406. American Sunday School Union. Used by permission.

forget this place for their prophets and other leaders frequently reminded them of its significance in their life. By way of parenthesis it may be said that this mount recurs at other times in the story of the Christian religion. Elijah, fleeing from Jezebel, found refuge at Mount Horeb. Some scholars, perhaps on insufficient grounds, believe that Paul repaired to this mountain during his years in Arabia after his conversion at Damascus. In the early centuries of church history it served as a sanctuary for persecuted Christians. Later on great numbers of monks and nuns lived in these quiet mountains. One of the most famous ancient manuscripts of the Greek New Testament was found here in 1859 by Professor Tischendorf and for this reason this manuscript bears the title of Codex Sinaiticus.

When the Hebrews were ready to depart the pillar of cloud and fire moved in front to indicate their route. It is not possible now to identify all the places involved in this journey but the general route was northward and terminated at Kadesh-Barnea on the southern borders of Canaan. The main events of this jounrey were: Moses invitation to Hobab, his brother-in-law to join them; Hobab's refusal; the punishing of the people by fire because of their murmuring; the appointment of seventy elders to assist Moses; the supply of quail for food; the rebellion of Aaron and Miriam against Moses; and Miriam's punishment.

2. *Encamped at Kadesh-Barnea.*

At this point twelve men, one from each tribe, were commissioned to go up into the land of Canaan to secure and bring back vital information about the land. They were to ascertain what kind of land it was — its fertility and products, what kind of cities were in the country, and what kind of people inhabited the territory. They proceeded to the extreme northern boundary and returned probably by a slightly different route. The mission occupied forty days which was ample time for a thorough. survey of this small country. To demonstrate the fertility of the soil they brought back large bunches of grapes from Eschol.

Upon their return the people were assembled to hear their report. All twelve men were agreed that it was a good land, which was highly desirable for them. Upon the question of its conquest they were divided. Ten reported that they could not seize this country now, because of its walled cities and its giant fighting men. Two of the spies, Caleb and Joshua, reported that it could be done. "Let us go up at once, and possess it; for we are well able to overcome it." (Numbers 13:30.) In spite of the valiant efforts of these two faithful men the majority prevailed and the people would not undertake the conquest.

3. Breakdown of Faith.

This failure to exercise faith, when for every reason they should have trusted God who had so often delivered them in their need, was a grievous sin which must be punished. Except Joshua and Caleb every one of that generation (above 20 years of age) would die before they finally came into the Promised Land. The people were to wander in the wilderness forty long years. The ten unfaithful spies were instantly killed. It should be said in this connection that the Exodus should have been completed within at least two years; the forty years wandering was not a part of the original plan, but was punishment for their sin of faithlessness.

4. Tragedy of the Forty Years.

For every one concerned these were hard years. Suffering and death were the portion of the people much of the time. What questions must have arisen in their minds. Was it not a mistake ever to undertake this big venture? Would it not be better even now to return to bondage in Egypt where they could at least be sure of a home and of food? Was not this punishment too great to be endured? Could God still love them and let them suffer like this?

The lot of Moses was even harder. He was their leader who was actually responsible. He must endure the reproaches and deal with the rebellions of his own people. To see them suffer brought deep grief to him. He must experience the loss of his sister Miriam and his brother Aaron. Ultimately he is to be taken by death before he sees the realization of his dream, the fulfillment of his desire. These years were full of pathos for all the people.

5. Rebellion of Korah.

One of the significant happenings of these forty years was the rebellion against Moses and Aaron led by Korah, Dathan and Abiram. Two hundred and fifty princes of the people executed the uprising in which they charged Moses and Aaron with taking too much authority. The situation was a serious one involving a large number of people. The matter was referred to the Lord who answered by vindicating his two servants. The earth opened up and all the rebellious ones were swallowed up while the two hundred and fifty princes were consumed with fire. This was followed by a plague which took the lives of a great number.

6. Mistake of Moses and Aaron.

We shall not attempt to follow these people in their wanderings during these years. It will be sufficient to recount briefly two or three other big events that belong to this period. Returning at length to Kadesh, Miriam was taken by death and was buried in this memorable place. An event here brought unhappy consequences in the life of Moses. When water failed the people murmured bitterly. Moses and Aaron assembled them before a large rock with the assurance that upon their word water would flow from the rock. Wearied and impatient at their constant complainings Moses and Aaron committed a sin for which they were to be punished. "Hear now, ye rebels: shall we bring you forth water out of this rock." Upon saying this he smote the rock twice with his rod, and an abundance of water gushed forth. What was the sin of Moses? Some think it was his temporary loss of self-control. In all probability, however, it was his failure to give God credit for this miracle. Because of this sin he and Aaron were to be punished by being denied the privilege of leading the people into the Promised Land. It was a severe penalty and yet Moses made no complaint. Neither he nor any other man could expect exemption from the consequences of wrongdoing.

7. Death of Aaron.

The Israelites now began the last stage of their journey to Canaan. Between them and their objective lay the territory of the Edomites. To save time they requested permission to traverse this land giving assurance that their passage would be peaceable. But the Edomites refused their request and it was necessary for them to journey far to the south and then eastward before turning north again toward Eastern Palestine. At Mt. Hor near the impressive city of Petra, Aaron came to the end of his days. Moses, Aaron, and his son Eleazer climbed the Mount from which they could look northward to Canaan, and there Moses removed the official priestly robes from his brother Aaron and placed them on Eleazer. The beloved Highpriest was then taken by death and his body was buried at the place. The people observed a period of thirty days mourning for this honored leader before resuming their march.

8. Fiery Serpents.

Moving from Mt. Hor they entered the hot flat plains. "A dreary waste, sand hills beyond sand hills, tufted with broom and other bushes, affording excellent pasturage, but still a dreary solitude, a howling wilderness; while the Edomites from their black mountains, look down on them in scorn." (*Lord Lindsay's Letters.*) Here the people again complained bitterly. As punishment for this sin many of them were bitten by poisonous serpents and died. Repenting of their sin they begged for mercy. Moses was then instructed to erect a serpent of brass and to place it on an elevated staff so that all who looked upon it might be healed. This is the event to which Jesus referred in John 3:14.

SECTION V — ADVANCING TOWARD THE PROMISED LAND
      (Numbers 31-36, Deuteronomy 28-34).

1. The Territory of Sihon.

The hard journey to the south and east of Edom was at last completed and the Hebrews began advancing northward on the eastern side of the Dead Sea-Jordan River valley. They encountered no opposition until they reached the Arnon river which flows into the Dead Sea on the east side about half way between the northern and southern ends. This region was one of great beauty and fertility and to the Israelites, so long accustomed to the wastes of the desert, it would be most impressive and desirable. The area was famous for cattle, sheep, good pastures, and fertile fields. It was known as the territory of Sihon and was inhabited by an Amorite tribe. The Israelites requested peaceful passage through this territory but the Amorites, who were a savage, fierce-fighting people refused to grant their request. The Israelites engaged them in battle, and with divine aid, won a signal victory.

2. Kingdom of Og.

Having passed through the territory of Sihon they next faced the kingdom of Og, apparently to the north. This was a region of strong, fortified cities ruled by Og, king of Bashan. These people, protected by their fortified cities, were also hard fighters. However, the Israelites, more experienced now, and encouraged by the victory over Sihon, went to battle and again were victorious. This victory gave them possession of these sixty fenced cities and the fertile territory of Og.

3. Among the Moabites.

The Israelites next came to the homeland of the Moabites, a region directly east of the Dead Sea. Balak, king of Moab, learning of the two decisive victories just won by these Israelites was filled with fear. In consulting with the leaders of his neighbors, the Midianites, he decided to send for Balaam, a noted religious leader who lived east of the Euphrates river, to come and put a curse on this horde of invaders.

4. Balak and Balaam.

Leaders were dispatched at once with rich gifts to persuade Balaam to come to the assistance of the Moabites. Balaam, being instructed of Jehovah, refused to go. A second and more urgent invitation with larger gifts was made, and at last he agreed to go, but with the understanding that he would not speak against God's people. This strange story, with the ass talking, with Balaam refusing to curse the Israelites, his final acquiescence, and encouraging the very people he could not curse to engage in heathenish idolatry, is one which is subject to a variety of interpretations. Even though the Israelites were punished for their sin, they accomplished their purpose of getting beyond the territory of the Moabites and thus were able later to cross the Jordan and enter the Promised Land.

5. Defeating Midian.

After these strange experiences with the Moabites, it was necessary for the Israelites to deal with one other group, the Midianites. These people who were in the conspiracy with the Moabites were a real threat to the security of the Israelites. Moses selected a thousand men from each tribe who were sent to fight this opposing nation. In the battle they were successful in destroying the army of the Midianites. This victory left Moses and his people in a secure position in the territory east of the Jordan. Thus they were able at last to make preparations for the real conquests on the other side of the Jordan river. During this period of general planning there were a number of important events which we shall consider.

6. Settling East of the Jordan.

This territory won from Sihon, Og, the Moabites, and the Midianites was a fertile land very desirable for pasturage and good also for agriculture. When the conquest east of the Jordan was completed the tribes of Reuben and Gad, and part of the tribe of Manasseh, who were interested primarily in sheepraising, requested permission from Moses to settle in this area as their part of the Promised Land. Permission to do this was granted provided, of course, that the fighting men of these tribes would go over the Jordan and contribute their share in the task of conquering the future home of the other tribes. This was a fair requirement since all twelve tribes had done their part in obtaining the territory of Eastern Palestine. Since these two or three tribes readily agreed to this arrangement they secured as their permanent home the region east of the Dead Sea and the Jordan River almost as far north as the Lake of Galilee.

7. Selection of Joshua.

The time for the close of Moses' career was almost at hand. God directed him to select Joshua as his successor and to give to the new commander all necessary instructions. Joshua had been closely associated with Moses through the long years of the Exodus. He had assisted Moses in the battle against the Amalekites, he had been one of the two faithful spies, and in other ways had shown his ability and his loyalty. His selection seems to have met with public approval. Joshua had a difficult place to fill, and the experiences just after crossing the Jordan indicate that he undertook his work with hesitation and was in need of frequent encouragement in his duties. But unquestionably he was the man best equipped to follow in the footsteps of the great Moses.

8. The Farewell of Moses.

Among other things to be done by Moses before his final departure were the assigning of cities to the tribe of Levi, setting the boundaries of the Promised Land, giving final instructions to Joshua, numbering the people, and most important of all, publicly addressing the leaders of his people. His farewell address, or as some think, his series of addresses recorded in Deuteronomy, would be his last official act for his people. This must have been a memorable occasion, one filled with greatest solemnity and deepest sorrow. Here stood their great leader who had brought them through so many experiences, speaking his last words to them. How many scenes would be brought to mind as they gazed upon his majestic countenance and heard his gracious words. How selfish and ungenerous had been their treatment of him so many times. Here is their aged warrior laying aside his sword, their honored leader relinquishing his heavy responsibilities, their wise counsellor giving his last admonitions.

His impressive address had one chief purpose — to get them to realize how much God had done for them, how dependent they were upon him and the necessity of unswerving loyalty to him forever. The burden of this message was the penalties of disobedience and the rewards of obedience to God. They are to be obedient to him, not because he is an arbitrary God who can deal with them according to whim, but because obedience to God is the way of reason, truth, and justice! Disobedience brings its own penalties. The way of security, prosperity and peace for Israel for all time lies in their loyalty to Jehovah and all his commandments.

9. Death of Moses.

When he had finished his farewell address he was summoned to Mount Pisgah, high in the hills of Moab, where he was to see the glories of the land on which he was never to set foot. From this range of mountains the aged leader could look to the west across the deep ravine of the Jordan and see from south to north the future home of his people. One likes to think that his last look came in the afternoon as the lowering sun lighted up the chief features of the Promised Land. When the view had been completed the God whom he had so faithfully served quitely closed his eyes with the glories of the vision of Canaan still fresh in his mind. Here God took him home; here God placed his body in a tomb never to be known by men. "And he buried him in a valley in the land of Moab, over against Beth-Peor; but no man knoweth of his sepulchre unto this day." (Deuteronomy 34:6.)

> By Nebo's lonely mountain,
> On this side Jordan's wave,
> In a vale in the land of Moab,
> There lies a lonely grave;
> But no man built that sepulchre
> And no man saw it e'er;
> For the angels of God upturned the sod,
> And laid the dead man there.
> *Cecil Francis Alexander.*

10. An Appraisal of Moses.

It is impossible in brief space to make an adequate appraisal of a man so distinguished as Moses. He was the greatest man in Hebrew history. The long record of his achievements is still almost unbelievable.

It seems best to follow the customary procedure of considering first his *character* and then his *work*.

In character he was pre-eminent. He possessed almost all the qualities of personal greatness. Superb courage, patience, unselfishness, forgiveness, meekness (unselfish disinterestedness), integrity, vision, faith and loyalty are all nobly exhibited in the life of this remarkable man.

His work surpasses that of any Biblical character except Jesus Christ. By any standard he would be considered one of the most amazing men in human history. "The Hebrew lawgiver was a man, who, considered merely in a historical light, without any reference to his Divine inspiration, has exercised a more extensive and permanent influence over the destinies of his own nation and mankind at large, than any other individual recorded in the annals of the world."*

He was lawgiver, statesman, judge, warrior, prophet, priest, and poet. To him, more than to any other man, belongs the credit for molding and leading the Hebrew people into a nation. A lesser figure could not have accomplished this great undertaking. Before his departure he was able to look upon a mighty people ready now to enter the Promised Land where they could begin to fulfill their high mission as God's chosen people.

*Stanley: *Lectures on Jewish History, pp.* 199-200.

Chapter VIII

CONQUEST AND SETTLEMENT IN CANAAN

Joshua, Judges, Ruth

Section I — Introduction.

1. A Significant Period. 2. Conditions Favoring the Conquest. 3. Inhabitants of Canaan.

Section II — The Conquest of Canaan (Joshua).

1. Under the New Commander. 2. Eager for the Great Adventure. 3. Preliminary Precautions. 4. Crossing the Jordan. 5. The First Memorial in Canaan. 6. Jericho, the Key City. 7. Plan of Conquest. 8. Ai, Achan, Achor. 9. Israel at Shechem. 10. Battle of Gibeon. 11. Completing the Conquest. 12. Locating the Tribes. 13. Jealousy and Misunderstanding. 14. Joshua's Farewell Address. 15. An Appraisal of Joshua. 16. Religion and Culture of the Canaanites. 17. Israel's Cruelty to the Canaanites. 18. Problems and Perils Ahead.

Section III — The Period of the Judges (Judges, Ruth).

1. "Dark Ages" of Hebrew History. 2. History Repeating Itself. 3. Functions of the Judges. 4. List of the Judges. 5. Othniel and the Mesopotamians. 6. Ehud and the Moabites. 7. Deborah and Barak Against the Canaanites. 8. Gideon Against the Midianites. 9. Jephthah and the Ammonites. 10. Samson and the Philistines. 11. Three Sordid Stories. 12. Story of Ruth. 13. Hebrew Domestic Life. 14. Religious Life in the Period.

Conquest and Settlement in Canaan

JOSHUA 1-24, JUDGES 1-21, RUTH 1-4

SECTION I — INTRODUCTION.

1. A Significant Period.

This period of Hebrew history is a significant one. It extends over something less than 200 years (1250-1100 B.C.). The events of the period are confined to the narrow limits of the little land of Canaan. It is characterized by striking contrasts — brilliant, hard fighting at first, followed by weak compromises; high patriotic fervor in the conquest followed by a demoralization of ideals and purpose. After the hard years in Egyptian bondage and the long, weary wanderings in the wilderness they entered the long-awaited promised land. They were at home at last. After the hard fighting came the thrill of settling in their respective territories, the selecting of claims of land, the building of their homes. Patriotic enthusiasm was at high tide as they followed Joshua from victory to victory and then in solemn assembly pledged their fidelity to the law of Moses. At last their nation was on its way to the realization of its great mission. But this enthusiasm was soon chilled by weak compromises and easy surrender of ideals until the latter half of the period came to be known as the "Dark Ages" of Hebrew history. Toward the end of the period the dense darkness began to disappear with the activities of Samuel, the young man who was destined to lead the way to a better day for his nation.

2. Conditions Favoring the Conquest.

The conquest of the land of Canaan was a magnificent achievement. It was no small accomplishment for these people who were inexperienced in the art of warfare, to march successfully through the territory of several strong kingdoms and then in a series of brilliant battles wrest their new homeland from the fierce-fighting tribes that claimed it as their own. On what basis can this be explained? To be sure God was with them and provided miraculous help in their campaign. But there was another important factor in this great achievement. They came at an opportune time, a time when outward conditions favored such a conquest. The various nations surrounding Canaan and the tribes inside the land were not united in opposing the advances of an invading nation. Had Edom, Moab, Ammon and other nations outside Canaan formed an alliance and combined their fighting forces against Israel presumably they could easily have prevented them from ever reaching eastern Palestine. But their relationship with each other at this time was such that this could not, or did not occur. Somewhat the same condition prevailed in the region west of the Jordan. Here were several small, independent peoples living near each other, apparently as rivals but with no thought of combining their resources to fight off an invader. Had the Canaanites, the Gergashites, the Hittites, the Jebusites and other such groups formed a strong alliance and offered united and well planned opposition, the results might have been`different. Either they would not or could not do this. From the statements made to the spies sent by Joshua into Jericho these people had heard reports of the coming of this invading army of Israelites and were filled with fear at their approach. Thus it appears that the Hebrew people came to their new homeland at just the right time, a time when conditions were such as to make its conquest easier than it might have been at any other time.

3. Inhabitants of Canaan.

West of the Jordan lay the larger and better part of Canaan, the territory which was to be the real home of the Hebrews. At this time it was occupied by several fierce tribes, who naturally would resist the invasion by another people. In the Jordan valley, in the plain of Esdraelon and on the Mediterranean coast lived the *Canaanites,* the chief of these tribes. The fortress later to become Jerusalem was held by the *Jebusites.* Southern Canaan was occupied by the *Hittites.* The *Ammonites* occupied southeastern Judah, while the *Hivites* lived in central Samaria. The *Perizzites* dwelt near Carmel, while the tribe of *Jabin* lived in the mountainous region of Galilee. The *Philistines,* not challenged in the conquest, occupied the coastal territory between Judah and the sea. The *Phoenicians,* who likewise were not involved in the wars of conquest, lived on the narrow strip between the mountains and the sea in the extreme northern end of Canaan.

SECTION II—THE CONQUEST OF CANAAN (Joshua 1-24).

1. Under the New Commander.

It will be recalled that Moses, just before his death in Moab, did much in getting the Hebrews ready for the important venture of crossing the Jordan and conquering western Palestine. Joshua, the son of Nun, was selected and was instructed by Moses. A number of incidents illustrating his activity and loyalty are given in the Biblical account. (Exodus 17:10f, 23:13, 32:17; Numbers 13:8, 16, 14:38, etc.) Apparently he was the logical one to succeed Moses, the great leader now removed from them.

Upon the death of Moses Joshua assumed command and began at once his plans for the big task ahead. Considering the pre-eminent leadership of his predecessor it is no wonder that Joshua was keenly conscious of the heavy responsibility now thrust upon him. He was brave and competent, though he was frequently exhorted to be courageous in his great undertaking. It appears that the people accepted him and followed him with confidence. They were now in the hands of a new leader, younger and less experienced than Moses, but one who trusted in Jehovah and sought with all his powers to measure up to his heavy responsibilities.

2. Eager for the Great Adventure.

As the Israelites, encamped east of the Jordan, made final preparations for the last stages of their venture in getting their new home, there was an air of expectancy among them. At last, after the bitter years of bondage and wilderness wanderings they were on the threshold of their new home. Behind them were the years of wilderness hardships; ahead of them was the homeland. How eager they must have been to finish the conquest and settle their families in the new home which offered so much to them. No doubt some were too eager to proceed and were impatient at the delays necessary for successful conquest. Joshua, however, would not be rushed and wisely planned the details of the new adventure.

3. Preliminary Precautions.

Across the Jordan at the foot of the mountains of western Canaan lay the strategic city of Jericho. It commanded the main pass up into the mountains. It was necessary, therefore, that this strongly fortified city should be taken first. In order to proceed intelligently it was essential that Joshua have accurate and detailed information about this city and the regions roundabout. Accordingly two spies were selected and sent across the river to reconnoitre this strategic city. They gained access to the home of a woman named Rahab who fortunately co-operated with them. The king of Jericho got word of the coming of the spies and attempted to seize them. Rahab hid them in her home and enabled them to secure the needed information by bargaining with them for the saving of her family when the Israelites should conquer the city. She reported to them the fear which the inhabitants of Canaan had concerning this invading army which had so successfully defeated the nations east of the Jordan under the leadership of a God of such marvelous power. For this assistance the spies promised to spare the house of Rahab and agreed with her that her house should be marked by a scarlet cord in the window. They were then let down from the window outside the walls of the city and proceeded to make their way back across the Jordan to report to Joshua.

In the meantime Joshua was making final plans with his people. Food was provided, the order of the march was arranged, and the people were given instructions for any exigency ahead.

4. Crossing the Jordan.

The time had now come for the decisive move. The confident report of the spies from Jericho inspired Joshua and the people to proceed at once. Early in the morning, which was four days before the time of the Passover, they left their camp and came down to the Jordan. The priests bore the Ark marching three thousand feet in front of the people, and as they reached the banks and stepped into the waters of the river, which at this season overflowed its banks, "the waters which came down from above stood, and rose up in one heap a great way off at Adam, the city that is beside Zarethan; and those that went down toward the sea of the Arabah, even the Salt Sea, were wholly cut off; and the people passed over right against Jericho." (Joshua 3:16.) With the opening of the waters the priests moved to the middle of the river bed and held the Ark while the people passed by them to cross to the other side. When the crossing was completed and the priests had come up on the western banks, the waters of the river came rolling down and again overflowed its banks.

It is worthy of note that an old account by a reputable historian tells the story of another crossing of the Jordan river that was regarded as miraculous. According to this account in the year 1257 A.D. Sultan Bibers sent workmen to repair a bridge over the Jordan at this very point, in order to provide crossing for a Mohammedan army in retreat. It was the time for spring floods and they naturally expected that the Jordan valley would be flooded so they could not do their work. To their surprise, however, as they came to the river they discovered that the river bed was almost dry. They rushed their repair work and had barely finished it when the waters came pouring down from the north. Upon investigation they discovered that a great landslide up the valley had completely dammed up the waters of the Jordan.

This miraculous experience made a deep impression on the Hebrew people. Forty years earlier God had opened up the waters of the Red sea to provide deliverance from bondage and now again he opened up the waters to provide an entrance to their new homeland. The event must be kept fresh in their minds. In succeeding centuries prophets, poets, and other teachers would recount this experience to inspire greater faith in Jehovah. Even to our day the event is kept fresh in mind by the use of such hymns as "On Jordan's Stormy Banks I Stand," and "Guide Me, O Thou Great Jehovah."

5. The First Memorial in Canaan.

To commemorate this miraculous deliverance the twelve chief men brought from the bed of the Jordan twelve large stones with which to build a memorial at the place known as Gilgal on the western side of the river. "And Joshua spoke unto the children of Israel, saying, When your children shall ask their fathers in time to come, saying, What mean these stones? then ye shall let your children know, saying, Israel came over this Jordan on dry land . . . that all the peoples of this earth may know the hand of Jehovah your God forever." (Joshua 4:21-24.)

The rite of circumcision commanded of Abraham, but for a long time neglected, was performed. This was followed by the celebration of the Passover on the evening of the 14th day of Nisan. After this the supply of manna which Jehovah had provided ceased. The Exodus had come to an end.

6. Jericho, the Key City.

The important city of Jericho which stood some six miles west of the Jordan guarded the pass into the highlands of western Canaan. The ruins of this ancient city which are oval shaped and cover some thirteen acres, can be seen by travelers today. They are elevated about forty feet above the surrounding plains and are enclosed by a wall which excavators have studied with great care. This wall, some seven feet thick, was about sixteen feet high. On top of this stone wall another one about eight feet high, made of brick, was placed. On the north end was a citadel used by the inhabitants in defense of the city.

Naturally these walls have great interest for Bible students in view of the unusual story of the conquest of the city by the Hebrews.

Unfortunately, it is not possible for the archaeologists to give adequate answers to all the questions we have about the destruction of this ancient city. Despite the curse pronounced upon any who should attempt to rebuild the historic city, it was rebuilt again and again. It was in existence during much of the Old Testament history, and subsequently. In view of these several rebuildings it is difficult to reconstruct the original city as conquered by Joshua and his forces.

This "city of palm trees," set in beautiful surroundings, with springs of water and fertile plains, was famous for its balsam trees which produced a balm well known for its healing qualities. In Joshua's day a beautiful forest of palm trees some eight miles long and three wide, stood immediately east of the city. Thus Jericho was almost concealed between the steep hills on the west and the forest on the east. This elevated city with its high walls must have appeared well nigh impregnable to the Hebrews as they advanced westward from the Jordan. But the city must be conquered if they are ever to succeed in wresting their new homeland from the enemy since it was practically impossible to get up into the western highlands by any other route. It would be fatal to leave such a fortified city in the hands of their enemies. Jericho was indeed a key city.

Instructions for the capturing of the city were given to Joshua in a visit from a messenger of Jehovah. For six days the people of Israel were to march once each day around the walls of the city as they were led by seven priests who were to sound the trumpets. On the seventh day they were to march around it seven times after which the trumpets were to sound a long, loud blast. This was to be followed by a short blast after which the walls of the city were to fall down. Joshua and his forces were commanded to destroy every living thing in the city, except the family of Rahab in keeping with the contract previously made by the spies with her. All property was to be destroyed except the metal vessels which were to be kept for use in service to Jehovah.

These instructions were carried out and on the seventh day the proud city was reduced to ruins and the first step in the conquest of western Canaan was successfully taken. This removed the barrier to the pass up into the western highlands, their future home in Canaan.

7. Plan of Conquest.

By reading the records of succeeding encounters it is easy to discern the general plan of conquest decided upon by the Hebrews. Their strategy was to move directly west toward the Mediterranean Sea conquering a strip of territory through the center of the land. This would forestall any possibility of the peoples of the south and the north joining their forces to offer united resistance to the Hebrews. This plan to divide and conquer proved to be effective. Joshua's forces, upon completing their drive to the west, turned southward and eliminated their leading enemies in this direction, and later advanced northward, subduing their opponents in this area. The last real battle of the conquest was fought far in the north near the waters of the little lake (Merom) a few miles above the Sea of Galilee.

8. Ai, Achan, Achor.

Highly elated, and perhaps over-confident after their decisive victory at Jericho, the Israelites were soon to taste the bitterness of humiliating defeat. Moving westward up the mountain from Jericho their next objective was the stronghold of Ai, a city near ancient Bethel in the heart of western Palestine. They underestimated the strength of this city of some twelve thousand people and marched against it with only three thousand men. They were utterly defeated and driven back toward Jericho in great humiliation. This experience caused general consternation among them. Led by Joshua, they prostrated themselves before Jehovah, and were then informed of the cause of their defeat. Contrary to the specific command that none of the valuables of Jericho were to be saved or appropriated, one of their number had been guilty of stealing and hiding certain articles. Upon investigation it was discovered that a man named Achan, of the tribe of Judah, had hidden in his tent a rich Oriental robe, two hundred shekels of silver and an immense wedge or bar of solid gold. Confronted with the charges Achan publicly confessed his crime. Thereupon he and all his family were taken to a valley south of the ruins of Jericho where they were publicly stoned to death. A mound of stones was placed above the place and the name Achor (trouble) was then given to the valley of execution.

A second attack upon Ai was now to be made. This time their strategy, which has been employed many times since then, proved successful. During the darkness of night 5,000 men were placed in ambush behind the city. Joshua and the rest of his army next morning marched to attack the city. The king of Ai immediately moved to meet them in battle. Joshua's forces, according to plan, began again to retreat. The enemy rapidly pursued them, thus leaving their city unprotected. The 5,000 men in ambush then entered the city, set it on fire and set out in pursuit of the Aites. The forces led by Joshua now stopped their retreat and turned upon their pursuers who were caught between the two armies of the Hebrews, and were utterly annihilated. Ai was sacked and burned, the inhabitants were killed and their army was destroyed.

9. Israel at Shechem.

The victory at Ai seems to have secured Joshua's position in central Canaan, for he now called for an assembly of the people at the historic place called Shechem. Here were the twin mounts, Ebal and Gerizim, which stood close enough together to form a sort of natural amphitheatre which was ideally suited for an assemblage. The time had now come for the ratifying of the law which Moses had commanded. This law used on this occasion, was probably the Blessings and the Cursings found in Deuteronomy 27. One half the tribes ascended Mt. Ebal, the other six climbed Mt. Gerizim. In the space between these stood the priests, Levites and other leaders, with Joshua. As the Levites read aloud the curses the assembly of Mt. Ebal responded with a great Amen, while those on Mt. Gerizim replied in similar manner to the Blessings. In this impressive manner the Israelites publicly committed themselves to the keeping of the law of Moses. Had they remained loyal to their vows the subsequent history might have been quite different.

10. Battle at Gibeon.

A group of Canaanite kings, now thoroughly alarmed at Joshua's victories, were mustering their forces for a united stand against the Hebrew invaders. The people of Gibeon, one of the nearby cities, refused to join this alliance and were eager to make terms with Joshua for their own protection. By a cunning stratagem, wearing old, tattered clothes as if they had come from a great distance, and assuming an air of piety they deceived Joshua into making peace with them. Three days later the Israelites discovered that the Gibeonites were their immediate neighbors and had cleverly deceived them. However, they kept their word and did not kill the Gibeonites but did reduce them to servitude.

In the meantime the kings of five nearby cities (Jebus, Hebron, Jarmuth, Lachish and Eglon) having resolved to destroy the Gibeonites, marched against them in great force. These besieged Gibeonites sent an urgent appeal to Joshua, who was at Gilgal, to come to their defense against these strong opponents. Marching by night Joshua came unexpectedly upon these armies on the plains of Gibeon. In a fierce battle he put them to rout, driving them through the pass of Beth-horon into the valley below the heights. The five kings were taken from the cave where they had sought to escape death and were publicly beheaded. Joshua immediately hurried to the home cities of these five kings and destroyed their inhabitants. The effect was immediate. All opposition in southern Palestine now crumbled and thus, within a short time, the Hebrews were in possession of practically all of the land as far south as Kadesh-Barnea. The bigger part of the conquest was over.

11. Completing the Conquest.

The northern part of their land must now be wrested from the natives. Near the Lake of Galilee lived Jabin the strong king of Hazor, who had summoned several other local chiefs to form a confederacy against Joshua's army. Upon hearing of this Joshua set forth with his army to meet them in battle. He came upon them as they encamped near the small lake called Merom, in the northern end of the land. In this battle the northern kings were utterly defeated and their cities were possessed by the forces of Joshua. This victory was decisive. It led to the conquest of all northern Palestine and gave to the Hebrews possession of much of western Palestine.

12. Locating the Tribes.

The common task in which all were interested was the division of their new homeland among the various tribes. In a previous chapter we saw that Reuben and Gad and a part of the tribe of Manasseh, upon their request, had been assigned the territory east of the Jordan. The remaining nine and one half tribes were to be given their territory west of the Jordan. Joshua, assisted by Eleazar, the high priest, made assignments of most of this territory. It appears, however, that some groups with strong leaders went out and obtained certain localities for themselves. Caleb, reminding Joshua of the promise of Moses, secured his permission to claim Hebron in southern Palestine as his territory. He took with him a strong fighting force and in hard battle seized this region from the sons of Anak.

The casting of lots before the tabernacle was the plan used for determining the locality to be occupied by the nine and one half tribes. The first tribe to receive its assignment was *Judah,* the strongest of all. This was a large territory which stretched westward from the Dead Sea across the western highlands to the borders of Philistia.

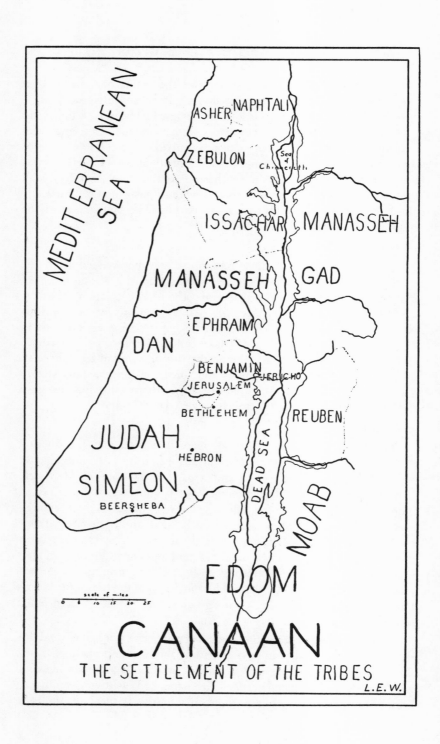

CANAAN

THE SETTLEMENT OF THE TRIBES

Much of it was rugged wilderness and barren hill country, but it was strategically situated and made a good home for the sons of Judah. *Simeon* was given the territory southwest of Judah which was a sandy hill country, whose borders varied from time to time. Just northwest of Judah in the hill country sloping down to the sea, the tribe of *Dan* was first located. At a later date, however, this tribe moved to the far north above the lake of Galilee. *Benjamin* was given the land immediately north of Judah in the western highlands. This territory was much smaller than Judah's, but it was a choice location. Benjamin, while not so large in numbers, was very prominent in national affairs and contributed more than her share of leaders in subsequent years.

Immediately north of Benjamin on the high ridge and extending over east to the Jordan and west to the coastal plains was the region given to *Ephraim* and half of *Manasseh*. The territory, known later as the plain of Esdraelon and Galilee, was assigned to four tribes. *Issachar* received the fertile plain between Galilee and Samaria. This is the most historic area in Palestine and was the scene of many important events in both Old Testament and New Testament times. The people of Issachar, however, seem not to have been very prominent in the life of the nation afterwards. To the far north were located *Zebulon, Asher,* and *Naphtali.*

The careful student will have noted that in these assignments no provision was made for the tribe of Levi. And there were good reasons for this. This priestly tribe was to be supported by the tithes of cattle and agricultural produce from the other tribes. In addition to these tithes each tribe was to furnish four cities as homes for the Levites. Included in these forty-eight cities were six cities of refuge, Kedesh, Galan, Shechem, Ramoth-Gilead, Bezer, and Hebron.

13. Jealousy and Misunderstanding.

The allocating of territory having been completed, the people of Reuben, Gad, and part of Manasseh were given permission by Joshua to return to their homes east of the Jordan as previously agreed upon. They began their journey homeward and upon coming down to the Jordan set up an altar as a perpetual witness that they were not divided from their brethren west of the Jordan in religion or national purposes. Word of the erection of this altar came to some of their brethren west of the river, who without good reasons, jumped to the conclusion that these tribes had erected the altar to worship foreign gods. They hastily concluded to make war upon these eastern tribes, but wisely resolved to learn the facts first. When they discovered the honorable intentions of their brethren an unfortunate civil war was averted.

14. Joshua's Farewell Address.

When the tribes had settled in their new homes the career of Joshua, the great soldier and leader, came to an end. Having been warned of the imminence of his departure, he called for an assembly of the chief officials and leaders of the nation at ancient Shechem. In his wisdom he foresaw some of the dangers that lay ahead for his nation. He and other trusted men like Eleazar and Caleb must pass on and leave younger men in charge. These new leaders should be prepared and tested. He saw the danger of gradual mingling and even intermarriage with the pagan people, so many of whom were still left in their land. The Hebrews had not yet conquered much of the territory occupied by these foreign tribes who constituted a menace to their faith in God. They needed to become familiar with the law of Moses for their guidance. They needed also to pledge themselves publicly to observe these laws since the welfare of the nation depended upon their loyalty to the principles enunciated in them.

In his address on this impressive and historic occasion Joshua reviewed hurriedly the big events in their national history and traced the protection and guidance of Jehovah their God in their life as a nation. He then challenged the people to pledge themselves anew to the service of Jehovah, their God. The people solemnly renewed the covenant whereupon Joshua set up a stone pillar as a memorial of this event. The people then departed to return to their respective localities.

15. An Appraisal of Joshua.

Shortly after the assembly at Shechem Joshua, now 110 years of age, came peacefully to the end of his days. He was buried in his home city, Timnath-Serah in Ephraim. After this the Israelites buried the body of Joseph their great preserver which, in keeping with their promise to him, they had brought with them from Egypt.

Joshua had served his people with great devotion at a critical time in their history. He followed Israel's greatest statesman, Moses, and naturally was somewhat overshadowed by him, but his contribution was exceptionally valuable and in his own name he stands out as a very remarkable man. As a soldier he was brave and resourceful, showing unusual gifts in strategy. As a civic leader or statesman he exercised fine foresight and sound wisdom. As a man he was genuine, courageous and honorable. In religious matters he was humble, genuinely faithful to Jehovah and was uncompromising in his efforts to lead his people to whole-hearted loyalty to the law of Moses. The life of Israel might have been vastly different without the wise and able leadership of Joshua during the critical years of conquest and settlement in Canaan.

16. Religion and Culture of the Canaanites.

In another connection we have spoken of the various pagan tribes which occupied Canaan at the time of the conquest. Of these peoples the Canaanites were the most powerful. With them, more than any others, the Hebrews were to be involved in the next century. They were a cruel, fierce-fighting people whose moral and religious practices were exceptionally wicked and repulsive. The Biblical account (Leviticus 18:21-30, Deut. 12:30-32) tells something of these abominable practices. The discoveries of the archaeologists have given most impressive corroboration to the Biblical record. The work of Dr. Macalister at ancient Gezer, a Canaanite city, was especially revealing. Uncovering this ancient mound layer by layer, he came upon the stratum belonging to the time of Joshua. Here he found the high place, the area where the Canaanites carried on their worship. The great high place at Gezer had its foundation in the second stratum below the Israelite. It was, therefore, one of the Canaanite high places. It contained ten monoliths or upright pillars, the tallest of which was ten feet and nine inches and the lowest five feet and seven inches. These pillars ran in a curved line in the general direction of north and south. All of these except one, were of the kind of stone found in abundance around Gezer. These had been taken from the immediate neighborhood and bore no marks of a tool. The sacred one (worn smooth in places by the continuous rubbing and kissing of devotees) was of stone found around Jerusalem. The excavators are of the opinion that these were erected about the time of Abraham, and were used with frequency each year until the time of the Exile 587 b.c. Hard by were two large caves connected by a narrow, crooked passage so that they could be used for the giving of oracles. The area of this high place seems to have been about 150 feet by 120 feet. Apparently no buildings were connected with it.

The whole area of this high place was a cemetery for new-born babes. In all probability they were first-born children sacrificed to the deity. These were enclosed in jars with the body put in head first.

Two or three small vessels, usually a bowl and a jug, were put in with them. That these were sacrifices is shown by the fact that they were children. It could not have been a burial place since such was considered unclean and hence would not be near the place of worship. These gruesome discoveries of this high place make very real the horrible practices of the people just antedating the Israelites in Palestine.

The large collection of suggestive images of Astarte found in this place bears convincing testimony to the immoral worship that went on here. All these images were designed to foster in the worshiper that type of service described in Isa. 57:3ff. "Draw near hither, ye sons of the sorceress, the seed of the adulterer and the harlot — ye that inflame yourselves among the oaks, under every green tree, that slay children in the valleys. Upon a high and lofty mountain thou hast set thy bed, thither wentest thou up to offer sacrifice. Thou hast enlarged thy bed and made thee a covenant with them; thou lovest their bed where thou sawest it." So many of these suggestive images and sketchings were found that Prof. Macalister was led to say: "No one who was not at Gezer during the excavating can realize how demoralizing the whole atmosphere of such a worship must have been." Archaeology has revealed to us in a most vivid way the character of the worship against which the prophets of Jehovah had to contend.

The late Dr. J. P. Peters of the University of Pennsylvania in his book "The Religion of the Hebrews" fills out the picture and gives us some conception of the nature of this worship that proved such a temptation and snare to God's people in the days before they were finally led away captive. He says, "The Canaanite religion was the nature worship of an agricultural people. Baal gave grain, oil, wine. For this his worshipers prayed to him and for this they thanked him. Baal was identified with nature. Its yearly revival and death were a revival and death of the god. In this revival and death his worshipers took part. In connection with the latter it was their religion to mourn and mutilate themselves; in connection with the former to give themselves over to the most unbridled merrymaking. Baal was the giver of life; he was also the destroyer of life. As the latter, men sought to appease his wrath by offerings, even of their children; as the former men reveled in his bounty with the wildest orgies. The life of nature appeared to them to rest on the mystical process of generation, hence sexual immorality was a feature of their worship of the gods.

"Each city had a Baal as its god and in consequence of the likeness of the life of the various cities there was no great difference between these various Baals. They were distinguished in general by adding the name of the city or place in which they were worshiped. They were represented often by symbols taken from the animal world, bulls and lions, cows, doves and birds of prey, in which the generative force or the consuming ardor of the sun was represented.

"Along with the Baal was worshiped a Baalat or corresponding goddess. Throughout the religion of the settled Semites, as we find it in Babylonia, Canaan and among the settled Arameans, there was a duality of sex and a tendency to worship the goddess with immoral rites. At her shrines and in her name sexual license was permitted or commanded, and sometimes the sacrifice of female chastity was required in her service. At places strange and unnatural lust formed part of her worship; and both female and male prostitutes inhabited her temples and served at her shrines."*

Such was the worship universally practiced in Palestine at the time when Israel entered her promised home. In the conquest the devotees of this worship were not destroyed but, instead, a policy of compromise was adopted which allowed these evil practices to continue, and to corrupt the religious life of the Hebrews as it flourished in subsequent years. Every generation from their settlement in Canaan to the Exile witnessed the old, yet ever-new, struggle of Jehovah worship against Baal. This was not a far-off, unreal, imaginary evil, but was real, ever-present, alluring and challenging.

17. Israel's Cruelty to the Canaanites.

Some students have been puzzled by the command of God to exterminate the Canaanites. We should remember that the experiences in these cruel, barbarous days were more than 1300 years removed from the ethical ideals and standards of Jesus. We must judge them by the day in which they lived. We should keep in mind also the fact that by the standards of that day loyalty to the command of their god called for the extermination of all enemies of their god.

In view of the very wicked and licentious practices of these Canaanites we may ask the question, Was not the complete extermination of such people the only safeguard for the future life of his chosen people upon whom so much depended? The grave danger was that the Israelites might become amalgamated with these pagan people, gradually adopt their practices of vicious paganism and lose

*Peters, J. P.: *The Religion of The Hebrews*, pp. 112-113. The Atheneum Press — 1940. Used by permission.

all that they had been commissioned to give to the world. Indeed, this very thing did take place to an extent that was exceedingly dangerous. One wonders how much better it might have been had all these evil influences been removed so that the Israelites might have had an opportunity to develop without these insidious and inviting practices all about them. It might have saved them from the "Dark Ages" which followed the death of Joshua (Lev. 18:24-28).

18. Problems and Perils Ahead.

It was natural for the Hebrew people to assume that with the settlement of the tribes in their new home the most difficult problems and hardest days were over. Gone were the hardships of slave life in Egypt, the dreary years of wilderness wanderings and the hard battles of conquest. The days of struggles and problems were over! Unfortunately this was not the case. There were several very real dangers ahead for these people in their new home.

There was much of the land, both strong cities and open country, still in the hands of these enemy tribes. The conquest was far from complete. A very real peril was the natural inclination to relax too early, to compromise with the enemy rather than conquer him. These strong forces left within their land constituted a danger which might finally lead to the extinction of the whole nation.

Social contacts with these alien tribes provided a real danger. It was easy to look upon these peoples at first as harmless neighbors, then to trade with them, then social relations would lead to marriage, and ultimately to amalgamation. With this occurring they would lose their identity, and forfeit their mission as a distinct race with a special mission to the world.

There was the danger also of the loss of their distinctive religious ideals. The alluring religious practices of the Canaanites would ensnare many of the Hebrews and cause them to stray away from the strict law of Moses.

It will be remembered that originally the Hebrews were a shepherd people. Now that they were in their new home they must adjust themselves to another type of life demanded of a settled agricultural people. This adjustment would not be easy.

Finally, they must work out some plan of governing themselves. This would call for a certain amount of experimenting in which there would of necessity be some mistakes.

With these problems and dangers ahead the future was by no means secure.

SECTION III — THE PERIOD OF THE JUDGES (Judges 1-21, Ruth 1-4).

1. Dark Ages of Hebrew History.

The period which we now enter is known as the "Dark Ages" of Hebrew history. It is characterized by such words as apostasy, decline, disorder and demoralization. It was a time of decline in all areas of life, economic, political, social, moral and religious. It was a time of compromise and acceptance by many of God's people of the ideals and standards of their pagan neighbors. The oft-recurring statement in the book of Judges is "The children of Israel did that which was evil in the sight of Jehovah."

2. History Repeating Itself.

The book of Judges relates the stories of a number of leaders called "Judges." Each story follows the same pattern. It may be called history repeating itself in four stages or steps. (1) The people of God doing evil. (2) Jehovah sending an oppressor to persecute and enslave them. (3) The people in distress praying for deliverance. (4) God raising up a Judge or deliverer to defeat the enemy and deliver the people.

3. Functions of the Judges.

The chief function of these Judges was to serve as military leaders to deliver the people from their oppressors. In some cases their work continued as statesmen or political and judicial leaders after the crisis was past. In some instances they served as religious leaders. In most cases these Judges seem to have passed off the stage shortly after the crisis was over.

It should be remembered that the Judges are not represented as men of ideal character. Indeed, their weaknesses are frankly recorded. For example, Jephthah, an illegitimate son, was a crude, barbaric person who evidently believed in human sacrifice; Samson was weak in religious ideals and moral character. We should judge them in the light of the day in which they lived.

These men served very largely in local crises. They were not leaders of all twelve tribes, and were not, like kings, elected to succeed each other. It is probable that there were times when no judge was serving while at other times two or more might be practically contemporary.

4. List of the Judges.

The number of these depends somewhat on the classification one accepts. For example, some students include both Ruth and Samuel as Judges while others do not.

Usually the number is listed as follows: (1) Othniel of Judah, (2) Ehud, a Benjaminite, (3) Deborah, the prophetess, and Barak, (4) Gideon from Manasseh, (5) Abimelech, son of Gideon, (6) Jair of Gilead, (7) Tolar of Issachar, (8) Jephthah of Gilead, (9) Ibzan from Bethlehem, (10) Elan of Zebulon, (11) Abdon, (12) Samson of Dan, (13) Shamgar.

Of these, six are regarded as leaders. We shall consider these as follows: Othniel, Ehud, Deborah and Barak, Gideon, Jephthah and Samson.

5. Othniel and the Mesopotamians.

Chronologically Othniel came as the first deliverer, and apparently served not many years after the death of Joshua. The people of Judah had yielded to the temptation of indulging in the wicked ceremonies of Canaanite worship, having forsaken the worship of Jehovah. From far-off Mesopotamia a king, Cushan Rishathaim, was sent as an oppressor. For eight years his oppression grew steadily worse until the people called upon Jehovah. Othniel, the nephew of Caleb, rose up as deliverer and in an encounter, the details of which are not given, defeated the enemy, drove them out and thus delivered the people of Judah.

6. Ehud and the Moabites.

The next invader came from Moab east of the Jordan valley. Eglon, king of Moab, crossed the Jordan, captured Jericho and for eighteen years oppressed the tribes east of the Jordan as well as the people of Benjamin and probably of Judah. Ehud, a left-handed warrior from Benjamin, went to the palace of Eglon and asked for a private interview with the king. When he was left alone with Eglon he whipped out his dagger and stabbed him, hurried from the room, locked the door and quickly crossed the Jordan to Mt. Ephriam. Here he organized his army with which he seized the fords of the Jordan and blocked the retreat of the now panicky Moabites as they sought to return to their home. According to the Biblical account he slew ten thousand of the enemy and allowed not one to escape.

7. Deborah and Barak Against the Canaanites.

The Canaanites, who occupied much of the valley of Esdraelon, were the next foe to oppress the Hebrews. Jabin, their king, with his fighting forces threatened the very life of Ephraim and the other tribes in central Canaan. Deborah, a prophetess who dwelt in Ephraim, served as an agent for rallying an army to fight these invaders. She persuaded Barak to undertake to raise an army. He agreed to do this and to lead the fight, provided she would assist. To this she consented with the understanding that in the event of victory credit should go to her. Barak was able to assemble an army of ten thousand men on Mt. Tabor overlooking the valley of Esdraelon. His army met that of the Canaanites on the banks of the river Kishon in Esdraelon. Sisera, with his nine hundred war chariots, led the forces of king Jabin. The Hebrews led the attack and threw the Canaanites into confusion. Just then a furious storm broke over the valley rendering the bows of the Canaanites useless. The rapidly rising waters descending with flood proportions caused the heavy iron chariots to bog in the mud. In this hopeless confusion Sisera leaped from his chariot and fled to the north. The victory against the Canaanites was decisive.

Sisera in his flight came to Kedesh in Naphtali, was given shelter in the tent of a woman named Jael, the wife of Heber, the Kenite. Exhausted, he fell asleep. Then Jael took a long tent pin, drove it through his head and fastened him to the ground in death.

After the overwhelming victory Deborah composed her famous song which was used in celebrating this impressive deliverance. The student should read carefully this beautiful poem (Judges 5:1-31) which is one of the earliest songs of the Hebrew people.

8. Gideon Against the Midianites.

This oppression and deliverance, which is recorded at length, is perhaps the most familiar story in the book of Judges. The foes were the Midianites, the Amalakites, and probably Arab tribes who came from the east under the leadership of Zebah and Zalmunnah with the two chiefs Oreb and Zeeb. They destroyed the crops and inflicted the severest sufferings on the Israelites for seven years.

Gideon, the deliverer, came from the tribe of Manasseh. While threshing wheat he received divine commission to slay the Midianites. Upon his request for a sign to corroborate this commission his offering was miraculously consumed with fire. Later the Lord appeared

to him in a dream and commanded him to destroy the altar of Baal
and in its place to erect an altar to Jehovah. He was then commissioned
to gather an army to fight his enemies. Sending men to the tribes of
Asher, Zebulon, Naphtali, and Manasseh, he sought further proof
of the leadership of the Lord. This was given in the familiar incident
of the wet and dry fleece. He mustered an army of thirty-two thousand
men near Jezreel, but was informed by the Lord that this was too large
a force, lest such an army claim credit to itself for the victory.
Accordingly he proposed that all those who desired to go home should
do so. More than twenty-two thousand then returned home. But ten
thousand were still too many. So when these ten thousand were brought
to the spring to drink Gideon discovered that all but about three
hundred of them, forgetting to be vigilant, got down upon their knees
and greedily slacked their thirst. The three hundred continued to
watch as they dipped water with their hands and lapped the water
with their tongues. These men were selected as his army.

Gideon and his company of three hundred spent the night on the
hill overlooking the valley where the Midianites were encamped.
In the darkness he and his armor-bearer crept down to the enemy's
camp where he overheard two Midianites telling of a dream which
they had and which they interpreted as a certain prediction of the
defeat which the Midianites were to suffer at the hands of Gideon.
He and his companion stealthily returned to their camp and quickly
prepared for their attack. Dividing his group into three equal com-
panies, he gave each man a horn, an earthen pitcher and a torch.
Quietly they crept down the hill to the enemy camp. At the given
signal the three hundred horns were blown, the jars crashed and the
torches blazed. The Midianites, taken completely by surprise, assumed
that their foes were a large army. In the confusion they turned on
each other and then fled in disorder toward the Jordan, hoping to
cross to safety. The two chiefs, Oreb and Zeeb, were captured. The two
kings with a large force succeeded in crossing the river but after a
long chase were captured and their army defeated. Gideon then
returned in triumph to his home.

9. Jephthah and the Ammonites.

Again the people of Judah, Benjamin and Ephraim were guilty
of idoltary and were oppressed by another tribe of fierce fighters,
the Ammonites from the borderland of the desert east of the Jordan.
This oppression was so severe and so prolonged that at length they

cried out for a deliverer. This liberator was found in the person of a crude Gileadite chieftain, Jephthah, an illegitimate son who was without respectable standing. Upon being asked to deliver them from the hands of the Ammonites he agreed upon the promise that if he were victorious he would be given proper recognition among his people. He recruited an army with which he met the Ammonites in the forests of Gilead. He decisively defeated them and took twenty of their strong cities.

Before going to battle Jephthah foolishly and unnecessarily vowed to Jehovah that if he should be victorious he would upon his return home sacrifice whatever should first come out of his house to meet him. After his victory as he approached his home, his only child, a daughter, came out to meet him. He kept his vow and sacrificed his child. Should he have kept his vow? Some students claim that he did right in carrying out his pledge. Others will as vigorously disagree. He should never have made such a vow in the first place since there was nothing in the law of Moses to encourage or sanction it. This incident certainly is not an argument for human sacrifice among the Hebrew people.

10. Samson and the Philistines.

Samson is one of the strangest and most disappointing characters in the Bible. It is not possible in this connection to relate the details of his remarkable exploits which culminated in his tragic death.

The Philistines had long been a serious threat to the Hebrews in central and southern Palestine. They now came forward to oppress the Israelites, especially the people of Dan, whose territory was nearby.

Samson, set apart for his work even before his birth, was endowed with supernatural strength. As one reads the story of his youth, his determination to marry a Philistine girl, his frivolous behavior, the prodigal use of his powers for his own selfish purposes, his indulgence in forbidden pursuits, his immoral conduct, and finally, his capture by the enemy and his death, a sense of keen disappointment comes over him. In all these experiences there is no sign of genuine piety, no evidence of his comprehending his possibilities as a saviour of his people. He never understood his mission; he never measured up to the greatest opportunity of his generation. One can not help wondering what he might have done for his people if he only would. The long bitter struggles with this enemy nation which the Hebrews had to endure for the next hundred or more years might have been averted if Samson had been the right kind of man. Perhaps the chief value of these stories is to show the tragedy of selfish indulgence and wasted opportunities.

11. Three Sordid Stories.

The book of Judges closes with three stories which for lawlessness, idolatory, lust, cruelty, and murder have but few equals in the Bible or elsewhere. These are the story of Micah's image, the moving of the Danites and the crime of Gibeah. We need not relate these stories in this connection. It may be that they are included with impartiality and frankness in the Biblical record to show the degree to which the Hebrew people during this period succumbed to the low standards of the peoples by whom they were surrounded.

12. Story of Ruth.

It is a distinct relief to turn from the depressing and sordid stories of the latter part of the book of Judges to the bright, wholesome and lovely story of Ruth. Critics differ on the question of the exact date of this book. Some feel that it belongs at the very end of the period of Judges (1100 B.C.) while others insist that it should ge placed earlier in the period. Still others would put it as late as 500 B.C. The purpose and value of the book however, are in no way affected by the date.

It is the story of Elimelech and his wife Naomi and their two sons who lived in the vicinity of Bethlehem. During a severe famine the family left their ancestral home and took up their abode in Moab, east of the Dead Sea. While sojourning in this land Mahlon and Chilion, the two sons, married two Moabite girls, Ruth and Orpah. Elimelech, and later the two sons all died in Moab, leaving Naomi and her daughters-in-law in the land. In due time Naomi decided to return to her old home. Her daughters-in-law offered to go with her. Naomi kindly remonstrated, explaining that such was not necessary or expected. Orpah returned to her family but Ruth declared her purpose to accompany her mother-in-law. "Entreat me not to leave thee, or to return from following after thee; for whither thou goest, I will go; and where thou lodgest, I will lodge; thy people shall be my people, and thy God my God. Where thou diest, will I die and there will I be buried; the Lord do so to me, and more also, if ought but death part thee and me."

Upon their arrival in the old home they faced the necessity of making a living. Ruth found work gleaning in the fields of Boaz, a rich farmer. She and Boaz came to love each other and, after a time, were married. This delightful story closes with the account of the birth of a baby boy named Obed. "And Naomi took the child, and laid it on her bosom, and became nurse unto it." This boy, Obed, became father to Jesse who was father to David the great king of Israel. Since Jesus was of the line of David, Ruth the Moabitess was an ancestress of Jesus Christ, the Messiah.

This story of happy, wholesome home life is one of the classic love stories of all ages. It indicates that even in the darkest periods there are always some homes where the choicest values of life are preserved.

13. Hebrew Domestic Life.

During this period the people gradually became settled farmers, though pastoral life was not altogether abandoned. Their farms were small, usually owned by the head of the family. Their products were various kinds of grains, such as wheat, barley and millet; the fruits of the orchard, grapes, figs, apples and olives. No doubt they produced a variety of garden vegetables also. In addition their herds would furnish meat, milk, butter and cheese.

Social life was simple. Visiting between families was then, as always, a delightful custom. Business transactions were simple and involved but little travel and intercourse with foreign peoples.

Government was largely local, each community and tribe furnishing its own leadership. In cases where the interests of all the tribes were involved they seem to have had a sort of assembly of elected representatives called "The whole congregation of Israel." They had no national government and apparently were not keenly conscious of their mission as a nation.

14. Religious Life in This Period.

Considered as a whole, religious life during this period was not of a high order. The general air of decline and compromise affected their worship. Frequently we read of their participation in the idolatrous practices of their neighbors. Faith in an invisible God sustained by prayer and spiritual exercises like that of Abraham, Jacob and Moses apparently had but little appeal to most of the people of this period. Toward the end of the period the light of a better day began to dawn. In the genuine piety and devout faith of Hannah, the mother of Samuel, we see portents of better things. Samuel, trained by his devout mother, proved to be the prophet of a new and better era. However, his story properly belongs to the period to be considered in our next chapter.

Chapter IX

THE UNITED HEBREW MONARCHY

From Samuel to the Death of Solomon
I Samuel, II Samuel, I Kings 1-11, I Chronicles 10-29,
II Chronicles 1-9

Section 1 — Introduction.

1. A Significant Change in Hebrew Life. 2. Material Strength and Splendor. 3. Samuel, Leader in the Transition. 4. Early Years of Samuel. 5. Call of Samuel. 6. Growth of Samuel. 7. The Philistine Upsurge. 8. Statesman, Prophet, Priest.

Section II — The Reign of Saul (I Samuel 9-18).

1. The People's Demand for a King. 2. Election of Saul. 3. Saul's Qualifications. 4. His Great Opportunity. 5. His Relationship with Samuel. 6. Saul's Military Campaigns. 7. Battle of Micmash. 8. Saul's Mistakes. 9. Saul's Plight. 10. Saul and David. 11. David's Behavior Toward Saul. 12. Death of Samuel. 13. Death of Saul. 14. An Appraisal of Saul.

Section III — The Reign of David (I Samuel 19-31, II Samuel 1-24, I Kings 1-2, I Chronicles 10-29).

1. David's Background. 2. Coming into Public Favor. 3. A Fugitive From Injustice. 4. Among the Philistines. 5. Tribute to Saul and Jonathan. 6. King of Judah. 7. Ishbosheth, Abner, Joab, Mephibosheth. 8. King of All Israel. 9. Jerusalem, the New Capital. 10. The Ark and the Temple. 11. God's Message to David. 12. Conquering Surrounding Nations. 13. David's Government. 14. His Sin. 15. Courageous Prophet. 16. Disgrace in the Royal Family. 17. Conspiracy of Absalom. 18. Hushai and

Ahithophel. 19. Defeat and Death of Absalom. 20. Rebellion of Sheba. 21. David in Jerusalem Again. 22. His Last Days as King. 23. An Appraisal of David.

Section IV — The Reign of Solomon (I Kings 1-11, II Chronicles 1-9).

1. The New King and His Kingdom. 2. His Auspicious Start. 3. Solomon's Government. 4. His Wisdom. 5. Building the Temple. 6. Dedication of the Temple. 7. Solomon's Other Buildings. 8. Commercial Enterprises. 9. Solomon's Sins. 10. Beginning of the End. 11. His Character and Contribution.

CHAPTER IX

The United Hebrew Monarchy

From Samuel to the Death of Solomon
I and II Samuel, I Kings 1-11, I Chronicles 10-29, II Chronicles 1-9

Section I — INTRODUCTION (I Samuel 1-8).

1. A Significant Change in Hebrew Life.

The period which we are now to consider covers something more than one hundred years. It began with the closing years of the Judges and terminated with the death of Solomon around 950 B.C. Its significance, however, is out of all proportion to its length. During this period the life of the Hebrew nation underwent a very radical change. In the beginning they were a group of scattered and unorganized tribes, having but little vital connection with each other, living almost as separate peoples. At the death of Solomon the Hebrew nation had attained its highest rank as a nation of wealth and fame. All areas of life — economic, educational, political, social, and religious — were genuinely affected and altered during this time.

2. Material Strength and Splendor.

Under the reigns of her kings, particularly David and Solomon, Israel emerged as a strong and influential national group of the time. When Saul was anointed king the territory occupied by the Hebrews was only about one half of Canaan itself. At the death of Solomon, this kingdom extended from Mesopotamia to Egypt and from the desert to the Mediterranean Sea, an area of some fifty thousand square miles. All bordering nations had been subdued and were paying heavy tribute. A strong army guaranteed protection to the nation. A well organized government functioned in the magnificent buildings erected in the city of Jerusalem. Trade alliances with foreign peoples, together with tribute exacted from subdued peoples, had made Israel a wealthy nation. The glorious reign of David and the wit and wealth of Solomon had made this little kingdom known and respected among all contemporary nations. During this century the Hebrews reached their greatest position of material splendor and fame.

3. Samuel, Leader in the Transition.

The transition from the dark and chaotic days of the Judges to the glorious era of the Kings was not a sudden nor an accidental one.

It came gradually and was effected largely through the life and influence of one man, Samuel. He is called by some the last of the Judges. Others think of him as the first big figure in the new era. Really he was both. He spanned the chasm between the two, closing one period and opening another. He rendered a very valuable service to his nation. In many respects he was the greatest leader between Moses and David.

4. The Early Years of Samuel.

The story of the birth, the boyhood and training of this future prophet is inspiring and encouraging. It centers around the devout and noble mother, Hannah. Eli, the aged priest, ministered in the sanctuary at Shiloh in the highlands of Ephraim. Here, on his elevated seat, the priest observed the worshipers as they came to offer their prayers and sacrifices. Among those who came regularly was Hannah, one of the two wives of Elkanah. Peninnah, the other wife, had several children, but Hannah had none. Because of this she was taunted by her rival. On a certain day Eli watched her in prayer and observed that her lips moved, but hearing no audible words he was puzzled and hastily concluded that she was drunk. Upon being rebuked, however, she told him her story, her deep yearning and her earnest prayer for a baby boy. Eli then apologized and gave her his blessing after which she returned to her home in the country nearby.

At home she prayed most earnestly, vowing to the Lord that if he should give to her a boy she would dedicate him to the Lord for all his life. Her prayer was answered within the year and she gave to her boy the name Samuel (asked of God). When the boy was weaned his mother kept her vow, brought him to the sanctuary and turned him over to Eli to become his helper. The story of Hannah's periodic visits to Shiloh to see her boy, bringing him clothing and loving gifts, is one that always warms the heart. Hannah, the devout mother, kept her vow and prayed for her son and the cause he was to serve.

Eli, the priest, had two sons, Phinehas, and Hophni, who, with their greedy and lustful actions, brought shame to their father and reproach to the worshipers of Jehovah. Their sins, unrestrained by their father, brought a stern warning to Eli that his sons should not succeed him but that death should claim both of them on the same day and that the priesthood should be transferred to another one. Even this seems to have been ineffective as they continued their wicked practices.

5. The Call of Samuel.

This delightful story is a familiar one. One night while asleep the boy Samuel heard a voice which naturally, he assumed to be that of Eli. He reported to Eli but was surprised to learn that the priest had not called him. Twice more the experience was repeated. Then the aged priest suggested to the boy that perhaps it was Jehovah speaking to him, and bade him respond, should the call come again. Samuel, running to his bed again heard the voice and replied as Eli suggested, "Speak, Lord, for thy servant heareth." God spoke to the child to tell the dread news that Eli's sons would be slain and that he (Saumel) was to become the priest. Being encouraged by the aged Eli, the boy told him the substance of his revelation from God. The priest accepted these tidings of disappointment for himself and his sons with the statement, "It is the Lord, let him do what seemeth him good."

6. The Growth of Samuel.

It is not difficult to imagine the main outlines of the life of the boy Samuel as the attendant or helper of Eli at Shiloh. He was by nature, and through the teachings of his mother, respectful and devout in spirit. He was industrious and willing to learn. He could serve the aged priest in numerous ways and could learn many things which later he would be called upon to do. His "call" came when he was probably about twelve years old. Since he was conscious now of his mission in the future, his work would take on new meaning. As Eli grew more feeble and his sons continued in their wicked course, people began to turn to the promising young man. About twenty years passed, and we see Samuel acting as leader of the Israelites in their great assembly at Mizpeh. He was the leader of a religious reformation and was accepted as a prophet of deep spiritual life. He was now ready to lead the nation in the crisis caused by the advance of the Philistines.

7. The Philistine Upsurge.

The Philistines advanced toward ancient Jebus and in a battle killed four thousand Israelites, whereupon the Hebrews resolved to take the Ark into battle against the Philistines in the hope that it would guarantee victory. Phinehas and Hophni accompanied the Ark. In a fierce battle the Philistines, with renewed determination, succeeded in capturing the Ark and in killing 30,000 Israelites. Among the number killed were Phinehas and Hophni, the sons of Eli.

Tidings of the battle were taken back by a runner who privately reported to Eli, sitting by the roadside, that the Ark was in possession of the enemy and that his sons were killed in battle. Upon hearing this Eli fell backward, broke his neck and died. The wife of Phinehas, as she learned of the death of her husband and of the priest, gave birth prematurely to a son, who was given the name Ichabod (the glory has departed), just before her own untimely death.

This victory seemed for a time to be decisive and the Ark remained among the Philistines. However, its presence there was the cause of continued troubles to them. Passed from one city to another, it brought plagues upon them until finally it was returned to the Hebrew people in Bethshemesh in Dan, from whence it was later taken to Kirjath-Jearim the home of Abinadab.

In the meantime Samuel, now an acknowledged prophet and leader, was urging the people to renounce idolatry and return to the worship of Jehovah, their God. The movement gained headway and caused the Philistines to come forth again in battle. Samuel offered sacrifice and, as the Philistines attacked, a sudden storm and earthquake took place. In alarm the Philistines fled, but were pursued by the Israelites who killed many of their number. To commemorate this signal victory Samuel placed on the very spot where twenty years earlier the Philistines had won such a great victory, a large stone which he called Ebenezer (stone of help).

8. Statesman, Prophet, Priest.

During these years Samuel had displayed such qualities of character and strength that he now was the acknowledged leader of all Israel. He stood forth as the one big figure of his time, a man to whom all turned for judgment and guidance. He served as judge or statesman, as priest to direct their worship and as prophet to speak to them the word of God.

As judge, naturally he was chief adviser in all political and judicial questions. He proved himself an able statesman, well informed on all issues, fair and impartial in his decisions. He enjoyed the unquestioned confidence of all the people which placed him in a position to exercise far-reaching influence on the destinies of his nation.

As priest and prophet he was the responsible leader in the religious life of his people. His home was at Ramah but he established "offices" at three other nearby centers, Bethel, Gilgal and Mizpeh. He made regular visits to these cities like the Methodist "circuit riders" of a later day. Upon these official visits he served in both capacities, political and religious, and gave decisions upon all such questions. During this time he foresaw the coming of better days for his people, particularly in religious life. A man of genuine piety and sincere devotion to Jehovah, he gave active leadership to the religious life of the people. At his official posts, Ramah, Shiloh, Gilgal and Mizpeh, he established schools of the prophets. In this way promising young men were brought together to live and study under the direction of a prophet or teacher. Presumably they studied the law of Moses, sacred music and poetry. Under able and experienced teachers they would learn much that would enable them to go back to their respective communities as the harbingers of better days. Undoubtedly these schools were largely responsible for the improved conditions that were to come in the political, moral and religious life of the people of Israel.

SECTION II — THE REIGN OF SAUL (I Samuel 9-18).

1. The People's Demand for a King.

As Samuel grew older there developed a new notion among the people, a desire and even a demand for a change in government which would provide for them a king. There were several reasons for this. Samuel had two sons who proved disappointing to their father and to the nation. The nations bordering on Israel now gave signs of renewed uprisings to threaten the life of the people. The Philistines on the west and the Ammonites from the east of the Jordan were particularly threatening. The leading men of Israel felt that their security demanded a strong military leader. There was an urgent demand for a king who could lead their forces to battle and who could be welcomed with lavish Oriental display upon his victorious return from battle. Finally, they wanted a king in order to be like other nations. Already the pomp and splendor of an Oriental court was making an appeal to them. In this they forgot that Jehovah was really their king which arrangement should have been sufficient for all their needs.

The desire for a king was so general and so urgent that a delegation appeared before Samuel in Ramah to make their request. At first the prophet was displeased. He saw at once the danger of forsaking their God and he knew the perils of such a type of government. But since the demand was so widespread, Samuel gave serious consideration to their petition. After prayer it was revealed to him that he should not refuse, even though this procedure apparently meant the rejection of Jehovah. Samuel was to convene the leaders and point out the real dangers of such a step. This was done but despite the prophet's earnest warnings, they were insistent in their demands. Again Samuel prayed and was told to hearken to their demand. This was a momentous decision. It entailed vast changes in government for the nation. Far-reaching developments were now in the making.

2. *The Election of Saul.*

Samuel warned the people of the dangers in an Oriental monarchy and told them the price they would have to pay, though he agreed to their demand. Shortly afterward the prophet was informed that on the next day the future king would be sent to him. In the meantime, a man named Kish, of the tribe of Benjamin, sent his son, Saul, with a servant to find some asses which had strayed from the pasture. The young man Saul and his attendant came to Ramah and while there decided to call upon the noted prophet. Samuel invited Saul to the feast, gave him special honors and afterward in a long, private conversation, gave him the assurance that he was to be the first king of Israel. He then privately anointed his head with olive oil.

Shortly afterward, in an assembly of Israel's leaders at Mizpeh, Saul was selected by lot to become king. In his modesty he had concealed himself during the casting of lots but was brought out and before the assembly was acclaimed king. The prophet with great foresight carefully explained to them the laws of the new kingdom as contained in Deuteronomy 17:14-20 and caused the people to pledge themselves in writing to observe these laws. After this anointing he then returned to his home in Gibeah. A third anointing was to come at an assembly a short time later.

3. *Saul's Qualifications.*

It will be well at this point to consider the qualifications of this new ruler of Israel. What kind of man was he? He possessed several admirable qualities. He was a man of large physique and attractive appearance. "He was higher than any of the people from his shoulders and upward." "There is none like him among all the people." When he first appeared he was modest and humble. He did not seek the office and apparently was not eager to serve. In the beginning his humility and obedience to God were very commendable. Undoubtedly he had qualities of real leadership. He had the ability to organize and to execute. He was an able military leader as indicated by his decisive victories early in his career. He made a good beginning.

4. His Great Opportunity.

The situation offered him a great opportunity. He was the first king, the one to blaze the trail, to set the pattern for later rulers. He was all but unanimously accepted. He had all the authority of his kingly office. He had the benefits of the wise counsel and the valuable experience of Samuel, the honored and respected leader for so many years. He stood on the threshold of a new day.

Shortly after his public election a situation developed which offered him an ideal opportunity to prove his worth and to establish himself with his people. The Ammonites east of the Jordan, under their king, Nahash, surrounded the city of Jabesh-Gilead. The people of the city hastily offered to make a covenant with Nahash, but he insultingly refused to consider it except on condition that the right eye of all the men of Israel be put out. A seven day's truce was arranged. In this time the Jabeshites sent messengers begging for help from the tribes west of the river. When word came to Saul he accepted the challenge and quickly assembled an army of three hundred and thirty thousand men. He led this army against Nahash and, in an early morning attack, utterly defeated the Ammonites. This decisive victory caused all Israel to turn to their new king with undivided loyalty. He had proved himself.

5. His Relationship With Samuel.

It will be recalled that Samuel gave his approval to the demand for a king and gave his promise of support to Saul with the definite understanding that the new king would recognize always his dependence upon God, and would be obedient to the will of God as conveyed to him by the prophet Samuel. At first Saul kept his word. The secret of his tragic failure at the end was his refusal to be obedient to God. It is worthy of note that in every instance the prophet kept his word and always proved his integrity in his dealings with Saul. When Saul's disobedience and vanity finally forced Samuel to renounce him one can feel in his stern rebuke nothing but pity for the conceited and doomed Saul.

After Saul's great victory when the people were assembled at Gilgal, the aged Samuel witnessed the final inauguration of Saul while the people rejoiced. In this connection Samuel formally stepped aside and relinquished his official leadership of the nation. In a moving address he challenged any and all of the people to name any instances of dishonesty or faithlessness during the years of his service. He then gave his final exhortation for them to remain loyal to Jehovah in the years ahead. His words were ratified by a miracle, a thunderstorm in the midst of the summer, the "dry season" when no rains fall in Palestine. This formal retirement of the honored prophet must have been an impressive occasion. Perhaps none of them ever dreamed that the fatal mistakes later to mar the career of their new king would call forth this honored leader in his old age to serve his people again.

6. Saul's Military Campaigns.

According to the Biblical record Saul led in seven military campaigns. 1. Against the Ammonites at Jabesh-Gilead. 2. Against the Philistines. 3. Several against Moab-Edom and Zobah. 4. Against the Amalekites. 5. Against the Philistines under Goliath. 6. His long and unjustified pursuits of David. 7. Against the Philistines at Mt. Gilboa, which resulted in his death.

7. The Battle of Micmash.

In the first campaign against the Philistines we see Saul in real difficulties. It was a genuine campaign for deliverance from the recurring attacks of his enemy. He took an army of only three thousand men, gave his son Jonathan charge of one thousand of these, and stationed himself with his two thousand men at Micmash, just north of Jerusalem. Jonathan made an unplanned attack on a company of Philistines and defeated them, but this caused a general attack by the enemy which drove back all the army of Saul in defeat to Gilgal. In this defeat the Israelites were bewildered and discouraged. The Philistines, now in possession of central Palestine, inflicted terrible sufferings upon the Israelites. In this crisis Saul sent for Samuel to offer sacrifice in preparation of his army for battle. The prophet delayed his coming and Saul rashly offered the sacrifice himself, thus assuming the perogatives of a priest. Immediately afterwards Samuel appeared and rebuked the king for his sin.

Again Jonathan acted hastily, bursting unexpectedly upon the Philistines at Micmash and again he was surprisingly successful in putting the enemy to rout. Saul was forced to join the pursuit. The enemy, now in utter confusion, fled from Micmash down the slopes to the passes of Ajalon. This was a temporary victory which delivered the Israelites from Philistine oppression and further strengthened Saul's position as king.

8. Saul's Mistakes.

Already the willful and rebellious spirit of Saul was beginning to assert itself. His first sin, mentioned above, was his failure to wait for

Samuel and his assuming the role of the priest. For this Samuel sternly rebuked him and told him that ultimately the kingdom would be taken from his family. The occasion for his second sin, which proved decisive, soon presented itself. After successfully defeating Moab, Ammon and Edom, Samuel appeared to Saul with the command that he should go to war against the Amalekites, their bitter and cruel enemy in the south. He was to administer decisive defeat upon them, even to "slay both man and woman, infant and suckling, oxen and sheep, camel and ass." Saul went as commanded and was completely victorious in the campaign. He carried out the instructions to the letter except for sparing the life of Agag, the king, and saving the best of the cattle. Upon his return he erected a memorial of his victory at Carmel and then proceeded to Gilgal where he met Samuel. He lied to the prophet, professing to have carried out his order in detail. The lowing of the cattle gave him away, as did the presence of Agag. When reprimanded, Saul further betrayed his rebellious and self-sufficient attitude. "The people spared the best of the sheep and of the oxen, to sacrifice unto Jehovah, *your* God." It was necessary now for Samuel to pronounce the doom awaiting the disobedient and deceptive king. "And Samuel, said, Hath Jehovah as great delight in burnt offerings, as in obeying the voice of the Lord? Behold, to obey is better than sacrifice, and to hearken than the fat of rams. For rebellion is as the sin of witchcraft, and stubbornness is as iniquity, and idolatry. Because thou hast rejected the word of Jehovah he hath rejected thee from being king." (I Samuel 15:22-23.)

9. Saul's Plight.

His rejection naturally proved to be a disastrous blow to the king. Even though he was allowed to remain king until his death, his last years were tragic ones. His mind was affected by some sort of madness. His judgment and actions were no longer normal. Periods of deep depression and gloom came upon him. To restore him to sanity, a youthful musician, the boy David, was brought to the court to play the harp to soothe his frenzied soul. This story is the basis for Browning's immortal poem, *Saul*. In this incident we are introduced to the boy who later was to become the famous king of Israel. Another account tells the story of Samuel's secret anointing of David in Bethlehem to become the next king. Directed by the Lord, he called at the home of Jesse who was the descendant of Ruth and Boaz. Jesse had eight sons, one of which was to be anointed. The first seven of these were examined and still God had not indicated his choice. Upon inquiry, Samuel learned that the eighth son, only a lad, was watching the sheep out in the fields. Samuel asked for him to be called in and when this attractive lad appeared it was immediately revealed to the prophet that he was to be chosen. So David was anointed by the prophet to be the next king.

10. Saul and David.

Apparently Saul was unaware of the fact that this boy had been selected to succeed him, for his treatment of the lad who played the harp for him was cordial and friendly. However, a dramatic event took place which caused the king to change his whole attitude toward the boy. Again the Philistines gathered their forces for war against the Israelites. They were led by a giant named Goliath who openly defied any of the Hebrews to fight him. Not even Saul would accept the challenge and all the people were "dismayed and greatly afraid." David, now a young man, came forward to accept the challenge and to announce to Goliath that he was going to kill him in the name of Jehovah the God of the Hebrews. "This day will Jehovah deliver thee into my hand; and I will smite thee, and take thy head from off thee; and I will give the dead bodies of the host of the Philistines this day unto the birds of the heavens, and to the wild beasts of the earth; that all the earth may know that there is a God in Israel." (I Samuel 17:46.)

The story of his dramatic slaying of Goliath is too familiar to be recited here. The effect of it was immediate. The Philistines fled in disarray, to be utterly smitten by the Israelites. David at once became the popular hero of all the people. He was welcomed home with loud acclaim. "The women sang one to another as they played, and said:

> Saul hath slain his thousands,
> And David his ten thousands."

This praise of David inflamed the soul of Saul and he became insanely jealous of young David. "And Saul was very wroth, and this saying displeased him; and he said, They have ascribed unto David ten thousands, and to me they have ascribed but thousands; and what can he have more but the kingdom? And Saul eyed David from that day and forward." (I Samuel 18:8-9.)

11. David's Behavior Toward Saul.

The experiences of David in fleeing from the anger of Saul will be given in the next section of our studies, but it will be well at this point to notice the exemplary behavior of this young man, especially at the magnanimity of soul he exhibited toward Saul, now his enemy. "And David behaved himself wisely in all his ways; and Jehovah was with him. And when Saul saw that he behaved himself very wisely, he stood in awe of him. But all Israel and Judah loved David, for he went out and came in before them." (I Samuel 18:14-16.) Twice during the hard years when he was forced to flee from the king, David had opportunity to kill his enemy, but did not do so. He steadfastly refrained from inflicting any injury upon the king and even made an exile of himself to save his life, but without any criticism of Saul. Finally upon learning of the death of the king he composed a beautiful poem extolling his virtues.

12. The Death of Samuel.

Seemingly during the time when Saul was chasing David, the aged and honored Samuel came to the end of his days. The people came together and buried him in his home at Ramah, the scene of so many historic events in his life. His had been a long and distinguished career. He had guided his people in the crucial years of establishing the kingdom. By his unimpeachable integrity, his unwavering loyalty to Jehovah, his wise counsel and sound judgment he had made a contribution to his nation which few have surpassed.

13. The Death of Saul.

The unhappy situation of Saul grew steadily worse until it culminated in his tragic death on Mount Gilboa. These closing years witnessed a rapid decline in his service to his people and in his own personal fortunes. Instead of following up his early victories over his enemies and devoting himself to constructive planning for his kingdom, he wasted his time in pursuing young David. The sympathy and support of the people were gradually transferred from him to David. In the meantime the Philistines, sensing the unhappy situation in Israel, came again with a great army for the knockout blow. David was a refugee in Philistia, but did not join with them in the war against Saul. With a small army, poorly organized and greatly discouraged, the king must face the mighty hosts of the Philistines. He was in desperate straits. In addition to these difficult circumstances Saul's inward plight was extreme. The spirit of rebellion and self-sufficiency was bearing its bitter fruit. He tried to pray but in disappointment turned despairingly to an outlawed witch at the nearby village of Endor. This strange story, variously interpreted, reveals Saul's desperation. It is worthy of note that he was eager to converse with Samuel, the prophet whom he had so often flaunted. Be it said to the credit of Saul that he got himself together and prepared to fight the next day despite the announcement of certain defeat.

The battle took place next day on Mt. Gilboa. The meagre and discouraged army of Saul was soon put to rout. The Philistines pursued Saul and his sons and killed three of these, including Jonathan. The wounded Saul besought his armor-bearer to kill him. When he refused the king fell upon his own sword and died in the midst of his enemies. "So Saul died, and his three sons, and his armor-bearer, and all his men, that same day together."

The Philistines found the bodies of Saul and his sons, cut off the head of the king, stripped off his armor and sent it back as a trophy to Philistia. They then took his headless body, together with those of his sons, and fastened them to the wall of the city of Bethshan near the Jordan. The people of Jabesh-Gilead, whom Saul had saved in his first great battle as king, now showed their appreciation. Coming by night to Bethshan they removed the bodies from the wall, took them to Jabesh, burned them and then gave honorable burial to their bones.

14. An Appraisal of Saul.

Thus ended the career of the first king of Israel, a career which began well and might have closed in glory. His great weakness was his spirit of rebellion and self-will. He used his power to forward his tyrannical purposes. Resisting steadily the spirit of God he reaped the bitter fruits of his own folly.

However, he rendered a distinct service to his people, and laid some foundations that made possible the brilliant achievements of David his successor. His career was not altogether a failure, but might have been far more glorious, but for his own stubbornness and egotism.

SECTION III — THE REIGN OF DAVID (I Samuel 19-31, II Samuel 1-24, I Kings 1-2, I Chronicles 10-29).

1. David's Background.

In the preceding section we have considered some of the early events in the career of David, since his story is closely interwoven with that of Saul. However, because of the exceptional importance of David's work we shall look further into the background of this remarkable man.

To begin with he came from the large and important tribe of Judah which occupied the prominent place in the history of the Hebrew people. He was the son of Jesse, who was a pious and eminent descendant of Ruth and Boaz. He was born in Bethlehem, a little city six miles south of Jerusalem. This little city, too, has had a prominent place in the affairs of Israel.

The boy is introduced to us as a shepherd lad. As such he would develop self-reliance, courage and a meditative spirit. From the first he seems to have been devout and worshipful in spirit. He was clean in his habits and is described as attractive in appearance with a ruddy complexion. He must have had an unusual combination of desirable qualities — modesty, sincerity, warmth, piety, faith, courage, and a brilliant mind. Many scholars rank David as the foremost character in the Old Testament.

2. Coming Into Public Favor.

David's anointing was in secret and probably was known by only a few. However, he was brought to the king's court as a musician, and while there seems to have served also as Saul's armor-bearer or attendant. The killing of Goliath naturally made a national hero of him. He was now before all Israel and was respected and loved by his people.

This heroic exploit caused the king to become insanely jealous of David, and to begin at once plans to kill him. As a member of the king's court Saul made several attempts. (1) He urged Jonathan and his servants to kill him. (2) He cast a spear at him. (3) He sent for David when he was ill in bed. (4) He sent men to Ramah to seize him. (5) He himself went to Ramah to get him. However, while Saul was seeking to destroy him, other members of the king's family became his fast friends. Merab, the oldest daughter of Saul evidently was friendly to him since her father promised her to him as his wife, though Saul broke the promise. He married Michal another daughter of Saul, who, incidentally, helped him escape from the anger of her father. But the friendship between Jonathan and David was one of exceptional strength and beauty. Indeed, this has become a classic in the annals of friendship. It was mutual, was utterly unselfish and lasted until death overtook Jonathan on Mt. Gilboa. David's lament and tribute to Jonathan is one of his most beautiful poems.

3. A Fugitive From Injustice.

These attempts on his life made it necessary for David to flee for safety. This period of his life when he was being chased by Saul is sometimes referred to as his "outlaw" life. We should remember that he was fleeing, not from justice, but from injustice. This period covered several years and since the limits of space will not permit giving details of these, we shall point out very briefly only the leading experiences.

He fled first to Nob, not far distant, and there was befriended by the high priest. We find him next at Gath where he thoughtlessly exposed himself to his enemies, the Philistines, by going to the home city of Goliath whom he had slain. By feigning madness he escaped from Gath and took refuge in the cave of Adullam in Judah. He went later to the wilderness of Judah but was forced to move on when Saul, learning of his whereabouts, sought him there. The wilderness of Ziph was his next destination and here he had an interview with Jonathan. He stayed in Maon only a short time and then went to Engedi, a small oasis on the western shore of the Dead Sea. He took refuge here in a great cave and generously saved the life of Saul, who, unaware of David's presence, spent the night in the same cave. We find him later at Carmel in southern Judah. While in this vicinity he had his unhappy experience with Nabal, who was punished by death, and whose widow, Abigail, David later married. At Hacilah, evidently not far distant, David was generous enough to spare the life of Saul again. Twice he had refrained from killing the king whose treatment of him was so unjust, because he hoped by such clemency that he might win the king from his foolish course.

4. Among the Philistines.

It is likely that David by this time realized that he could expect no mercy from Saul, and growing weary of the life of a fugitive, he decided to go to the Philistines and ask to be received as a refugee. Upon his request they received him and gave to him the little border city of Ziklag as his home. Here he remained for more than a year. During this time the Philistines were gathering their forces for the great battle against Saul. David was summoned to the king for a decision as to whether or not he should join his enemies, who now gave him refuge, against his own people led by Saul. However, the difficult decision was made for him when the Philistine leaders ruled against his going with them.

While he was away from Ziklag, the Amalekites from the south country came up for a sudden raid on the town. They took away all David's family and possessions and then burned the city. David led his army in pursuit, finally overtook the Amalekites and in a long, fierce battle his men completely defeated them, regained their wives and property and in addition captured much booty to take back home.

5. *Tribute to Saul and Jonathan.*

The outcome of the battle between the Philistines and Saul on Mt. Gilboa near the plain of Esdraelon has already been related. David was in Ziklag when a messenger brought the news of the death of Saul and Jonathan. This messenger claimed credit for killing Saul, hoping to be rewarded by David. To his consternation, however, David ordered him to be killed. In genuine grief David then composed his beautiful song in tribute to Saul the king and Jonathan his son and David's greatest friend.

> "Saul and Jonathan were lovely and pleasant in their lives
> And in their death they were not divided."

To appreciate its beauty the student should read this entire poem. (II Samuel 1:19-27.)

6. *King of Judah.*

The death of Saul left the Israelites without a king. What should David do? After praying to God he was told to go to Hebron where the leaders of Judah would make him their king. In this ancient city, so prominent in the lives of his forefathers, David set up his kingdom and for seven and one half years ruled over Judah. His first act as king was to express to the people of Jabesh-Gilead his appreciation for the honorable burial which they had given to Saul and his sons.

7. *Ishbosheth, Abner, Joab, Mephibosheth.*

After the death of Saul only one son, Ishbosheth, survived. Under the leadership of Abner, a very influential military figure in Saul's regime, Ishbosheth was made king of all the tribes except Judah. He set up his kingdom at Mahanaim, a city east of the Jordan. Naturally there was rivalry between the two kingdoms, and this occasioned a number of skirmishes. Before long a serious difference broke out between Ishbosheth and Abner, because Abner, confident of his position, had taken one of Saul's concubines as wife. When rebuked by the king, Abner angrily announced that he was deserting Ishbosheth and would take the eleven tribes to David. He proceeded at once to Hebron to carry out his design. After a conference with David, Abner departed but was called back by Joab, the crafty military leader of David. Holding Abner responsible for the death of his brother Asahel, and jealous of the enviable position this new ally of David's might occupy, he murdered Abner in the gate of the city. For this unjustifiable cruelty David severely rebuked Joab.

Shortly after Abner's death Ishbosheth was murdered in bed by two of his minor officers, Baanah and Rechab. After their vile deed these two assassins hurried to David hoping to be rewarded for removing his rival. They were doomed to disappointment, however, for David severely censured them for this murder and had them executed.

Of the family of Saul there remained now only one man, Mephibosheth, the son of Jonathan. David, desiring to show his gratitude to Jonathan, sought out this young man, who had been crippled in boyhood and who now lived in Lo-Debar, a little town on the edge of the desert, and invited him to come to the king's court to live permanently "for Jonathan's sake."

8. *King of all Israel.*

With the death of Ishbosheth it was natural that all the tribes should turn to David as their king. When representatives appeared before David offering him kingship over all Israel he accepted and was publicly anointed. At last, after years of trial and disappointment, he was the official ruler of the entire nation. He was the people's choice, he had their hearty support and was now ready to begin a reign which was destined to be a most glorious one.

9. *Jerusalem, the New Capital.*

Now that he was king of all Israel, David faced the need for a new capital city. Hebron was not easily fortified and was not centrally situated. In looking around for a desirable place he came upon an ancient citadel, Jebus, situated in the center of the western highlands and ideal for fortifying. However, since this city was still in the hands of the Jebusites it would have to be taken. David proposed that the man who led in the capture of this city should be commander of his forces. Joab was able to enter the city, probably by following the underground tunnel leading from the Virgin's Fountain outside its walls to the inside of the fortress. The city was taken, though the inhabitants were spared.

This new capital was ideally situated. Located in the center of western Palestine it stood twenty-seven hundred feet above sea level and 4000 feet above the Dead Sea. The city occupied four hills shaped somewhat like a horseshoe with the opening toward the north. It was surrounded on the east, south and west by ravines. On the east was the deep Kidron brook while the Hinnom valley began at the northwest corner and ran south on the west side and flowed east to join the Kidron just southeast of the city. On each side the mountains rise up above the city. The Mount of Olives, the most famous of them, lay just across the Kidron valley to the east of Jerusalem.

Under David this new city was called Zion, city of David, but later took the name of Jerusalem. From now on this lovely city was destined to play a prominent part in the life of the Hebrew nation and of many other peoples, even up to the present time. To millions of people who never saw Mt. Zion it has come to have peculiar significance. It has become enshrined in the hearts of multitudes and somehow symbolizes the dreams and hopes of all spiritually minded men. It is the "Holy City" of history.

10. The Ark and The Temple.

Having secured his capital, David planned to make it headquarters for the religious life of the nation also. The ark, symbolizing the presence of Jehovah, had been for some time at Kirjath-Jearim. After one unsuccessful attempt to bring it to Jerusalem, which resulted in the death of Uzzah, three months later he made elaborate preparations for bringing it to his new capital to be placed in the new tabernacle which he had erected especially for it. The long procession was led by the king himself, accompanied by joyous music for the occasion. When the ark was safely deposited in its new home special sacrifices were offered and the multitude returned to their homes.

It was the sincere desire of David to build a glorious temple for the worship of Jehovah. However, it was revealed to him that this honor should not be his because he was a man of war, but would be reserved for his son as a man of peace. Even though Solomon was to build it, David made all preparations for it, including the actual plans of the building.

11. God's Message to David.

Shortly afterwards God sent Nathan, his prophet, to the king with a special message indicating his pleasure in him and promising to prosper his reign and to make him great among men. "I took thee from the sheepcote, from following the sheep that thou shouldest be prince over my people; over Israel. . . . And I will make thee a great name, like unto the name of the great ones that are in the earth." (II Samuel 7:8-9.) The divine messenger further assured him that the kingship should not depart from his house, but that he would even "establish the throne of his kingdom forever." Immediately following the reception of this memorable message the devout king offered a long prayer of humble thanksgiving. To understand the deep spiritual mind of David the student should read carefully this remarkable prayer. (II Samuel 7:18-29.) Indeed this king of Israel was an unusual servant of God.

12. Conquering Surrounding Nations.

David now inaugurated a series of campaigns for the conquest of the surrounding nations. In these campaigns he was eminently successful. The record of these significant conquests is a very brief one but the effects were far-reaching. These conquests included: (1) the subjugation of the Philistines, (2) conquest of Moab, (3) defeat of Hadadezer of Zobah, (4) subduing Edom, and (5) finally, conquering the Ammonites and the Syrians. With the completion of these conquests he had secured dominion over a vast territory extending from the Euphrates to Egypt, a kingdom some fifty thousand square miles in area. At no other time did the Hebrew kingdom attain such an extended area.

13. David's Government.

With a kingdom expanding in size and wealth, a well organized government with responsibilities assigned to different groups or officers was necessary. From the various references made to these officers it appears that David organized his government somewhat as follows;

1. The king was chief justice, holding court for all the people. He served also as director of all religious services.

2. The king had a cabinet made up of heads of various departments: (1) Joab was head of all military affairs. (2) The king's personal counsellor or private adviser. (3) The official recorder or clerk. (4) The private secretary or scribe for the king.

The army was reorganized by David. His soldiers were divided into twelve divisions of twenty-four thousand each, the entire army being under the direction of Joab. It appears that he had a royal body-guard under Benaiah, and another special military order called "Heroes" or "Mightymen" which was headed by David's nephew, Abishai.

14. His Sin.

When the king was at the height of his power and fame he fell victim to temptation and in an hour of weakness committed a gross sin which brought shame and fearful consequences to himself and his family. The temptation came in a period of idleness. His army was across the Jordan fighting the Ammonites while the king rested in his palace. He became infatuated with a beautiful woman, Bathsheba, the wife of Uriah, one of his soldiers on duty with the army. His sin of adultery with her illustrates the common weakness of man. The story of his sin is told with absolute frankness and at great length in the Biblical record. The fact that such experiences may have occurred frequently in Oriental court life does not exonerate David, the man of God.

Like so many men before and since his day, David attempted to cover one sin by another. Realizing his difficulty, the king ordered Joab to arrange for the death of Uriah by having him placed in the front ranks where death would be certain. This done, David then took Bathsheba as his wife. One wonders at the feelings of Bathsheba in this sordid episode. Was she an innocent victim of the king's passion and cruelty, or did she have some part in initiating and carrying out this unwholesome and tragic occurrence?

15. The Courageous Prophet.

Such a sin on the part of the king must have caused wonderment and shame among his people who idolized him. But such behaviour was not to pass unnoticed. God sent his faithful prophet Nathan, who previously had brought God's message of approval to David, to rebuke him for his sin. This man of God tactfully presented the matter to David by the use of a story which is now very familiar. As the king listened to the account of the poor family whose only lamb was taken by the rich man who had many, David's sense of justice was aroused. He immediately declared: "The man that hath done this thing shall surely die!" Then the fearless Nathan announced: "Thou art the man!" With this declaration Nathan then proceeded to point out the enormity of this sin and to announce the penalty that God would impose. In true humility the great king confessed his guilt, declared his willingness to suffer, and then prayed for the forgiveness of God. He was forgiven, but the fearful consequences of his sin must follow. In this experience of confession and repentance David passed through a period of intense distress and suffering of soul. To understand the depth of his suffering one should read carefully the entire 51st Psalm which he wrote on this occasion and which is still the classic expression of the guilty sinner pleading for forgiveness.

When he was fully forgiven and restored by the grace of God he expressed his relief and gratitude in the familiar words of Psalm 32.

16. Disgrace in the Royal Family.

The effect of one's transgression is never confined to the life of the guilty party. The consequences of David's wrong-doing were tragically reflected in the life of the royal family for years to come.

In due time Bathsheba gave birth to this child "conceived in sin." Ere long the child fell ill, lingered for awhile and then died. This illness and death David interpreted as a punishment for his sin. In this experience the king, after learning of the child's death, gave utterance to the famous expression generally interpreted as his belief in immortality. "Can I bring him back again? I shall go to him, but he shall not return to me" (II Samuel 12:23). Later his wife Bathsheba bore him a second son whom David called Solomon (the peaceful one).

In the meantime David's army under Joab's leadership had utterly defeated the Ammonites and David went out to lead the victorious army home. The conquests of the king were now complete and his regime had reached its zenith of fame and power. From now on the clouds gathered and storm after storm broke over the later years of his reign.

Domestic troubles came thick and fast. The seed which the king had sown bore a harvest of shame in the lives of his own family. His son Amnon became infatuated with Tamar, his half-sister, and forced her in the sin of fornication. Her brother Absalom avenged her disgrace by killing Amnon. Absalom, fearing the anger of his father, David, fled to Syria and remained in exile for a number of years.

17. The Conspiracy of Absalom.

Absalom was a favorite of his father who yearned for his return, even though his crime demanded punishment. Finally through the offices of Joab, Absalom was permitted to come back to Jerusalem "on probation." This return, however, resulted in tragedy for the king. Absalom, treacherous and unscrupulous by nature, soon set into operation his wicked plot to steal the kingdom from his father. By flattery and misrepresentation he won the hearts of many of the people. Carefully laying his plans he soon picked his leaders. When the time was ripe he secured permission from David to go to Hebron under the pretext of worship and there his henchmen met him and proclaimed him king. Ably supported by leaders from all parts of the kingdom he was able to win the majority of the people. David was caught completely off guard, so that it was necessary for him to flee from Jerusalem to save his own life.

18. Hushai and Ahithophel.

With his bodyguard and some faithful friends David hastened from the city down to the Jordan. In his flight he met his trusted friend, Hushai, who swore allegiance to him and offered his services. David urged him to return to Jerusalem, pretend to be the friend of Absalom and in the conference of Absalom's advisers to counteract the counsel of Ahithophel who possessed valuable information which might be used against David. In the conference Hushai was admitted, apparently without suspicion. When called upon for his opinion as to what should be now done, Ahithophel advised that they proceed at once to overtake the fleeing king before he could organize an army for battle. This seemed good to Absalom, but he then called upon Hushai for his opinion. Skillfully Hushai offset the recommendation of Ahithophel by arguing that it would be far better to prepare themselves adequately before attacking David who was an experienced warrior who might be better equipped than they supposed. The scheme worked. Absalom accepted the counsel of Hushai and thus David was given more time to prepare himself for battle. Thereupon Ahithophel, being discredited, went out and committed suicide.

19. The Defeat and Death of Absalom.

In the meantime David and his men hurried across the Jordan to the old city of Mahanaim where temporary headquarters were set up. Joab mustered his army, a larger one than at first appeared possible, and prepared to meet the forces of Absalom. David wanted to lead his men in battle but was dissuaded by Joab on the ground that should he die in battle it would be fatal to their cause. As the men went forth to battle the aged king urged them to deal gently with the young man Absalom, his enemy, but also his son.

The armies met in the forest of Ephraim. It soon became apparent that the forces of Absalom were no match for David's men under the direction of Joab. In the heat of the battle the fighting men of Absalom turned in flight. Absalom himself sought to escape. Mounted on an ass he fled through the forest. As he passed under a large tree he was caught by the head in its branches and was left suspended in midair. One of David's men reported the plight of Absalom to Joab, who hurried to the spot and then ran his spear through the heart of the rebellious son of David. The body of Absalom was then taken down and buried in the forest of Ephraim. With the death of the leader the rebellion was at an end.

Stationed in the gate of the city of Mahanaim, David awaited with anxiety and mixed feelings the tidings of the battle. When the runner appeared with news of the battle the king's first question was, "Is it well with the young man Absalom?" Upon learning of the death of his son, David gave utterance to a lament which echoes the grief of every broken-hearted father:

"Oh my son Absalom, my son, my son Absalom!

Would God I had died for thee, oh Absalom, my son, my son."

David was a king, but he was also a father.

Only after Joab reminded him of his obligation to his faithful warriors was the king able to shake off his grief and become king again. He must now prepare to return to Jerusalem and take up once more his duties as king of Israel.

20. The Rebellion of Sheba.

The defeat of Absalom's army did not end the troubles of the returning king. Another insurrection was led by a man named Sheba, of the tribe of Benjamin, whose grievance was that the ten northern tribes were not properly recognized in bringing David back to Jerusalem. He won quite a following from those tribes. Joab finally took charge of the forces opposing Sheba and soon put him to rout. Sheba and his forces fled to a little town, Abel-beth-maacah in Naphtali, far to the north. Joab and Abishai laid siege of the town and were ready to destroy it when the inhabitants in a conference agreed to deliver Sheba to them if they would call off the siege. These terms were accepted and shortly afterwards they threw over the wall the head of the rebel Sheba. The trumpet was then blown, the siege was raised, and the army returned to Jerusalem.

21. David in Jerusalem Again.

After these two rebellions David, anxious to heal the wounds and regain his prestige as king, made certain concessions and endeavored to restore the unity and glory of former years. But old age and other troubles proved too great a handicap. A three year drought and famine occurred. The strange story of his numbering the people, probably with the idea of boasting of his military strength, was evidence of his failing judgment. Because of his sin in taking this census Jehovah was displeased and sent Gad, the prophet, to give him his choice of three penalties: seven years of famine, three months of defeat before his enemies, or three days of pestilence. David chose the last of these which resulted in the death of seventy thousand men.

22. His Last Days as King.

The close of the reign of David came rapidly. Not long before the end he summoned his son Solomon, and gave over to him all the supplies which he had gathered for building the temple, including even the detailed plans for its arrangement and construction. By this act he showed his preference as to his successor.

The three oldest sons of David were dead, so Adonijah, the fourth son, selected a strong body-guard, won the support of the high priest Abiathar and Joab, and then launched his program to usurp the throne. He came very near succeeding, but was thwarted by Nathan and Bathsheba. Upon the advice of Nathan, Bathsheba appeared before the king, told him of the plot and reminded him of his promise that Solomon should succeed him. Zadok and Beniah were hastily ordered, with Nathan, publicly to proclaim Solomon as king. When the new king was seated on his throne the shouting of the people was heard by Adonijah and his conspirators. Adonijah hurriedly prostrated himself before the new king, promised absolute obedience and begged for mercy. Solomon spared his life at this time but later was forced to order his death.

David, now seventy years old, was obviously coming rapidly to the end. In a solemn assembly he exhorted the new king to be faithful to Jehovah. With great sacrifices Solomon was anointed for the second time and publicly accepted as the new ruler of Israel.

Shortly after this David, the honored and beloved king, was gathered to his fathers, having reigned forty years. He was buried on Mt. Zion, in the city which he had made famous. Thus ended the career of Israel's famous ruler.

23. An Appraisal of David.

David was probably the most colorful character in Hebrew history. He occupies a place of greatness next to Moses in all of the Old Testament. And there are good reasons for this. He had many excellent qualities and was one of the most versatile men in Hebrew history.

He had many admirable personal qualities. From the very first people were attracted to him. He won his way into the affections of Saul's family; he was soon idolized by the public; he was a hero to all the outlaws who followed him in this period of his career; he was respected by his enemies; he was loved by all who came under the spell of his winsome personality.

On the whole his personal character was good. To be sure he stooped to cruel, inhumane acts in war, and he was guilty of immorality. But a careful analysis of his deeds will reveal many noble, courageous and unselfish acts which far outweigh his weaknesses. He was loyal, was honest, was a man of genuine integrity of character.

He was a capable musician, and unquestionably gave great encouragement to this fine art in the life of his people.

He is one of the best known and loved poets of any race or time. Whatever may be the exact number of Psalms composed by him, we can be sure that he wrote a sufficient number to make any man famous.

As a warrior and military man he was fearless and valorous. By his military achievements he made his nation great. No ordinary soldier could have accomplished what he did. No wonder he is still regarded as Israel's great warrior.

As a king he was without an equal in all the life of his nation. He seems to have had all the necessary qualifications. He knew how to select competent leaders, he had a genius for organization, he could judge the feelings and the needs of his people, he had an unselfish passion for the welfare and the glory of his nation.

As a religious leader he was exceptional. To be sure his conception of God and of real religion may fall short of the high ideals of New Testament standards, but he should be judged by the standards of his own day. However, an honest study of his deeds leaves one with the genuine conviction that he was doing what he thought was right and that he was honestly trying to be true to Jehovah as far as he knew. He was "a man after God's own heart."

All in all, it is remarkable that any man of his time could so nearly approach the spirit and ideals of the New Testament as his deeds and his writings reveal him to have done. Many of his writings will continue to be the favorite devotional literature for honest souls seeking a better understanding of and a closer walk with God.

SECTION IV — THE REIGN OF SOLOMON
(I Kings 1-11, II Chronicles 1-9).

1. The New King and His Kingdom.

In the preceding section we have recounted briefly the story of Solomon's succession to the throne of Israel. His coronation, though hastily accomplished, met with universal approval.

The new king was the son of David and Bathsheba. While we know but little of the experiences of his early life we may assume that as the son of the king he would have exceptional advantages and that he probably made good use of these opportunities. He had a good mind and certainly in the beginning of his reign was a man of sincere purpose and of a religious spirit.

He assumed direction of the nation at the time of its greatest material prosperity and splendor. This kingdom extending from Mesopotamia to Egypt, comprised some fifty thousand square miles of territory — the largest in its history. The people were united and at peace with each other and with surrounding nations. David had left an enviable heritage to his son.

Very early in his reign Solomon was forced to deal most severely with leaders who threatened his position as king. Adonijah, who earlier had been mercifully spared by Solomon, now became involved in another scheme which Solomon interpreted as threatening. The safe course seemed to be to get rid of this troublemaker, so the king ordered his execution. At the same time he determined to eliminate the cruel and unscrupulous Joab, who had been guilty of so many murders and had caused so much grief for David. If this seems heartless and brutal we should remember that Solomon was dealing with dangerous and unprincipled men and that the safety of his throne was at stake.

2. *His Auspicious Start.*

Early in his reign Solomon, with a large assembly, went to Gibeon, six miles north of Jerusalem, for the offering of sacrifices. At night Jehovah appeared to the king and said, "Ask what shall I give thee?" The young king, as yet humble in heart, asked not for riches nor long life, nor honor nor for the death of his enemies, but for an understanding heart to judge the people and to discriminate between good and evil. This pleased Jehovah who promised him not only what he had asked, but in addition to these both riches and honor and length of days, if he should walk in the steps of his father David. This was an auspicious beginning for any king.

3. *Solomon's Government.*

In general Solomon used the same plan of organization of his government as that of David, except that the cabinet was enlarged and more departments were added. He created the offices of court chamberlain and superintendent of slaves. The country was divided into twelve districts, nine west of the Jordan and three east of the river. Over each of these a supply officer was placed with the responsibility of providing regular supplies for the king's court, one district for each month of the year. The daily amount of these provisions is given and indicates the size and growing luxury of the court. As the years passed Solomon's court life reached a standard of luxury and extravagance unheard of in all Israel's history. This expansion necessitated an ever increasing number of officials on government pay. For example, it would require many men to take care of his "forty thousand stalls of horses."

4. His Wisdom.

It is traditional to think of Solomon as an exceptionally wise man. The degree to which we accept this view depends somewhat on our definition or understanding of the meaning of wisdom. Unquestionably he had a remarkable knowledge of the natural world, plants, and animals, as his proverbs will demonstrate. He seems also to have had a deep understanding of human nature. His famous decision in the case of the two mothers who claimed the same child illustrates this. Also he possessed an alert and ready mind and was especially gifted in phrasing proverbs. He must have been an entertaining conversationalist, quick at repartee and gifted with a sense of wit. He was a keen observer of human life and knew well the folly of sin and wickedness, and the wisdom of prudence and virtue.

However, a careful examination of his entire career leads one to question his wisdom, certainly in his behavior. If wisdom means the courage to practice his own precepts he failed notably. The latter years of his life witnessed the violation of many of the principles of wisdom which he so eloquently proclaimed.

Solomon acted as chief justice in his kingdom. The fact that he gained such a reputation for wisdom would indicate that he had keen insight and good judgment. His fame was made also by the magnificence and splendor of his buildings, his vast wealth and his extravagant court life. Certain it is that he dominated all the people of his court and was known even to far-off peoples, like the Queen of Sheba. "There came of all peoples to hear the wisdom of Solomon, from all the kings of the earth who had heard of his wisdom."

5. Building the Temple.

One of the first big undertakings of Solomon was to erect the temple which David had planned and had instructed him to build.

This was to be built on the site of the threshing floor of Araunah where the tent of meeting had stood. The site was enlarged in order to accommodate the new structure.

This was an ambitious venture, involving much planning, securing materials and providing workmen. Having no skilled architects and builders in his kingdom Solomon secured these from Hiram, king of Tyre. From Hiram he also obtained cedar timber for the temple. This was cut in the forests of Lebanon, then floated down the coast to Joppa whence it was taken overland up the mountains to Jerusalem. The stone was taken from quarries near Jerusalem, was cut and fitted and then moved to the site of the new edifice. All this work necessitated large numbers of workmen. We are told that there were thirty thousand men employed in cutting the cedars, ten thousand working each third month, eighty thousand cutters of stone and seventy thousand ordinary workmen, besides a large number of superintendents. All the materials were carefully prepared beforehand so that when they were assembled the great building was put up "without the noise of hammer." Gold, silver, bronze and all the other metals were imported.

The building was famous, becoming "the joy of all the earth," not because of its size, since it was comparatively small, but because of its magnificence and the quality of its materials. It was finished only after seven long years of work.

From the various statements given it is difficult to determine the exact detailed plans of this magnificent structure. It is but natural that scholars disagree on these details. However, the following sketch will give the student the most important features of it.

It was built in rectangular form, facing the east. The ground floor was surrounded by a wall facing the court known as the "Court of the Gentiles." One story above this court was another called the "Court of the Israelites," and on a still higher level, the "Court of the Priests."

The temple itself consisted of three general sections, the Porch, the Holy Place, and the Holy of Holies.

The Porch was some fifteen feet deep, thirty feet wide and forty-five feet high. It contained two immense pillars, Jachin (durability) and Boaz (strength) which were richly ornamented.

The Holy Place was thirty feet wide, forty-five feet high and sixty feet long. It was made of hewn stone, with cedar wainscoting and overlaid with gold. This room contained the Golden Altar of Incense, the Table of Shewbread, and the ten Golden Candlesticks.

The Holy of Holies on the west end was a perfect cube thirty feet in height, length and width. It was separated from the Holy Place by a beautiful and expensive veil. It contained the Ark and the huge Cherubim. This room symbolized the presence of the Holy God, Jehovah. It was to be entered only once each year and that by the high priest, who, after elaborate ablutions, entered on the Day of Atonement to atone for the sins of the people.

It is possible that the chambers of the priests, which were three stories high, were on either side of these courts.

6. Dedication of the Temple.

At last when the building was completed an elaborate program of dedication was observed. The priests, the Levites and the leaders of all twelve tribes were invited. The king, elevated in a chair of brass, presided over the ceremonies. The Ark was brought in and placed in the Holy of Holies as a cloud filled the house to hide the presence of Jehovah. The king blessed the great crowd of worshipers and then related the history of the building of this temple of Jehovah. Standing before the altar Solomon offered his long prayer of dedication. This prayer (I Kings 8:23-61) should be read carefully. It reveals an admirable spirit of devotion in the heart of Solomon. "That all the people of the earth may know that Jehovah is God and there is none else. Let your heart therefore be perfect with the Lord our God, to walk in his statutes and to keep his commandments, as at this day." The dedication lasted seven days and was then followed by the Feast of Tabernacles which was lengthened to two weeks instead of the usual one.

7. Solomon's Other Buildings.

After the completion of the temple Solomon set about the construction of a number of other buildings hard by the temple. This series of buildings has been called the "Palace Complex." It consisted of some five structures and required thirteen years for its completion.

Beginning at the south the first building was the "house of the forest of Lebanon" so named because of the forty-five cedar pillars which supported the upper part. It was one hundred and fifty feet long, seventy-five feet wide and forty-five feet high. It was used as a place for storing arms and probably as an assembly hall.

Next to this was a hall seventy-five feet long by forty-five feet wide which was probably an ante-room to the throne hall, where distinguished guests were received.

The throne room was exceptionally ornate and beautiful. The throne itself was made of carved ivory overlaid with gold. A stairway of six steps, with six standing lions at each end, led to the throne.

Next in order was the king's own palace. It was exceptionally large so as to accommodate the large number in his family, and was the last word in beauty and grandeur. Adjoining his own palace was the special apartment or residence for his Egyptian wife.

Upon completion, this series of buildings also was dedicated with great ceremony.

8. Commercial Enterprises.

Not all Solomon's building enterprises were in Jerusalem. To carry on effectively his vast trade enterprises he built up many store cities. Among these famous cities built by him were Tadmor or Palmyra, and Baalath, better known as Baalbek, in Syria. The ruins of these cities testify to the splendor they exhibited when built. In order to protect his kingdom he built up fortresses and accommodations for his army. The extent of all these public buildings is not surely known, but there were many which were scattered widely over his kingdom.

In Solomon's reign we see another new development in the life of the Hebrew people. He entered upon vast commercial enterprises with a number of nations. Some of this trade was probably handled by caravans of camels, but the most significant was his maritime enterprises. Some of this was done on the Mediterranean Sea through an alliance with Hiram of Tyre. His ships are said to have gone as far west as Spain, bringing back great stores of silver. Most of his maritime trade was through the seaport of Ezion-Geber at the head of the Gulf of Akabah. From here his ships sailed through the Red Sea to the Indian ocean and thence east in three year trips. One authority states that on one trip his ships returned with a cargo of gold alone valued at $12,000,000. Other imports from the East included silver, sandalwood, precious stones, ivory, apes and peacocks. Archaeologists have recently found an old silver mine in Abyssinia, or ancient Ethiopia, which they believe was used by Solomon as a source of silver for his kingdom.

It is impossible to say how much wealth came into Solomon's hands through these commercial activities. One scholar has estimated the yearly total at more than $100,000,000 We can be certain that it was stupendous. He secured vast amounts also through tribute exacted from surrounding peoples as well as by the heavy burden of taxes imposed upon his own people.

The accumulation of such wealth, together with the luxurious life of the court resulting from it, brought about a deplorable condition in his kingdom. Perhaps unconsciously Solomon became a typical Oriental despot. In his egotism he lost sight of the rights and welfare of his people. At last the exact situation which Samuel had predicted but which the people demanded, had developed. They had a wealthy and a famous kingdom, but at a terrible price!

9. Solomon's Sins.

The years of Solomon's reign brought a change, not only in the character of his government, but also in the ideals and the conduct of the king himself. Toward the end he had lost his spirit of modesty and humility and had become conceited, haughty and despotic. Riches and luxury had enslaved him and left him restless and unsatisfied. Surrounded by untold wealth and acclaimed as the world's wisest man he came to the end of his days a pathetic figure. Whether he wrote them or not, the words ascribed to him, "Vanity of vanities, saith the preacher, all is vanity," described his condition.

The great sin of Solomon was his loss of devotion to Jehovah. He brought into his court many wives and concubines from Egypt, Moab, Ammon and many other lands. These foreign wives made their demands on the time and attention of the king. For them he must provide, not only the usual courtesies of his court, but in addition, the facilities for enjoying their own national rites and customs. This included the practice of their pagan religious rites, which meant the worship of their idols. The result was the making of Jerusalem, indeed the very temple area itself which was dedicated wholly to Jehovah, the scene of worship of pagan idols and heathen gods. This practice ultimately dulled the king's own religious convictions and led finally to his approval and even his practice of idoltary. This was the sin that proved fatal to Solomon.

10. The Beginning of the End.

Some years before the death of Solomon the outlines of failure and disaster could be discerned. His own people, weary of the heavy burden of taxes for the support of his luxurious court, grew restless and finally rebellious. The surrounding nations who had been oppressed for so long began to gather their forces for rebellion. The collapse of his kingdom came from three directions. Hadad in Edom organized a revolt that was aimed at cutting off Solomon's trade from the Gulf of Akabah. This was a serious setback. In the north, Rezon, a Syrian, seized Damascus to endanger his holdings from that area. The most serious uprising came, however, from among his own people. Jeroboam of Ephraim, employed by Solomon as collector of taxes from Ephraim, saw the abuses and the oppression of the people. Divinely informed of his future place as king of the ten northern tribes, he was the object of Solomon's anger. He fled to Egypt where he remained until after the death of Solomon. However, the story of his return to Ephraim and of his leading the rebellion against Rehoboam, successor to Solomon, belongs to the next chapter.

Solomon's kingdom, while appearing outwardly as unified and strong, was, in reality, honeycombed with weaknesses that were to issue in the fatal division soon after Solomon's death.

11. His Character and Contribution.

After a reign of forty years "Solomon slept with his fathers, and was buried in the city of David, his father."

In many respects his character is a puzzle. There were many noble qualities in his make-up, particularly in his early years. To be sure he was swept off his feet by wealth, luxury and fame but there is no intimation of a lack of honor or integrity in his life. Unquestionably he was a far better man than the ordinary Oriental ruler of his time. We could only wish that he might have been strong enough to withstand the temptations which came to him.

His reign may be characterized by several features. Already we have considered the building and trade enterprises which made him rich and famous. In a word he made Jerusalem one of the most beautiful and notable cities of the ancient world. Solomon will always be regarded as a great builder. During his reign there was no war. He had a well organized army but he led no battles and was able to keep the peace throughout his entire administration. After the completion of the temple he seems to have done but little to promote the religious life of his people. There is no mention of his contact with any prophet or religious leader in all the years of his reign.

The contribution which he made to his nation and to the world was largely in the realm of the material. The impartial student surveying his administration is left with the feeling that here was a man who might have done infinitely better, one who knew what was right but who lacked the strength to measure up to it in his own behavior.

Chapter X

THE RIVAL KINGDOMS

Israel, the Northern Kingdom
I KINGS 11-22, II KINGS 1-17

Section I — Introduction.

1. Significance of This Period. 2. Sources of Information. 3. Chief Events. 4. Division of the Kingdom. 5. Two Rival Monarchies. 6. Relations Between These. 7. Capitals of Judah and Israel. 8. The Kings of Judah and Israel.

Section II — The Kingdom of Israel (From the Division to the End of Ahab's Line).

1. Changing Dynasties. 2. Summary of Leading Events. 3. Jeroboam, the Agitator. 4. Setting the Standards for Israel. 5. Nadab. 6. Baasha. 7. Elah and Zimri. 8. Omri. 9. Ahab and Jezebel. 10. Elijah, Champion of Jehovah Worship. 11. The Contest on Mt. Carmel. 12. Elijah's Reaction. 13. War With Benhadad. 14. Ahab and Naboth. 15. Death of Ahab. 16. Ahaziah. 17. Mesha and the Moabite Stone. 18. Jehoram of Israel. 19. Introducing Elisha. 20. Departure of Elijah. 21. An Appraisal of Elijah. 22. Miracles of Elisha. 23. Naaman, the Leper. 24. Renewed Conflict With Syria. 25. End of Ahab's House.

Section III — The Northern Kingdom (From Jehu to the End).

1. Jehu, the Bloody Reformer. 2. Jehu's Failure. 3. Jehoahaz and Jehoash. 4. Death of Elisha. 5. Jeroboam II. 6. Bloody Days in Israel. 7. Rise of Assyria. 8. Tiglath-Pileser III (Pul.) 9. Shalmaneser V. 10. Sargon II. 11. Sennacherib. 12. Downfall of Israel. 13. The Samaritans. 14. An Appraisal of the Kingdom of Israel.

CHAPTER X

The Rival Kingdoms

Israel, the Northern Kingdom
I KINGS 11-22, II KINGS 1-17

SECTION I — INTRODUCTION.

1. Significance of This Period.

The four hundred years of the period we are now entering were significant ones in the life of all the nations of southeastern Asia and Egypt. It was a time of international movements when various rulers dreamed of world conquests and sent armies forth to conquer rival nations. Syria, Assyria, Babylonia, Egypt and Palestine were all involved in these international struggles. For the Hebrew people it was a time of internal warfare and of severe struggle to survive in a world of shifting national powers. In this period they were in the very center of historically important movements.

2. Sources of Information.

The main events of this important period of Hebrew history are recorded in the books of Kings and the books of Chronicles. Since this is the era in which the greatest Hebrew prophets lived and spoke it is natural that we find much information in the books of prophecy. For example, there are important historical sections of Isaiah and Jeremiah. The prophetical books, however, give greatest assistance in interpreting these events, especially in their religious implications.

In the books of Kings the chief concern of the writer seems to be to show the religious aspect of the reigns of these kings. He passes judgment freely upon each of these. Some he regards as avowedly wicked, others as positively good, and still others as vacillating in their loyalty to God. Of every one of the nineteen kings of Israel, the northern kingdom, he used the same general statement, "he did that which was evil in the eyes of Jehovah." For the sins of their kings the northern kingdom was sent into captivity. Indeed, because of the great wickedness of Manasseh in Judah, which they were never able to overcome, Judah itself was led into Babylonian exile. The writer also gives much space to the work of the prophets, Elijah and Elisha. In this emphasis on the religious life of the nation he often dismisses important historical developments and events with but very brief mention.

3. *Chief Events of This Period.*

This period covers a long stretch of years. It opens with the split of the kingdom left by Solomon, around 950 B.C. and closes with the captivity of Judah 587-86 B.C. The rupture which resulted in two rival kingdoms is told in detail. The main story of these two kingdoms is woven into one account giving now the main developments in one and shifting quickly to outstanding occurrences in the other. The story includes the downfall of Israel with the capture of Samaria in 722 B.C. From this point the writer deals with the experiences of Judah alone, not mentioning Israel again, until Jerusalem is captured and the last group of exiles is taken to Babylonia in 587-86 B.C. Naturally, the record centers around the actions of the nineteen kings in Israel and the nineteen kings and one queen (who does not count) in Judah. A detailed historical record of all these events would fill a large volume.

4. *Division of the Kingdom.*

This event is so significant historically that it merits special consideration. The causes of this schism were both indirect and direct.

Indirectly the causes go back for some time. For many years there had been keen rivalry between the strong tribe of Judah in the south, with its capital city of Jerusalem, and some of the tribes further north. We have seen this showing up in at least two instances. Upon the death of Saul, Judah was quick to accept David as king while the northern tribes set up a rival kingdom under Ishbosheth. Later in the reign of David, Sheba, who probably knew of the old feeling of jealously, was able to launch a rebellion of the northern peoples against David which might well have succeeded. So the idea of division was not a new one.

The direct cause was the foolish behavior of Rehoboam who succeeded Solomon. When Rehoboam went up to Shechem for the confirming of his coronation the northern tribes under Jeroboam, who had hastily returned from Egypt after the death of Solomon, flatly demanded a statement of the new king as to his policy. They were tired of heavy taxes and tyrannical treatment by their king. Rehoboam wisely asked for time to prepare an answer. Three days were allowed for this. During this time the king sought advice from two groups. The older and wiser men urged him to be cautious and considerate, warning him of the real peril. The younger men, probably his friends in the court, advised that he treat the people harshly and put them in their place at once by a bold threat.

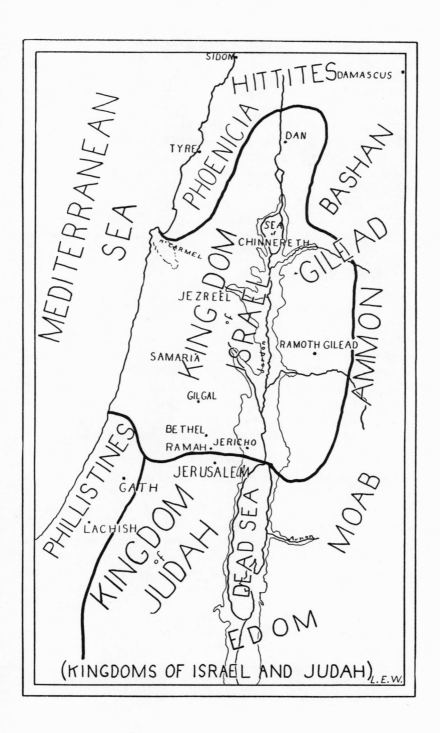

SIDON

HITTITES DAMASCUS

PHOENICIA

TYRE DAN

BASHAN

MEDITERRANEAN SEA

M. CARMEL

SEA of CHINNERETH

GILEAD

KINGDOM of ISRAEL

JEZREEL

RAMOTH GILEAD

AMMON

SAMARIA

GILGAL

BETHEL

RAMAH JERICHO

PHILLISTINES

JERUSALEM

GATH

KINGDOM of JUDAH

DEAD SEA

MOAB

LACHISH

Arnon

EDOM

(KINGDOMS OF ISRAEL AND JUDAH) L.E.W.

At the end of the three days the king appeared before the assembly to announce his decision. He had foolishly decided to follow the course recommended by his luxury-loving associates, and as the people faced him, he declared roughly: "My father made your yoke heavy, but I will add to your yoke: My father chastised you with whips, but I will chastise you with scorpions."

The reaction was immediate. Contrary to what Rehoboam probably expected, they shouted difiantly, "What portion have we in David? Neither have we inheritance in the son of Jesse: to your tents, O Israel: Now see to thine own house, David." The die was cast. The kingdom was split. Jeroboam set to work at once and the new kingdom became a reality.

5. *Two Rival Kingdoms.*

Since these two rival governments were to exist side by side for some 200 years it will be well to make a brief comparison of them. In size Israel was three to four times as large as Judah. In addition, the northern people had all the advantages economically. They were better situated for trade with other nations, and their territory, with its more fertile soil, was much better agriculturally. In one respect Judah was stronger. They had the capital city, Jerusalem, with all its magnificent buildings and the traditions gathered around it as the natural center of political and religious life. Certainly the temple, together with the Levites, gave Judah great strength religiously.

6. *Relations Between These Kingdoms.*

The relations between these two monarchies varied from time to time. For the first sixty years there was almost unbroken strife between them, for it took a long time to convince Judah that they could not ultimately force the rebellious tribes back into a united government. There was a long period when by intermarriage there was more or less peaceful relation between the two. With the destructive work of Jehu this cordial alliance was broken up and amicable relations were never successfully maintained afterwards.

7. *Capitals of Judah and Israel.*

For the southern tribes there was never any change in a capital city. Jerusalem, so splendid and beautiful, served without interruption as headquarters for its government.

The northern government had three different capital cities. At first governmental affairs were administered from the historic old city of Shechem. This was not altogether satisfactory, and for a time the capital was moved a few miles north to the little city of Tirzah. But this, too, proved unsatisfactory. Omri bought the hill of Samaria, admirably suited for this purpose, and on it he built a strong city called Samaria (Shemer's watch-mountain) which remained the capital city until it was conquered by the Assyrians in 722 B.C. With its fall the history of Israel as a kingdom came to an end.

8. *The Kings of Judah and Israel.*

For the convenience of the student we are giving a table of the kings of Judah and Israel, with the length of the reign of each, and the manner of his death.

KINGS OF JUDAH

Rehoboam	17 years	— Died
Abijah	3 years	— Died
Asa	41 years	— Died
Jehoshaphat	25 years	— Died
Jehoram	8 years	— Died
Ahaziah	1 year	— Slain
Athaliah (queen)	6 years	— Slain
Joash	40 years	— Slain
Amaziah	29 years	— Slain
Uzziah	52 years	— Died
Jotham	16 years	— Died
Ahaz	16 years	— Died
Hezekiah	29 years	— Died
Manasseh	55 years	— Died
Amon	2 years	— Slain
Josiah	31 years	— Slain in battle
Jehoahaz	3 months	— Egypt
Jehoiakim	11 years	— Died
Jehoiachin	3 months	— Egypt
Zedekiah	11 years	— Babylon

KINGS OF ISRAEL

*Jeroboam I	22 years	— Died
Nadab	2 years	— Slain
*Baasha	24 years	— Died
Elah	2 years	— Slain
*Zimri	7 days	— Suicide

*Omri	12 years	— Died
Ahab	22 years	— Slain
Ahaziah	2 years	— Accident
Jehoram	12 years	— Slain
*Jehu	28 years	— Died
Jehoahaz	17 years	— Died
Jehoash	16 years	— Died
Jeroboam II	41 years	— Died
Zachariah	6 months	— Slain
*Shallum	1 month	— Slain
*Menahem	10 years	— Died
Pekahiah	2 years	— Slain
*Pekah	20 years	— Slain
*Hoshea	9 years	— Prison

*Founders of Dynasties.

SECTION II — THE KINGDOM OF ISRAEL (From the Division to the End of Ahab's Line. I Kings 11-22, II Kings 1-10).

1. Changing Dynasties.

In the southern kingdom all the rulers except the usurper, Athaliah, were in direct line from David. There were no revolutions resulting in a change of dynasties. In Israel it was quite different. Nine different dynasties or ruling families occupied the throne in these 250 years. Revolutions were frequent; several kings were slain by usurpers who established their own dynasties. One ruler, Zimri, lasted only seven days; Shallum only one month; another, Zachariah, only six months. The following kings usurped the throne and set up new lines of rulers: Jeroboam I, Baasha, Zimri, Omri, Jehu, Shallum, Menahem, Pekah, and Hoshea.

2. Summary of Chief Events.

The sacred writer seems particularly interested in the character of the religious life of Israel. According to his record, all these kings were guilty of idolatry but some were worse than others. In general we may speak of this history under four periods. (1) The first half century (5 kings) was a time when idolatry flourished. (2) The second fifty years (4 kings) saw idolatry all but universally established. (3) This was followed by a time of more than 100 years (5 kings) when, through the work of mighty prophets, Baalism was effectively checked. (4) The last period of some fifty years witnessed the fruitage of idolatry, the downfall of the northern kingdom.

3. Jeroboam, the Agitator.

We shall now go back to look more carefully into the character and activities of Jeroboam I, the man who led in the formation of this new government. He was a capable young man who was originally employed by Solomon as collector of revenue for his native tribe, Ephriam. In this office he proved his capabilities and won recognition. On one occasion the prophet Ahijah, in a private interview, took his new robe, tore it into twelve pieces and gave ten of these to Jeroboam as a token that he would some day lead the ten tribes. No doubt the news of this came to Solomon who then sought to kill Jeroboam. The young man fled to Egypt to escape the threat of Solomon, and while there he seems to have won the friendship of Shishak (Sheshonk) the Pharaoh. It will be seen that when Rehoboam later went to war against Jeroboam and left the city of Jerusalem poorly defended, Shishak came up and took much wealth from the city, including many treasures from the temple. From this incident one may conclude that there was a friendly alliance between Jeroboam and Shishak.

Upon learning of the death of Solomon, Jeroboam hastened back to Ephraim and, no doubt, was a leader in the events which culminated in the division of the kingdom. He was a man of exceptional energy and ability, a natural leader around whom the angry tribes from the north rallied. The rebellion against Rehoboam was so strong and the leadership of Jeroboam so effective that it successfully withstood all the efforts made to break it up and to bring all the tribes together again into one government.

4. Setting the Standards for Israel.

Jeroboam had to start with but little since he had no capital city, no treasury, no cabinet and no kind of organization. He selected Shechem, prominent in the affairs of the people for several centuries, as the seat of his new government. This seems to have met the approval of .his subjects, though other cities were later selected. However, Jeroboam faced a real problem in the deeply intrenched practice of his people in going to the city of Jerusalem for the various religious ceremonies demanded of them. Naturally this glorious city with its temple was so strongly associated with the worship of Jehovah as to cause them to believe that worship could hardly be conducted elsewhere. In their revolt from Rehoboam's government there was no indication that they might not continue to go to Jerusalem at stated intervals for worship. In this practice, however, Jeroboam saw a very real danger to the future of his own government. With their regular return to this city the strong convictions which led to revolt might slowly disappear and thus they might gradually come to question the wisdom of having a separate kingdom. Public opinion might easily lead to union with Judah and the end of the northern kingdom.

To meet the situation Jeroboam set up two shrines for worship in his own territory, one at Bethel, only a short distance from his southern boundary, and one at Dan in the far north. His people were to repair to these shrines for worship and not to return to Jerusalem. Jeroboam's edict stated: "It is too much for you to go up to Jerusalem; behold thy gods O Israel, which brought thee up out of the land of Egypt." The establishing of centers of worship was not wrong; it was legitimate and convenient. The tragic mistake of Jeroboam was in the nature of the worship which he instituted in these places. Instead of Jehovah worship, it was idolatry. At these places he set up two calves of gold around which all worship was to center.

In this fatal policy Jeroboam set the standard for his government. Each succeeding king followed this policy which led to the downfall of the kingdom. Idolatry was never completely exterminated. Later the worship of Baal with all its horrible practices found a welcome and congenial climate in this kingdom.

Jeroboam was an able ruler showing great strength in organization and leadership. He reigned for twenty-two years in which time he made Israel a real nation. However, his lack of faith in Jehovah and his zeal in promoting idolatry earned for him the title, "Jeroboam, the son of Nebat, who made Israel to sin."

5. Nadab.

Jeroboam had two sons, Abijah and Nadab. Abijah died after a severe illness, as predicted by the prophet. Not long afterward, in a battle with the forces of Judah, Jeroboam lost several strong cities, including Bethel. The shock of this defeat affected Jeroboam so deeply that he died shortly afterward, leaving his throne to his son Nadab. Nadab had but a very brief reign. He went to battle against the Philistines but during this time Baasha of Issachar murdered him and all the other descendants of Jeroboam. During the two years of his reign Nadab seemingly accomplished nothing worthy of being reported.

6. Baasha.

Having destroyed all of the family of his predecessor, Baasha had no immediate trouble from inside his kingdom but was soon at war with Asa, king of Judah. Benhadad, king of Damascus, was persuaded by Asa to join him in an alliance against Baasha. War with these neighbors on the south and north kept Baasha occupied for most of the twenty-four years of his reign. Dissatisfied with Shechem as headquarters, he enlarged the little town of Tirzah, a few miles northward, and made it the center of his kingdom. He died a natural death and was buried in Tirzah.

7. Elah and Zimri.

Baasha's son, Elah, succeeded him on the throne. His reign of less than two full years came to an end in a drinking party at Tirzah when Zimri, one of his captains, assassinated him and all his family. Zimri can hardly be recognized as a king since his administration lasted only seven days. Omri was captain of the army and, upon hearing of the death of Elah, he hastened to Tirzah to seize the throne. Zimri, realizing that he had no chance, took refuge in the royal palace and burned it to the ground and lost his own life in the flames. Nadab, Baasha, Elah and Zimri followed in the steps of Jeroboam in practicing idolatry and caused Israel to sin.

8. Omri.

At first Omri had a rival claimant to the throne in the person of Tibni. He soon defeated Tibni and established himself for a reign which lasted twelve years. The Biblical record of Omri's work is very brief. His chief achievement in this record was the setting up of a new capital city. Tirzah was not an ideal city and was now in ruins. In looking over his territory he was attracted to the hill of Shemer not far distant. He purchased this and fortified it by great walls as a protection for the headquarters of his government. To the city he gave the name Samaria. This city was destined to become famous in Israel's history.

The reign of Omri is significant because of his relations with foreign powers, even though this is not mentioned in the Biblical account. He was known as a powerful and influential ruler by the Assyrian people, as their inscriptions indicate. These inscriptions designate Israel as the "land of Omri."

Omri established trade relations with a number of nations, including Phoenicia and Moab. Indeed, he reconquered Moab and as a result was

able to exact heavy yearly tribute from them which the writer of II
Kings enumerates as "one hundred thousand lambs and one hundred
thousand rams, with the wool." (II Kings 3:4.) His relations with
Moab, recounted on the famous Moabite Stone, would verify the
impression that Omri was one of the most important rulers of the
northern kingdom. It should be recorded that the policy of Omri
in religious matters was to walk in the path of Jeroboam and all other
kings of Israel; in fact the record states that he "did worse than all
that were before him." (I Kings 16:25.) Omri died and was buried
in Samaria and was succeeded by his son Ahab.

9. Ahab and Jezebel.

We know but little of the early years of Ahab who came to be
one of the most famous (or infamous) of Israel's kings. The order of
events in his career is not always easy to determine. Furthermore, his
whole character is puzzling. At times he seemed to have been possessed
by worthy motives. At other times he was guilty of unpardonable
offenses. Perhaps we could best characterize him as the vacillating
king. Certain it is that he was completely dominated by his strong-willed
wife, Jezebel. As a result, his reign was generally disappointing, and
altogether reprehensible, certainly from the religious standpoint.

Jezebel, whom Ahab should never have married, was the daughter
of Ethbaal, who by revolution had become king of Sidon (Phoenicia).
She was a most ardent devotee of Baal worship and from the start
seems to have determined to destroy the worship of Jehovah in Israel
and to supplant it with militant Baalism. To this end she devoted
herself most energetically and without scruples. Her husband was a
pliant tool through whom she came very near succeeding in her unholy
project. She brought her religion with its rituals and its priests, into the
land of Israel. Unscrupulous measures, including bitter persecution
and death, were employed by her. The prophets of Jehovah were
destroyed and the entire group would have been annihilated but for
Obadiah, servant of Ahab, who hid one hundred of these in caves and
fed them secretly. The case for Jehovah worship looked hopeless when
all of a sudden, Elijah, the prophet of God, appeared on the scene.

10. Elijah, Champion of Jehovah Worship.

Elijah appears on the scene as a full grown man, an uncompromising
prophet of Jehovah, one of the most powerful and colorful characters
in the Old Testament. We know practically nothing of his early life
except that he is called the Tishbite and that he came from Gilead

across the Jordan. He came first to the court and announced dramatically the coming of a severe drought as punishment for the sins of Ahab and Jezebel in their efforts to destroy Jehovah worship. "As the Lord God of Israel liveth, before whom I stand, there shall not be dew nor rain these years, but according to my word." No doubt they laughed at this crude, country prophet and dismissed him without serious consideration. Little did they realize how valiant a foe he was to prove in those next years. With a beautiful temple for her gods, with four hundred and fifty prophets of Baal and four hundred prophets of Astarte, all supported by the government and backed by the strong influence of the royal family, Jezebel felt no anxiety.

After his announcement Elijah disappeared from the court to await the fulfillment of his prophecy. He went to the brook Cherith, the location of which is uncertain, where for a time he was miraculously supplied with food and water. At length when the brook dried up he was directed to go to Zarephath, a little town between Tyre and Sidon in Phoenicia, the home of Jezebel, headquarters of Baal worship. While in this place two experiences took place according to the Biblical record. He found this area also suffering greatly from the drought and famine. Meeting a widowed woman, he asked for food, only to be told that she had but little meal and oil left and was even then preparing to cook this and then to starve. She generously offered to share this meagre repast with him. He accepted her hospitality, for which she was rewarded with an unfailing supply of meal and oil afterwards. Some time later the widow's son died and was restored to life by Elijah. In the meantime the ravages of the drought were widespread and serious. When three years were ended Jehovah commanded the prophet to show himself to Ahab.

Going forth to Samaria Elijah met Obadiah, the servant of Ahab, who remained faithful to Jehovah. Since the ravages of the drought had been so severe all Ahab's forces had searched for forage for the few cattle still living. Obadiah was commanded by the prophet to report to Ahab that he was ready now to talk to him. Obadiah at first hesitated, but Elijah assured him that he would meet him at that point; so the servant hurried to Ahab's palace and returned, bringing Ahab back with him. In a lively exchange of words Ahab blamed the prophet for all the sufferings of the drought, but Elijah asserted that Ahab's worship of Baal was responsible and then challenged him to a contest in which the real God of Israel should be determined.

11. The Contest on Mt. Carmel.

Elijah declared to Ahab that the time had now come for a showdown between Jehovah and Baal. He proposed a contest on Mt. Carmel, a high mount sloping up from Esdraelon toward the Mediterranean Sea. The four hundred and fifty prophets of Baal and the four hundred prophets of Astarte would assemble on one side while Elijah would represent Jehovah. They would each prepare an altar, place the sacrifice upon it and then pray to their god. The god who answered by fire to consume the offering would be the god of Israel. Ahab agreed to the proposition and these leaders, together with a great crowd of people, went up to the mount to witness the event.

Elijah insisted that his opponents should make their trial first. An altar was erected and the sacrifice was placed on it. Beginning at early morning their prophets, looking up, prayed "O Baal, hear us." Through the morning their prayers went unanswered. At noon time Elijah taunted them, urging them to pray louder since their god might be on a journey or only asleep. With increasing fervor they cut their bodies, and cried unto their god; but there was none to hear nor to answer. Late in the afternoon they accepted defeat and turned to watch Elijah in his petition to Jehovah his God.

The prophet' prepared the altar, slew the victim and placed it thereon. He then dug a trench around the altar and caused four barrels of water to be poured on it three times in succession till the wood was saturated and even the trench was filled. Then calmly and confidently, the strong prophet prayed to his God to vindicate himself. Fire descended, consumed the sacrifice and the wood on the altar and even licked up the water in the trench. Jehovah had spoken. The effect was electric. The people cried out, "Jehovah, He is the God, Jehovah, He is the God." The eight hundred and fifty prophets were taken to the river Kishon where they were slain. Elijah invited Ahab to join in observing the feast to commemorate the signal victory of Jehovah over Baal and Astarte.

The prophet, taking his servant, went to the top of the mountain, and while he engaged in prayer commanded the servant to look out over the sea. Six times the servant reported that he could see nothing, but the seventh time said he had seen a tiny cloud like a man's hand. "Get thee up, eat and drink; for there is the sound of abundance of rain." Ahab was then warned to start immediately for Jezreel, his summer home, before the rains descended. The heavens were soon overcast and the black clouds poured forth a heavy rain to break the long drought. Ahab and Elijah returned to Jezreel. The day had been a remarkable one for Elijah, and for Israel.

12. Elijah's Reaction.

If Elijah thought the matter was finally settled he was mistaken. Jezebel, who for some reason was not a witness to his victory on Mt. Carmel, was not defeated. Upon hearing the disastrous news she immediately sent word to Elijah to flee or take the consequences. The prophet must now find refuge outside the jurisdiction of Jezebel, so he fled southward until he came to far-distant Beersheba. Utterly exhausted in body and spirit, he fell to the ground and begged that he might die! He fell asleep to be awakened later by an angel who told him that he was to proceed to Mt. Horeb. Lodging in a cave of this mountain, he heard the voice of God saying to him, "What doest thou here, Elijah?" The discouraged prophet could only state his deep convictions of failure and express the feeling that it was all in vain. Whereupon God then spoke to him, not in the wind, not in the earthquake, not in the fire, but in a "still, small voice." The cause was not lost, not every knee had yet bowed to Baal. Elijah must return to Israel for work yet to be done. He was to see that Hazael was anointed king of Syria, Jehu of Ramoth-Gilead must be commissioned to destroy the family of Ahab and Jezebel, then Elisha must be prepared to succeed Elijah as prophet in Israel. The restored Elijah then proceeded to return home to his appointed tasks.

13. War With Benhadad.

In the meantime Ahab was having his troubles as king. Benhadad of Syria, with a large company of thirty-two kings which he probably had subdued, now invaded Israel. Approaching Samaria he sent an insulting message to Ahab demanding submission. Ahab refused to submit and was informed by a prophet that he would be victorious over the invader. It came to pass as prophesied and the Syrian king went home. However, he appeared next year resolved to fight only on the plains since he asserted that the Hebrew God was a God only of the hills and not the valleys. Accordingly he encamped in the plains of Esdraelon where the battle was fought. Again Ahab was divinely assured of victory because of Benhadad's statement that Jehovah could be victorious only in the hills. The victory was decisive and Benhadad fell into the hands of Ahab. Ahab played the fool, however, in listening to the persuasive speech of the Syrian king and spared his life and even formed an alliance with him, and allowed him to escape. For this mistake he was severely rebuked.

14. Ahab and Naboth.

While Samaria was still the capital city Ahab had built a summer palace at the beautiful little city of Jezreel in the valley of Esdraelon. Hard by his summer home was the vineyard of a man named Naboth, which Ahab wanted very much to add to his estate. He attempted to buy it but the owner refused to consider selling it since it was his ancestral property. Ahab sulked in disappointment until Jezebel took charge and "fixed" a false charge of blasphemy against Naboth and had him killed. In triumph she told her husband to go now to claim the property which he coveted. As he proceeded to carry out his plans, suddenly Elijah, his enemy of old, appeared and sternly announced: "Thus saith Jehovah, In the place where the dogs licked the blood of Naboth shall dogs lick thy blood, even thine." This prophecy was literally fulfilled.

15. Death of Ahab.

Benhadad soon renewed his war against Israel and Ahab persuaded Jehoshaphat, king of Judah, to join him in this campaign against the Syrian king. The battle took place at Ramoth in eastern Palestine. As the prophet Micaiah told Jehoshaphat and Ahab before they marched forth, the result was to be defeat for both of them. Ahab attempted to disguise himself, but "a certain man drew a bow at a venture" and the arrow found its way into the body of the king. His attendants held his body upright in his chariot, but his wounds were mortal and at evening time this vacillating and wicked king came to the end of his days. The blood of Ahab was washed from his chariot at the pool where Naboth was slain, as Elijah had predicted. A turbulent and bloody reign of twenty-two years had come to its end.

16. Ahaziah.

Ahaziah, the son of Ahab, now became king in Israel. He openly supported idolatry and when seriously ill sent to Baal-Zebub at Ekron to learn whether he should recover. Elijah openly denounced this preference for idolatry. The king, upon hearing this, made two attempts to kill the prophet; but in each instance God spared the life of Elijah. Later Elijah went to the king and denounced him for his sin and told him that he should not recover from the illness caused by his fall. Shortly afterward Ahaziah died, having made but little contribution to his country. "And he did evil in the sight of the Lord and walked in the way of his father Ahab who made Israel to sin."

17. Mesha and the Moabite Stone.

After Benhadad's victory over Ahab and Jehoshaphat, the Moabites, who had long been under the subjection of Israel, were encouraged to rise up in revolt against their oppressors. In this revolt they were successful and threw off their yoke. Mesha, king of Moab, who led the revolt, caused to be inscribed on a pillar the series of events connected with this accomplishment. This inscription is the famous Moabite Stone which was found at Dibon, directly east of the Dead Sea, in 1868. Fortunately, an impression of it was made at once, because the Arabs almost immediately broke it to pieces. The inscription was translated and later the broken pieces were collected and put together. This remarkable stone is now in the Louvre museum in Paris. Its significance is in its remarkable similarity to the account given in II Kings 3:4-27. A part of the inscription reads as follows: "I am Mesha, son of Chemosh . . . King of Moab, the Dibonite . . . Omri King of Israel oppressed Moab many days because Chemosh was angry with his land. And his son succeeded him, and he also said, I will oppress Moab. In my days he spoke, But I saw my desire upon him and upon his house, and Israel perished forever . . . Chemosh restored it in my days."

18. Jehoram of Israel.

Ahaziah's brother, Jehoram, succeeded him as king of Israel. He reigned twelve years before he and all the other descendants of Ahab and Jezebel were slain by Jehu. Thus Jehoram was the last king in the line of Ahab. His reign was important chiefly because of the work of the two prophets, Elijah and Elisha at this time.

19. Introducing Elisha.

It will be recalled that one of the tasks assigned to Elijah while at Horeb was to find Elisha as his successor. Elisha lived in the valley of the Jordan and was the son of a moderately wealthy man. Elijah found him at his work and gave him the invitation to follow him, which apparently he readily accepted. He was to be the helper and the student of Elijah and later, his successor. He probably served for several years as the helper to the great prophet.

20. Departure of Elijah.

It became apparent that Elijah's career was soon to come to an end. He tried to persuade Elisha to remain behind as he made his last journey but his attendant insisted on accompanying him as he went to Bethel and then to Jericho. The two went down to the Jordan while fifty other prophets remained behind to witness what was to take place. As they reached the river its waters divided, permitting the two to cross over to the other side. Elijah asked his successor what was his desire before he was left alone. The sincere Elisha made the unique request "Let a double portion of thy spirit be upon me." As they talked, a chariot of fire and horses of fire appeared to separate them and Elijah was taken by a whirlwind into heaven. Thus Elijah, the strong man of God, was removed from the scene of his notable labors and Elisha was left as his successor.

21. An Appraisal of Elijah

Elijah was a dramatic and colorful figure, a man of strong convictions, of unquestioned courage and great faith. His was not an easy task. It took tact and faith and courage to face the forces of evil and to challenge the entrenched idolatry of his time. His task demanded a stern and a bold spirit. His real achievement was in his effective checking of Baal worship and his keeping alive the religion of Jehovah at a time when it was perilously near to extinction. Life in Israel was hard enough with all that Elijah did to save it. One wonders how much worse it might have been without the contribution of this heroic servant of God.

22. Miracles of Elisha.

As successor to Elijah, Elisha continued to represent Jehovah in the land of Israel. In some respects he was like Elijah; though not as stern he was uncompromising. And yet he was quite different from his predecessor. He was not as dramatic, and had more of gentleness in his make-up. He was quieter, calmer and more persuasive, and yet fully as effective. He was active as a teacher of other prophets, working through the schools at Bethel, Gilgal and Jericho.

Much of his work was done by miracles, most of which were miracles of mercy. For the sake of brevity we are giving a list of the chief miracles attributed to him, without attempting to recount them in detail. All these are recorded in II Kings 2-6.

1. Healing the spring of water at Jericho.
2. Supplying water for Israel and her allied armies.
3. Providing oil for the widow.
4. Restoring to life the son of the Shunamite.
5. Removing the bitter flavor from pottage.

6. Multiplying the loaves for the people.
7. Healing Naaman of leprosy.
8. Making the axe head swim.
9. Leading the Syrians into Samaria.
10. Pronouncing a curse on boys who mocked him.
11. Punishing Gehazi with leprosy.

23. Naaman, the Leper.

One of the most remarkable of Elisha's experiences was the healing of Naaman, the captain of the army of Syria. Naaman lived in Damascus and was a brave and a famous man, "but he was a leper." He was a victim of that dread disease which has been the curse of the Orient. The disease is still incurable, except in its early stages. In his home he had a little servant girl who was a slave brought back from one of his invasions into Israel. This girl told him of the mighty prophet in her land who could perform miracles and who might be able to cure him. Resolved to explore this hope he secured a letter of introduction from Benhadad and taking rich presents with him he called upon Jehoram, king of Israel. Jehoram, suspicious of his motives, declared he could do nothing for him. Elisha then commanded the king to send Naaman to him in order to prove that there "was a prophet in Israel." Naaman with his company went to Elisha's home, but to his surprise he was not formally received by the prophet but was told through a servant to go to the Jordan river and dip himself in its waters seven times. In great anger Naaman declared he would not do such a foolish thing. It he needed to bathe he could do it in the clear, mountain streams of his own land, but not in the muddy waters of the Jordan. However, one of his servants persuaded him to try it, since he had come all this distance. Accordingly he did as commanded and was immediately cleansed so that his flesh was restored "like the flesh of a little child."

Being a gentleman, he then returned to thank the prophet and to make gifts to him. Elisha refused the gifts and sent his distinguished visitor on his way. Gehazi, the servant of Elisha, who coveted some of Naaman's rich gifts, hurried after him and begged for "two talents and two changes of raiment." These were given to him, but Elisha, knowing of Gehazi's avarice and deception, sternly rebuked him and caused him to become a leper "as white as snow."

24. Renewed Conflict With Syria.

Again Benhadad invaded Israel and sought to entrap Jehoram. Warned by Elisha, the king escaped again and again. Learning that the prophet was acquainting Jehoram with his plans to capture him, Benhadad sent a large force of men to Dothan to make Elisha a prisoner. These men were smitten with blindness and led away. Elisha generously intervened and saved their lives when Jehoram wanted to slay them.

Benhadad made still another effort to capture the king of Samaria. With a large army he laid siege to the city for three years. In this time the people of the city suffered extremely from hunger and thirst. So desperate was their condition that they resorted to eating human flesh. One is shocked to read the story of the two mothers who resolved to eat their own sons rather than to starve. In despair the king went to Elisha with the question as to how any one could continue to worship Jehovah in view of such want and suffering. Elisha then prophesied that food could be bought in Samaria next day. That night four lepers, isolated from the city, in desperation went to the camp of the Syrians for food. To their great surprise they found the camp deserted. Having satisfied their hunger they reported their discovery to the officer who in turn informed Jehoram. The king sent officers to look into the matter and upon their return they announced that the Syrians had fled and the siege was over. The forces of Benhadad in the night had heard mysterious sounds of chariots and horses and concluded that the armies of the Hittites and Egyptians were coming to the rescue of the city. To save themselves from this imaginary force they fled in confusion. Thus Samaria narrowly escaped capture by the Syrian army.

25. End of Ahab's House.

After the city of Samaria had been miraculously saved Elisha visited in Damascus where he was received with honor. During the time of his visit Hazael, an officer in the king's army suffocated Benhadad in bed and seized the throne to become the ruler of Syria.

Still another war against Israel was launched by Syria. In a battle at Ramoth-Gilead, Jehoram was wounded and was carried to his summer home at Jezreel to recuperate. His kinsman Ahaziah, king of Judah, came to the palace to visit him during his illness.

In the meantime Elisha sent a messenger from among the prophets to anoint Jehu of Ramoth-Gilead king of Israel and to commission him to go at once to Jezreel and to slay Jehoram and all the other descendants of Ahab and Jezebel.

Section III — THE NORTHERN KINGDOM (From the Accession of Jehu to the Capture of Samaria) II Kings 10-17.

1. Jehu, the Bloody Reformer.

Jehu was a captain in Jehoram's army and at the time was engaged at Ramoth-Gilead. Elisha's messenger sought him out, anointed him and commanded him to proceed at once to destroy the family of Ahab. Without delay he mounted his chariot and with his soldiers drove across the Jordan toward Jezreel. Watchmen from the tower in Jezreel spied him at a distance as he "rode furiously." Jehoram the king, accompanied by his guest Ahaziah, king of Judah, went out to meet him. Without delay he shot an arrow into the heart of Jehoram which caused his death on the estate of Naboth. Ahaziah fled in terror and was able to get only as far as Megiddo where he too was killed. In short order Jehu had slain the kings of Israel and Judah, since both kings were descendants of Ahab. Riding back into Jezreel, Jehu ordered the eunuchs with Jezebel on the housetop to throw her down to the street. Her broken body was devoured by the scavenger dogs so that when the servants went out to get her body for burial they were able to find only her skull, her feet and the palms of her hands. Elijah's prophecy that "in the portion of Jezreel shall the dogs eat of the flesh of Jezebel" had been literally fulfilled.

Jehu's program of slaughter was not yet finished. In rapid order seventy sons of Ahab were slain in Samaria, and in the same place the brothers of Ahaziah were slain. A little later all the priests and followers of Baal were ordered to assemble in their temple at Samaria "for worship." The doors of the temple were locked and the entire group was murdered to a man. In short order the entire house of Ahab and Jezebel. which had been responsible for so much wickedness in Israel, was wiped out in blood.

2. Jehu's Failure.

The new king of Israel had proved himself a ruthless destroyer. He had dealt a severe blow to Baal worship. However, as king he proved a disappointment. He not only showed no concern for Jehovah worship, but actually gave his hearty support to the worship of the calves at Bethel and Dan as set up by Jeroboam. We could hardly rejoice in the work of such a man and naturally are not surprised at the reactions which set in. No wonder that the prophet Hosea condemned his actions of unjustifiable cruelty. (Hosea 1:4.)

During the latter part of Jehu's reign he lost most of his holdings in eastern Palestine to the Syrian king Hazael. The Assyrian monuments state that Jehu had to pay tribute to the Assyrian king, Shalmaneser II. The sacred writer summarizes the character of his reign with the familiar words. "But Jehu took no heed to walk in the law of Jehovah, the God of Israel, with all his heart; he departed not from the sins of Jeroboam, wherewith he made Israel to sin." After a reign of twenty-eight years he "slept with his fathers" and was buried in Samaria.

3. Jehoahaz and Jehoash.

Jehu's son, Jehoahaz succeeded him on the throne. Hazael, the cruel king of Syria, who had successfully contended against Jehu, soon came again to ravage the territory east of the Jordan and to massacre its people. He compelled Jehoahaz to cut his army down to fifty horsemen, ten chariots and 10,000 infantry. There is nothing good reported of his reign of seventeen years. He died leaving the throne to his son Jehoash (Joash).

Joash followed the practice of his predecessors in supporting idolatry in spite of the warnings of the aged Elisha. When Elisha was stricken with his last illness, Joash called on him and wept at the prospect of death for the prophet. Elisha told him to open the window facing the east and to shoot his arrow in that direction. He shot three arrows, but was told by the dying prophet that in not shooting a larger number he had limited his victories to three. After the death of Elisha, Joash gained three victories over the Syrians and recovered the cities formerly taken by them. There is also a statement to the effect that Joash "fought with might against Amaziah, king of Judah." Being challenged by Amaziah to come and "let us look one another in the face" Joash accepted the challenge and "Judah was put to the worse before Israel; and they fled every man to his tent." Joash went to Jerusalem, broke down part of the wall and "took all the gold and silver, and all the vessels that were found in the house of Jehovah, and in the treasures of the kings house," and then returned with hostages to Samaria.

Jehoash reigned for sixteen years and "slept with his fathers and was buried in Samaria."

4. Death of Elisha.

The aged prophet died as a result of the illness on the occasion of Jehoash's visit to him. His career covered a long and eventful period of years, beginning before the ascension of Jehu and continuing for forty-five years after that revolution. He had served well as a counselor of kings and other leaders as well as with the common people. His calm, confident manner, his wise counsel and his uncompromising loyalty to Jehovah made him a powerful force in the life of the nation. The prophets trained by him exerted a strong influence for good among the people. He was held in honor among all the people and his death must have been the occasion for deep grief by all Israel.

5. Jeroboam II.

The first king of Israel, Jeroboam I, was a man of exceptional leadership. Likewise Jeroboam II, the son and successor of Jehoash, was a king who accomplished much for his kingdom. The Bible record speaks briefly, but the record of his political achievements is remarkable. He came to the throne at an auspicious time, a time when other powers were in a weakened condition. He thus had an ideal opportunity to enlarge the borders of his kingdom. This he did from the "approach to Hamath in the extreme north to the Dead Sea in the south." As a result of his conquests the territory occupied by Israel was practically equal to that of the glorious days of David and Solomon. These conquests brought added revenues in tribute and trade so that his reign was characterized by almost unparalleled prosperity and military glory. This tide of material prosperity brought with it serious abuses and real decline in moral and religious life. It was an age of riches without religion and money without morals. The sins attendant upon this era of prosperity were bitterly denounced by two of the strongest prophets, Amos and Hosea, whose work we shall consider in another chapter. After a long reign of forty-one years Jeroboam "slept with his fathers." Religiously, he like all the other kings of Israel, "departed not from the sins of Jeroboam, the son of Nebat, wherewith he made Israel to sin." He was succeeded by his son Zachariah.

6. Bloody Days in Israel.

We now enter an era of anarchy and bloodshed when "the dagger was the symbol of the immediate future." The religious apostasy and moral collapse resulting from the prosperity under Jeroboam II had weakened the nation and destroyed the moral fibre of the people. Henceforth, even to the end of the kingdom (722 B.C.), it was an era of revolution and murder. In the last fifty years there were five different ruling families on the throne, most of which came by revolt and assassination. It was indeed a time when, as the prophet declared, "blood toucheth blood."

Zachariah, the son of Jeroboam II, succeeded his father but occupied the throne only six months before he was assassinated by Shallum, who reigned for only one month, before he was deposed by Menahem. After ten years as king, Menahem died leaving the throne to his son Pekahiah. Pekah, a captian of Pekahiah's guard, slew him after a reign of only two years. Hoshea, the last king, gained the throne at the end of twenty years reign by Pekah. Hoshea was king when the Assyrian army laid siege to Samaria and finally conquered it in 722-21 B.C. This last half century of Israel's history was indeed a dark and bloody era.

7. Rise of Assyria.

During these last fifty years a great empire was rising like a black cloud in the east. Assyria had at this time a number of able and aggressive kings. These kings, understanding the weakness of Syria, Israel and Judah, began to plan the conquest of western Asia so that they would be in an advantageous position against Egypt. For nearly a century this ambitious, cruel, hard-fighting nation was engaged in numerous wars in western Asia. They came very near realizing their dreams of wide conquest. Only Jerusalem, and that by miraculous intervention, was able to escape conquest by them.

8. Tiglath-Pileser III (Pul.).

This mighty warrior came to the throne of Assyria in 745 B.C. His first war was against Babylon. In this he was successful, thereby enlarging his kingdom in the southeast. In 743 B.C. he marched toward Syria but was interrupted in this campaign for a while by other developments. In 740 B.C. he conquered Arpad in northern Syria. He then turned toward Armenia where he was engaged for a time, but in 739 B.C. had to return to Syria to suppress a revolt led by a certain Azriyuh (probably Azariah of Judah). In II Kings 15:19 we are told that Israel was forced to pay Tiglath-Pileser an enormous indemnity, the equivalent of one and one half million dollars. Tiglath was now master of Syria and had Israel, weakened and disunited by anarchy, at his mercy. Well satisfied he now returned to Nineveh for three years (738-735 B.C.).

Pekah of Israel attempted to form a coalition with Rezin of Damascus against Assyria. Evidently these two counted on Ahaz of Judah to join them, but he refused. These two then besieged Jerusalem to force Ahaz, but were unsuccessful. In the meantime Tiglath was marching down the Mediterranean coast to settle the rebels. Ahaz, in a panic, threw himself upon the mercy of Tiglath who made such heavy demands upon him as to result in practical slavery for Judah. Tiglath continued southward along the coast into Philistia where he captured Ashkelon and Gaza. Going around Judah he made terms with an Arab tribe south of the Dead Sea to seal this territory against any enemy from that direction. He then sent his armies through the plain of Esdraelon and cut off and ravaged all the northern part of Israel as well as part of Eastjordania.

Having crippled Philistia and Israel he now marched against Damascus and crushed it in short order in 732 B.C. From Damascus he carried away large numbers of its population into captivity and put Rezin to death.

9. Shalmaneser V.

Tiglath died in 727 B.C. and was succeeded by Shalmaneser V. We know but little about him except his dealings with Israel. The death of Tiglath caused Hoshea, last king of Israel, to entertain hope of throwing off the heavy Assyrian yoke imposed by Tiglath. Hoshea attempted to form an alliance with Egypt against Assyria and began his new policy toward Assyria by withholding from them the heavy tribute which Israel had been paying. Shalmaneser hurried to Samaria in 725 B.C. to quell this rebellion. He took Hoshea prisoner, though what actually became of him we do not know. He laid siege to Samaria in 725 B.C. and for nearly three years the city withstood the rigors of the siege.

10. Sargon II.

In 722 B.C. while Samaria was still unconquered, Shalmaneser died and was succeeded by Sargon II. Shortly after Sargon's accession the city of Samaria fell (722-21 B.C.) and the northern kingdom came to an end. Hardly had his armies won their victory at Samaria before Sargon was forced to march homeward to quell rebellions in other parts of his empire. The Elamites, led by Merodach-Baladan, captured Babylon, and Sargon was never able to regain this important territory. About the same time revolt broke out in Syria. Arpad and Damascus attempted to break his hold upon them. Sargon met and defeated them decisively in the battle of Karkar in 720 B.C. Sargon died in a battle with some desert tribes in 705 B.C.

11. Sennacherib.

Sennacherib, the son of Sargon, now became king of Assyria. In the beginning he was forced to deal with rebellions in several parts of his empire. The campaign of chief interest in our studies is his expedition to Palestine in 701 B.C. to set in order the affairs of his empire in that area. We shall not deal with this campaign at this point since it is a part of the story which belongs to the fortunes of the southern kingdom.

12. The Downfall of Israel.

We return now for a brief glimpse of the last days of the northern kingdom. As we have already seen, this collapse came with the downfall of Samaria, besieged by the Assyrians from 725-722 B.C. Starved into submission the little group of Jews gave up and Sargon took over.

The Biblical record of this important event is very brief. "Then the king of Assyria came up throughout all the land, and went up to Samaria, and besieged it three years. In the ninth year of Hoshea, the king of Assyria took Samaria and carried Israel away unto Assyria, and placed them in Halah, and on the Habor, the river of Gozan, and in the cities of the Medes." (II Kings 17:5-6.)

However, Sargon in his inscriptions gives a specific record of this significant event. "In the beginning of my reign, in my first year (December 722) Samaria I besieged, I captured. Twenty-seven thousand two hundred and ninety persons of its inhabitants I took captive; fifty chariots for my royal equipment I chose; I made it (Samaria) greater than it had been before; people of the lands (I had conquered, I settled there. I appointed my governor over them). Tribute, taxes, I imposed upon them as upon Assyrians."

Thus ended the kingdom of Israel, founded in revolt nearly 250 years earlier. Those captured and taken unto Assyria — a small number for what was once a populous kingdom — are not mentioned again in the record. What became of these captives? Many interesting speculations have been made concerning them but actual proof from historical records is wanting. Many of them perhaps were amalgamated with the peoples of their new home. It is reasonable to suppose that some of these were absorbed, but, with the spirit of exclusiveness and tenacity characteristic of Hebrew people, that many kept together and later joined other groups of Jews. It is to be remembered that when the Jewish people were allowed to return from Babylonian exile under Cyrus, king of Persia, in 536 B.C. to go back home, remnants of all twelve tribes were included in these groups.

13. The Samaritans.

It was a policy of Assyrian rulers to transport peoples from one land to another in order to keep down uprisings. By taking the

Israelites to Assyria he left much of this territory unoccupied. He brought in people from other areas to settle in northern Palestine. He imported "men from Babylon, and from Cuthah, and from Avva, and from Haneath, and Sepharvaim, and placed them in the cities of Samaria instead of the children of Israel." Naturally these brought their gods with them. In his records Sargon mentions still others which he brought into Samaria. "The tribes of the Tamud, Ibadid, Marsiman, Khayapa, distant Arabs, who inhabit the desert, who recognize no overlord who had paid tribute to no king, I smote in the service of Ashur, my lord, the remaining inhabitants I carried them away and settled them in Samaria."

All these conglomerate groups placed in Samaria lived with the remnant of Israelites left there. As time passed these associated with the Jews, intermarried and later formed social units with a common language and a religion made up of various elements and ideals. Out of this group grew the Samaritan people and religion. Racially and religiously they were a mixture. They built their faith around the Samaritan Pentateuch, in many respects similar to the Old Testament faith.

The Samaritans, as they were later called, were already a vigorous group by the time of Nehemiah (445 B.C.) since they gave him so much trouble in his work of rebuilding the walls of Jerusalem. In New Testament times they were a rather large and influential group living in the very heart of Palestine. The Jews despised them as a mongrel race and had "no dealings with them." A small remnant of this group still lives in Nablus, ancient Shechem.

14. An Appraisal of the Kingdom of Israel.

The two hundred and fifty years of history covered by the northern kingdom was a period of great importance, particularly in religious life. Despite the constant policy of idolatry followed in Israel, which caused its destruction, there were some wholesome influences. In the north there was a freer, more democratic spirit than in the conservative kingdom of Judah. The great social, political and religious problems in Israel brought forth some of the greatest prophets and teachers of all Hebrew history. The ministries of Elijah, Elisha, Jonah, Amos and Hosea, all in this period, gave to the world a rich heritage of truth needed for the social and religious problems of each generation. Their messages are both timely and timeless. Indeed, we may say that the failure of this northern kingdom to produce an abiding material kingdom was a small matter compared to the fine contribution made by her prophets. It is ironical that the very wickedness of its people should be the means of calling forth prophets whose condemnation of their own sins should constitute the chief glory and contribution of the kingdom.

Chapter XI

THE RIVAL KINGDOMS (Continued)

Judah, the Southern Kingdom

I Kings 11-22, II Kings 1-25, II Chronicles 10-36

Section I — From Rehoboam to Manasseh.

1. The Kings of Judah. 2. Strength of Judah. 3. Rehoboam. 4. Abijah. 5. Good King Asa. 6. Jehoshaphat. 7. Wars of Jehoshaphat. 8. Jehoram of Judah. 9. Ahaziah. 10. Athaliah, the Usurper. 11. Jehoash and Jehoiada. 12. Joash as King. 13. Amaziah. 14. Uzziah's Long Reign. 15. Jotham of Judah. 16. Ahaz. 17. Hezekiah's Significant Reign. 18. The Siloam Inscription. 19. Hezekiah and Assyria. 20. Hezekiah's Sickness. 21. International Intrigues. 22. Sennacherib's Invasion. 23. Prophets of Judah. 24. Close of the Period.

Section II — From Manasseh to the Captivity of Judah.

1. Long Reign of Manasseh. 2. Manasseh and Esarhaddon. 3. Manasseh's Last Days. 4. Amon. 5. Good King Josiah. 6. Josiah's Reformation. 7. Jeremiah the Prophet. 8. The Entrance of Egypt. 9. Death of Josiah. 10. Assyria and Babylon (Chaldea). 11. Jehoahaz and Jehoiakim. 12. The Coming of Nebuchadnezzar. 13. Jehoiachin. 14. Zedekiah, Judah's Last King. 15. Destruction of Jerusalem. 16. Captives Taken to Babylonia. 17. People Left in Judah. 18. End of the Kingdom of Judah.

The Rival Kingdoms

(Continued)

Judah, the Southern Kingdom

SECTION I — FROM REHOBOAM TO MANASSEH (I Kings 11-22, II Kings 1-20, II Chron. 10-32).

1. The Kings of Judah.

In the preceding chapter the list of the kings of Judah was given. We have seen that all of these rulers, except the usurper queen Athaliah, were in the line of David. Athaliah's brief reign as queen is considered only parenthetically in the Biblical record. The whole history of Judah is in reality the lasting influence of David. In this period of about three hundred and fifty years with one line of kings, backed by the tremendous prestige of David and Solomon, Judah enjoyed a distinct advantage over her rival in the north.

While the northern kingdom lasted a little more than two hundred years and had nineteen kings, Judah continued another one hundred and thirty-four years after the end of Israel, and yet had the same number of kings. This means, of course, that on the whole, the kings of Judah not only had more peaceable reigns but longer ones. To be sure some of these were brief, two of them only three months, but others were very long. Two of them, Uzziah and Manasseh, each reigned more than fifty years. Certainly, from the standpoint of religion, Judah's kings were far superior to those of Israel. A few of these, like Manasseh, were openly wicked, some were indifferent to religion, but many were exceptionally devoted to the worship of Jehovah.

2. The Strength of Judah.

The northern tribes had a great advantage over Judah in size, in economic resources, and in a more progressive policy or outlook. On the other hand, Judah had several distinct advantages. Her territory was more secluded, which made invasion much more difficult. This fact saved the people from defensive warfare a number of times. Then too, she had a unity of government not found in Israel. She was bound together by strong bonds, national ideals and social interests. The people of Judah, with the temple and the priesthood centered in

Jerusalem, naturally had a religious interest or purpose that proved a blessing to them in the crises of their history. This centralized worship of Jehovah was a source of national unity. The very presence of the temple with a system of worship already established was instrumental more than once in keeping the people from going off into the practice of idolatry as in the northern kingdom.

3. Rehoboam.

Rehoboam's "suicidal policy" in losing the ten northern tribes left him in a greatly weakened condition. No doubt he failed to realize the seriousness of the situation and felt that he could "bluff" these rebels. Realizing too late what had occurred, he made desperate efforts over a period of several years to regain control over these revolting tribes. In fact there was almost constant warfare between the two kingdoms for some time. The king was further humiliated by the disastrous invasion of Shishak (Sheshonk) of Egypt. It is likely that Jeroboam made friends with Shishak of Egypt while he was a refugee there during the last days of Solomon. Probably Jeroboam was responsible for the coming of his friend from Egypt against their common enemy, Rehoboam. At any rate Shishak with an enormous army, came up against Jerusalem and forced Rehoboam to pay him off with many treasures from his palace and the temple.

At the beginning Rehoboam apparently tried to walk in the ways of Jehovah. Before long, however, he fell into the same sins as his father Solomon. He took a number of wives and concubines and set up altars to their gods in his kingdom. "He set up images and groves on every high hill and under every green tree." The latter part of his reign was comparatively uneventful. At the end of seventeen years' reign he died in Jerusalem.

4. Abijah.

Abijah, the next king, was the son of Rehoboam and Maacah, the daughter of Absalom. He lived only three years after his accession, but these years were significant ones because of his continuous war with Jeroboam of Israel in an effort to recover the ten tribes. In one decisive battle with only 400,000 soldiers he defeated the army of Israel with 800,000 warriors. As a result of this battle he took the towns of Bethel, Jeshanah and Ephraim. Jeroboam never fully recovered after this severe loss. The Biblical record states that Abijah walked in the sins of his father, his heart not being perfect with Jehovah.

5. *Good King Asa.*

Asa, the son of Abijah, deserved the designation "good" since from the very first he began his program of destroying idolatry and re-establishing Jehovah worship in his realm. He expelled the Sodomites and destroyed the idols erected before his time. He even demoted his idolatrous queen mother, Maacah, from her position and publicly burned her idol. He made strong public appeals to his people to turn from heathen worship and to set up the worship of Jehovah, their true God. His zeal in this effort was contagious and a real reformation took place.

Asa proved to be an able warrior and statesman also. He fortified many cities in his territory and his standing army was numbered at 580,000 men. In the early years of his reign an Ethiopian prince, Zerah, (identified with Osorkon I of the Lybian Egyptain dynasty) came up against him with a mighty host of 1,000,000 men and 300 chariots. By the help of Jehovah Asa was able to defeat him disastrously in battle and to drive him home. After this decisive victory Asa was approved by Oded, the prophet of Jehovah, and then publicly called upon all his people to dedicate themselves wholly to Jehovah worship.

The latter part of his reign was marred by some unhappy events, with the intimation that Asa himself lost some of his faith in God and his zeal for his cause. Baasha, king of Israel, began to fortify the cities in the southern part of his realm. Asa became unduly alarmed and without faith in God hastily appealed to Benhadad, king of Syria, urging him to break his agreement with Baasha and attack Israel on the north. "Let there be a league between me and thee . . . So I have sent unto thee a present of silver and gold; go break thy league with Baasha, king of Israel." Benhadad did as he requested and sent his army against some of Baasha's cities in the north, forcing him to take his men from building the fortresses near Judah in order to fight Benhadad in the north. Then Asa sent his own men to destroy Baasha's fortresses and in their place to build up two strong bulwarks at Geba and Mizpeh.

In this episode the prophet Azariah rebuked Asa for not trusting Jehovah in the crisis. Another prophet, Hanani, rebuked him for his alliance with the Syrian king. For this rebuke Asa, in great anger, put Hanani in prison. In his latter days Asa suffered from a serious foot disease and "he called not on the Lord, but on the physicians." The latter years of his reign seem to be marked by a general breakdown of his faith in God. He died after a long reign of forty-one years which, taken as a whole, was a good administration. He was buried with great mourning by his people in Jerusalem.

6. Jehoshaphat.

Asa was succeeded by his son Jehoshaphat who ruled over Judah twenty-five years. He was an able king, both as a statesman and a religious leader. Indeed, he is rated as one of the best of all Judah's kings. He was vitally interested in the worship of his people and showed his interest early in his reign by a nation-wide program of teaching the people. This was followed by a tour through his kingdom to revive religious interest and loyalty to Jehovah. He received many gifts from neighboring states because of the prosperity which attended his religious program.

He built up a very large army, more than one million men, under competent officers. He fortified a number of cities in Judah and Ephraim. He restored many of the offices of government created by David. His reign was one of genuine prosperity.

7. The Wars of Jehoshaphat.

Evidently he was concerned over better relations between Israel and Judah. At any rate he accepted the invitation of Ahab of Israel to form a military alliance with him against the Syrians. Jehoshaphat's famous reply to Ahab was: "I am as thou art, my people as thy people, my horses as thy horses." The battle between these two confederates and the Syrians took place in Ramoth-Gilead. The Syrians still held this city in their possession, much to the chagrin of Ahab. These kings did not succeed in their effort to get it from Syria. Their forces were routed, Ahab received a fatal wound and Jehoshaphat barely escaped. Upon his return home, Jehoshaphat was rebuked by a prophet named Jehu, for going into this alliance.

Later Jehoshaphat was compelled to go to war against a large army of men from Ammon, Moab and Edom which had advanced against him from the south along the western shore of the Dead Sea. His army, singing psalms, advanced to meet their foes, but there was no occasion to fight. The enemy had engaged in a bitter quarrel among themselves which led to their slaying each other. When Jehoshaphat's army came to the field they found it strewn with the bodies of the slain. For three days his army gathered booty from the field and then returned home.

After twenty-five years' reign Jehoshaphat died, having previously designated his son Jehoram as his successor.

8. Jehoram of Judah.

With Jehoram we enter a dark period of Judah's history — a period in striking contrast to the peace and spiritual prosperity under Jehoshaphat. The alliance between Jehoshaphat and Ahab went further than mere military matters. His son Jehoram married Athaliah, the daughter of Ahab and Jezebel. In this way the pernicious influence of Baalism entered the kingdom of Judah. The new king not only renounced Jehovah and openly practiced idolatry, but he murdered all six of his own brothers and other possible rivals to the throne. For his brazen sins he received bitter chastisement. Edom and Libnah revolted and refused to pay the customary tribute. Later the Philistines and Arabians raided his kingdom and carried away immense treasures and numbers of his people, including all his sons except the youngest. After only eight years on the throne he died with an illness of the stomach, in dishonor even among his own people. His people would not permit his body to be buried in the tombs of the kings.

9. Ahaziah.

The only son of Jehoram left was Ahaziah, the youngest. At the age of twenty-two he became king of Judah. It was only natural that he should follow the ways of his father and his wicked mother Athaliah. It was but natural also that he should ally himself with Jehoram of Israel, his uncle (Athaliah's brother), in his next attempt to take Ramoth-Gilead from the Syrians. This attempt resulted not only in failure but in the death of both kings. Jehoram of Israel was wounded and was taken to Jezreel where Ahaziah went to visit him. It was at this time that Jehu, King of Israel, came and killed them both.

10. Athaliah the Usurper.

Upon hearing of the death of Ahaziah, his mother Athaliah now gave such an exhibition of cruelty and wickedness as to make her one of the most despicable women in history — worse even than her mother Jezebel. "It would be speaking too favorably of this woman to compare her to Lady Macbeth of Scotland" (Blaikie). She proceeded at once to destroy all of the seed royal and all her grandchildren except a tiny boy Joash, the son of Ahaziah, whose rescue was unknown to her. She then took over the throne and for six years Judah had to suffer under her wicked rule. Not many details are given but one can imagine what such a reign must have been.

11. Joash and Jehoiada.

Joash, the next king of Judah, escaped the slaughter of Athaliah through the alertness of his aunt Josheba, the wife of the priest Jehoiada.

This infant of one year and his nurse were rescued and hidden carefully by this devoted couple who planned for a change in Judah in later years. For six years they kept this future king in hiding and no doubt gave him instruction in preparation for the role he was later to play. When he was seven years old — the legal coronation age — the revolution was staged. Jehoiada was in control of the temple worship and Josheba was training the future king. Jehoiada shared his great secret with the soldiers who promised to assist in the scheme. The council of officers approved the coronation of the little prince and the time for it was set for the Sabbath day at an hour when the change of guards would put all the men on the temple area. The lad was brought out, placed on a platform, anointed and crowned as king. The people applauded and shouted "Long live the king."

Athaliah, unaware of what was taking place, heard the shouts of the people and attempted to get to the temple. She got near enough only to see the new king and to cry, "treason!" "treason!" before the guards slew her between the temple and the royal palace. At last Judah was rid of this wicked daughter of Ahab and Jezebel. The house of Baal in Jerusalem was wrecked, its altars destroyed and the priest slain. Joash was placed on the throne as king of Judah. The revolution was completed and a better day was at hand.

12. Joash as King.

During the first part of the reign of young Joash, Jehoiada was virtually the ruler of Judah. The priesthood was the dominant element in the government. Hence it was only natural that a religious reform should be inaugurated. The temple was repaired and Jehovah worship reinstituted. Joash ruled the people well as long as Jehoiada lived, and they prospered. But upon Jehoiada's death at one hundred and thirty years of age a decided change came into the government. Joash forsook Jehovah, revived the worship of Baal and caused the faithful prophet Zachariah, who had the courage to reprove him, to be put to death. The last words of the prophet: "Jehovah look upon it and require it" soon were fulfilled. Hazael, king of Syria, came down the Mediterranean coast, captured Gath (Philistia) and then hastened up to Jerusalem where the frightened Joash bribed him with treasures taken from the temple. In this cowardly act he lost the respect of his people. After forty years on the throne, a bitter and disappointed man, he fell ill. His own servants carried out their conspiracy by murdering him on his sick bed. He was not buried in the tombs of the kings.

13. Amaziah.

Amaziah, the son of Joash, now became king of Judah. One of his first acts was to punish the murderers of his father, though he spared the lives of their children. His first war was with Edom which had rebelled against him. In this he was successful to the extent of capturing the city of Petra. Returning home he established, for some strange reason, the idols of the Edomites. This idolatry brought a severe rebuke from one of the prophets. He next made war on Israel but was defeated and brought back to Jerusalem by Jehoash, king of Israel, who took back with him many treasures from the temple. Amaziah was discredited and despised to such an extent that he decided to flee to Lachish. His flight did not save him since the determined conspirators overtook him there and assassinated him. His body was brought back to Jerusalem for burial "with his father." The length of his reign is given as twenty-nine years.

14. Uzziah's Long Reign.

When only sixteen years of age Uzziah (Azariah), the son of Amaziah, was taken by "All Judah" and made king. His was a long and distinguished reign of fifty-two years. He was an able organizer and administrator and was well informed in agricultural matters. He possessed unusual knowledge of engineering as was shown in the erection of forts and in perfecting an engine for projecting stones. He reorganized the government and strengthened the walls of Jerusalem. He built Elath down on the Gulf of Akabah, built store houses in the wilderness and dug many cisterns to increase the supply of water. He was successful in wars against Philistia, Edom and the Ammonites.

The developments of resources at home, and the conquest of neighboring peoples, together with his ability as a businessman, brought great prosperity to his people. We are told that his fame went abroad among other nations.

In his early years he was loyal to Jehovah and was zealous in his efforts to establish true worship among his people. However, he like others of his predecessors, became vain and self-sufficient. Assuming the role of priest he went into the temple to burn the incense. Eighty priests publicly protested and immediately leprosy broke out upon his forehead. He was forced to spend the remainder of his days in isolation.

15. Jotham of Judah.

Jotham, the son and successor of Uzziah, was likewise an able man. He did much building, including several new cities, together with towers and castles and houses in Jerusalem. He waged successful war against the Ammonites from which he received heavy tribute. He seems to have had very weak convictions in religious matters. It appears that the people continued to practice idolatry and that there were serious moral and social sins in this period. The length of his reign is listed as sixteen years.

16. Ahaz.

The next ruler of Judah was Ahaz, the son of Jotham, whose reign was marked by far-reaching events. He openly rejected Jehovah worship, adopted the idolatrous practices of Israel and even of surrounding nations, including the sacrifice of children. He closed the temple, placed pagan altars all over Jerusalem and inaugurated the unspeakably immoral rites of the Canaanites.

Early in the reign of Ahaz, Pekah of Israel and Rezin of Damascus formed their alliance against Tiglath-Pileser. Ahaz evidently refused to join them and they invaded his realm, carrying away large groups of people. In a panic Ahaz appealed to Tiglath-Pileser for help. To make his situation even worse, the Edomites had retaken Elath on the Gulf of Akabah and the Philistines recaptured their cities previously taken by Amaziah. So he sent messengers to Tiglath-Pileser with the confession: "I am thy servant and thy son; come up and save me out of the hand of the king of Syria and . . . Israel." In addition to this he sent him presents of much gold and silver from the temple and his palace. In his successful invasion the Assyrian monarch conquered much of Palestine. Ahaz, along with others, was taken to Tiglath's new capital, Damascus. While here Ahaz completely prostrated himself before the Assyrian king. One of his first acts upon returning to Jerusalem later was to remove the altar of Jehovah and put in its place one like that of Tiglath's at Damascus. By further decrees and practices he brought the worst influences of paganism into his kingdom.

At the end of sixteen years of disgraceful rule Ahaz, evidently to the relief of all Judah, came to the end of his days.

17. Hezekiah's Significant Reign.

With the accession of Hezekiah better days began to dawn for Judah. He was a man of sincere piety and devotion and a great leader. At once he began a reform in religious practices. He destroyed all the altars to foreign gods erected by Ahaz, reopened the temple and thoroughly cleansed it. He then summoned the priests and ordered them to prepare for the reinstituting of proper worship. He offered sacrifices with the priests and Levites officiating. This caused great rejoicing among the good people of his kingdom.

He went further in his program of reform, attempting to re-establish all the Mosaic program of worship. He sent out invitations to the people in every part of his realm to observe the Passover feast. This was so successful that the feast was lengthened to include two full weeks.

This good king proved his ability by other activities in his kingdom. He built towns and fortresses; he constructed storehouses for surplus products; he encouraged trade and agriculture. He saw the necessity for an additional water supply for Jerusalem and to provide this completed an amazing piece of engineering for his time.

18. The Siloam Inscription.

This enterprise was the cutting of a tunnel from the Virgin's spring under the east side of the City of David to the pool of Siloam within the walls of the southern part of the city. This tunnel was seventeen hundred and fifty-eight feet long, six feet high, and was cut through solid rock. Workmen started at either end and worked toward each other. The two groups met near the halfway point in this underground passageway. So well executed was this task that when they met the two cuttings were almost exactly in line with each other. On the wall of the Siloam end of the tunnel a very remarkable inscription was cut to tell the story of the meeting of these two groups of workmen. The story of the discovery of this inscription is a most interesting one. In 1880 a school boy, who had decided not to attend school for the day, was roaming around the walls of Jerusalem. He found what he thought was a cave and with the typical adventurous spirit of a boy entered this cave to find that it was really a tunnel. He waded through the mud far enough to feel on the walls what he concluded was some writing cut in the stone. He reported this to some friends, with the result that archaeologists equipped with torches, entered the tunnel and found this famous inscription. The part of the wall containing the inscription was carefully cut out, removed, and later translated. It was taken to the Imperial Ottoman Museum in Constantinople where it has remained.

This inscription is translated as follows: "The boring through is completed. And this is the story of the boring through: while yet they plied the drill, each toward his fellow, and while yet there were three cubits to be bored through, there was heard the voice of one calling unto another, for there was a crevice in the rock on the right hand. And on the day of the boring through the stone cutters struck, each to meet his fellow, drill upon drill; and the water flowed from the source of the pool for a thousand and two hundred cubits, and a hundred cubits was the height of the rock above the heads of the stone-cutters." This inscription is the oldest known piece of Hebrew writing in existence.

19. Hezekiah and Assyria.

It was at this time that the ambitious and mighty Assyrian kings were making their conquests in Syria and Israel. In 722 B.C. Sargon II captured Samaria and took Israel into captivity. Apparently Hezekiah was not molested at this time by Sargon who had to hasten to another part of his kingdom to quell a rebellion. About 712 B.C. the king of Egypt laid plans for an invasion of the newly conquered territory of Assyria and for this purpose he formed an alliance with the king of Philistia. Sargon's inscriptions state that Judah, Moab, and Edom joined in this alliance, but were utterly defeated.

20. Hezekiah's Sickness.

It was about this time that Hezekiah's serious illness befell him. He was the victim of a very painful and serious skin disease. In his distress he called upon Isaiah, the great prophet, who told him that his illness would be fatal. In deep humiliation he prayed for forgiveness of his sins and for relief from his sickness. God then sent the prophet to tell him that his prayer was heard and that his life would be extended for fifteen years. A poultice of figs was applied to his body and he was cured. Isaiah records a very moving prayer of thanksgiving uttered by good king Hezekiah for the sparing of his life (Isa. 38:10-20).

21. International Intrigues.

We have already noted the fact that Merodach-Baladan had seized the city of Babylon from the Assyrian king. Sargon was now getting ready to march against this city to recapture it. Merodach in his anxiety sent messengers to Hezekiah — ostensibly to congratulate him on his recovery, but really to spy out his resources and to attempt to enlist his aid against Sargon. Hezekiah was gullible enough to be "taken in" by this scheme. With great pride he showed off all his treasures. For this Isaiah rebuked him and foretold the later captivity of Judah by Babylonia. In the meantime Sargon quickly defeated Merodach and recaptured Babylon.

Egypt again invited Judah to join in a concerted move against Sargon. With the greatest of effort Isaiah was able to keep Hezekiah from joining this unholy alliance.

22. Sennacherib's Invasion.

Sargon was killed in battle in 705 B.C. and was succeeded by his son, Sennacherib. It was a time of shifting international alliances. Hezekiah at last yielded to the temptation to join the enemies of Assyria. He thus greatly reduced his tribute to Sennacherib (a tribute which presumably went back to the days of Ahaz). All southwest Asia was now in virtual revolt against Sennacherib. This emergency caused the Assyrian monarch to hasten to this area to settle matters. Omitting details we may recount only the fact that he came down the Mediterranean coast with a large force and swept all opposition aside until he got to Lachish in Philistia where he was delayed for awhile. This city finally fell. In the meantime many of these little rebel states quickly surrendered to Sennacherib. Hezekiah, seeing the danger for Jerusalem, sent messengers to Lachish to tell Sennacherib: "I have offended; return from me; that which thou puttest on me will I bear."

A deal was made whereby Hezekiah was to pay vast amounts — a sum of approximately $1,500,000 — to Sennacherib. Hezekiah was able to secure this huge gift only by the most desperate measures. He thought this tribute would appease Sennacherib but the greedy Assyrian decided to demand in addition, the surrender of Jerusalem itself.

Space does not permit giving all the details of the events which followed. We can trace only the most important developments. The graphic account of Sennacherib's threat to Jerusalem is given in the tenth chapter of Isaiah. He sent three messengers and an army to Jerusalem. These messengers met three envoys sent out by Hezekiah. In the conversation, which the Assyrians insisted on conducting in the Hebrew language so all by-standers could hear, they taunted Israel and defiantly suggested surrender. "We will furnish two thousand horses if you can furnish riders for them" — an expression of their confidence in the weakened condition of the Jews. Hezekiah's envoys reported this desperate news to the king, who then relayed the news to the great Isaiah. In supurb confidence the prophet assured Hezekiah that the city should not fall to Assyria. "Be not afraid of the words which thou hast heard . . . he shall return to his own land; and I will cause him to fall by the sword in his own hand." The messengers of Sennacherib returned to Lachish without having accomplished their mission.

It appears that later Sennacherib sent another message to Hezekiah, stressing the utter hopelessness of his position in Jerusalem, since even Jehovah his God could not save it now. Again Hezekiah, after the most earnest prayer, turned to Isaiah, and again the prophet assured him that this haughty Assyrian, who had defied God would be unable to conquer the city. God had spoken: "I will put my hook in thy nose, and my bridle in thy lips, and I will turn thee back by the way which thou camest." (II Kings 19:28.) This prophecy came to pass. According to Isaiah's record (37:36) "The angel of Jehovah went forth and smote in the camps of the Assyrians 185,000. And when men arose early in the morning, behold, these were all dead bodies." The famous poem by Lord Byron describes this terrible catastrophe.

> "The angel of death spread his wings on the blast
> And breathed on the face of the foe as he passed;
> And the eyes of the sleepers waxed deadly and chill,
> And their hearts but once heaved, and forever were still.
> "And there lay the steed with his nostrils all wide,
> But through it there rolled not the breath of his pride;
> And the foam of his gasping lay white on the turf,
> And cold as the spray of the rock-beating surf.
> "And then lay the rider distorted and pale,
> With the dew on his brow and the rust on his mail;
> And the tents were all silent, the banners alone,
> The lances unlifted, the trumpet unblown."

There are many theories as to just how this disaster occurred. Suffice it to say that it was done as Isaiah predicted. On the inscriptions of Sennacherib, now deciphered by scholars, there are a number of references to Sennacherib's experiences in Palestine but this disaster is not mentioned. This is but natural since the purpose of the inscriptions of these vain kings was not to preserve an accurate historical record of important events, but to record those exploits of their own which would minister to their pride and assure them a place of honor in the history of their people. We certainly should not expect him to make a record of this humiliating defeat.

Sennacherib returned to Nineveh and later, as he was worshiping in his temple, two of his sons slew him with the sword.

23. Prophets of Judah.

In this chapter we have already referred to Isaiah a number of times. In another chapter we shall deal more fully with his work. As a prophet and a statesman he was the most influential man of the time. He began his work in the year that king Uzziah died (750 B.C.) and continued his ministry for some fifty years during the reigns of Jotham, Ahaz and Hezekiah. He counseled freely with the kings and advised them on the course of Judah in the toughest international problems which the kingdom faced. He was the messenger of God who served well in this crisis of the nation's history. Contemporary with Isaiah, the great city prophet, was Micah, known as the prophet from the country. But he too was a powerful influence for good and along with Isaiah helped to save the nation in one of its real crises. Nahum belongs to this period also. The chief burden of his work was to foretell the ultimate downfall of Assyria with its capital city, Nineveh.

24. The Close of the Period.

Hezekiah died after an eventful reign of twenty-nine years. Manasseh, his son, now came to the throne to open a new era, a period of wickedness and idolatry. The story of these frightful events, however, belongs to the next section of our studies.

SECTION II — FROM MANASSEH TO THE CAPTIVITY OF JUDAH (II Kings 21-25, II Chronicles 32-36).

1. The Long Reign of Manasseh.

With the death of good king Hezekiah, Isaiah and the other prophets, there was a radical change in the life of the nation. Manasseh succeeded his father, Hezekiah, when he was a lad of only twelve-years of age. He was very unlike his father, particularly in his religious affiliations. It may be that he had fallen under the influence of pagan-minded advisers in the court. At any rate he turned immediately away from the religious practices of his father and went completely over to idolatry. He set up in Jerusalem and other places the shrines of Baal, Astarte, Moloch and other heathen gods. He even practiced child sacrifice as required in the worship of Moloch. Wizards, familiar spirits, enchantments and other superstitious practices also were instituted. To make these pagan practices universal, he persecuted the prophets and leaders of Jehovah worship. He refused to hear the admonitions of the faithful and to heed the warnings of the prophets. His new program of worship went to disgraceful extremes and brought about a condition never seen in Judah before or after his day. "Manasseh shed innocent blood very much, till he had filled Jerusalem from one end to another; besides his sin wherewith he made Judah to sin." (II Kings 21:16.)

2. Manasseh and Esarhaddon.

At the time of his death Hezekiah was still paying annual tribute to Assyria. Evidently this was continued by Manasseh, since his name is included on the Assyrian inscriptions in the list of kings paying tribute. Upon the death of Sennacherib in 681 B.C. his son Esarhaddon came to the Assyrian throne. Two or three years after his accession he began a long and signally victorious campaign down into Palestine and all southwest Asia. He conquered Phoenicia and practically all other opponents and actually succeeded in conquering Egypt down to Thebes. He was the first Assyrian to gain a foothold in this coveted land. He had done what his predecessors for more than a century had dreamed of doing. Upon the death of Esarhaddon 668 B.C., his son Asshurbanipal became the ruler of Assyria. He, too, made one or more trips to the Mediterranean countries to quell uprisings. Against Egypt and some of the other rebel nations he had to use brutal and powerful forces. In all these Assyrian campaigns it appears that Judah was allowed to keep her independence, though, no doubt, many captives were taken away. Finally, however, Assyria gained access to Jerusalem and Manasseh was carried to Babylon as a captive.

3. Manasseh's Last Days.

For some reason Manasseh was allowed to return from captivity to his home land. He seems to have been given authority over Samaria as well as Judah, probably upon the understanding that he would remain loyal to Assyria and thus serve as a block to the rebellious Egyptian kingdom.

Upon his return to Jerusalem the aged Manasseh immediately turned from all the former idolatrous practices and became a very energetic and sincere advocate of Jehovah worship. In all sincerity he attempted the impossible task of undoing all the wickedness of his early years. He made determined efforts but apparently discovered that it was impossible to turn back the tide. After fifty-five long years on the throne he died and left the kingdom to his son Amon.

4. Amon.

Amon, whose name was that of an Egyptian god, was twenty-two years old when he became king. His policy was exactly that of his father Manasseh in the beginning of his reign. He went to work to undo the last reforms of his aged father and went to excess in his enthusiastic advocacy of idolatry. His behavior was so disgraceful that his own servants slew him in the second year of his reign.

5. Good King Josiah.

Josiah was one of the best of Judah's kings, a man loved and honored because of his character and achievements. He came to the throne when only eight years old, having been trained by God-fearing friends. His loyalty to Jehovah was well known and was soon demonstrated by his efforts to clear out idolatry and to strengthen the worship of Jehovah.

One of his most important enterprises was the repairing of the temple which had been neglected for so long. Money was collected for the undertaking and workmen were employed. Hilkiah the priest was in charge of the work. In clearing out the temple they found a roll or a book, probably the Pentateuch, in one of the closets. Shaphan the scribe, read this book the contents of which were so startling that he carried it to the king. This document predicted disaster to the wicked city. Huldah, the prophetess, then predicted that the city of Jerusalem would ultimately be destroyed, but not until after the death of Josiah. Josiah was so deeply moved that he called for an assembly of the priests for the reading of this book. Thereupon it was agreed to institute a reform movement in order to carry out the requirements stated in the book.

6. Josiah's Reformation.

Assisted by the influence of the prophet Jeremiah, the king set in motion plans for a nationwide reformation. The first step was the utter destruction of all forms of pagan worship in the land. This program of destruction was most thoroughgoing. Even the priests who ministered at these altars were slain. Having cleaned out all idolatry, they next proceeded to replace it with a comprehensive program of real worship services. The whole nation was called upon to observe the Passover feast. This was done with elaborate sacrifices and great ceremony. Outwardly at least, the reformation was complete. There were, however, too many of his subjects who were sympathetic with idolatry for this reform to accomplish fully its intended purpose. Josiah did his best but the sins of Manasseh could not be completely eradicated.

7. Jeremiah the Prophet.

Allusion to the forceful prophet, Jeremiah, has already been made, and we shall give a fuller discussion of his work in another chapter. However, since he was so closely identified with the historical record in these last years of Judah it will be well to speak briefly of his work at this point. He was a native of Anathoth, a little village not far from

Jerusalem. His ministry covered a period of approximately fifty years. He began his work about the time of Josiah's reformation and throughout the closing years of the southern kingdom he was a powerful, though unpopular, force in this period. He fearlessly condemned the wickedness and treachery of kings. Finally, he openly declared that captivity was inevitable and should be accepted. He was the one steady and reliable influence in these unhappy years.

8. The Entrance of Egypt.

During the reign of Josiah significant international movements took place. Assyria, after more than a century of cruel domination, was fast coming to an end of her control of southwest Asia. Egypt, ambitious for a larger place in world affairs, unwisely lined up with Assyria. Babylonia was on the threshold of a period of ambitious expansion while Media was backing her up. Babylonia, now supported by the Medes, made ready for the knock-out blow to Nineveh, the capital of Assyria.

In 616 B.C. an Egyptian army had gone to Syria to assist Assyria in her struggle against the advance of Babylon and Media. In 612 Nineveh fell under the siege of her enemies. Pharaoh Necho of Egypt felt that he must get additional help to Assyria at Carchemish before his ally was completely crippled.

9. The Death of Josiah.

In order to get to Assyria's relief Necho must pass through Palestine. For some reason Josiah refused to give him permission to go through his territory. There are various theories as to why Josiah made this refusal, but, at any rate, he was determined to block the passage of Egypt's army. He hurried to Megiddo and attempted to stop Necho. In the encounter he was killed. The body of this beloved king, so honored and respected by his people, was brought back to Jerusalem for burial. There was universal sorrow at the untimely death of the good king. Jeremiah, in deep sorrow, paid tribute to him.

10. Assyria and Babylonia.

In the meantime, the shift of power in the east was about complete. Without attempting to relate all the details it will satisfy our purposes here merely to state that Assyria was finally conquered and that Babylonia was to be the dominant world power in the east for about one hundred years. The battle of Carchemish (605 B.C.) finally established the supremacy of Babylon. Necho, who had gone to the aid of Assyria, was now in a precarious position because of his loss in the gamble. Egypt now had but little part in the affairs of southwest Asia.

11. Jehoahaz and Jehoiakim.

Upon the death of Josiah, Shallum his youngest son, was put on the throne by popular demand. His name was changed to Jehoahaz. Pharaoh-Necho now summoned the young king before him, put him in chains and sent him to Egypt as prisoner, possibly because of his suspected disloyalty to Egypt.

Necho then placed Eliakim, the oldest brother of Jehoahaz, on Judah's throne. This new king took the name Jehoiakim, and at best was but a puppet king under Necho. He had great ambitions and built extravagantly for which he was reproved.

When Necho lost in his gamble for power because of the victories of the Babylonian king, Jehoiakim came under the control of Nebuchadnezzar II, the new king of Babylonia. Jehoiakim had been loyal to Egypt, and now to transfer his loyalty to Nebuchadnezzar, his former enemy, must have been very awkward and embarrassing. For a while he did this and Judah was not molested. A bit later the group in Jehoiakim's court who favored Egypt grew stronger and evidently forced the king to ally himself with them so that he deliberately failed to pay his customary tribute to Nebuchadnezzar. About this time the neighboring nations, Ammonites, Moabites, Chaldeans, and Arameans invaded Judah and caused unrest and destruction of property.

12. The Coming of Nebuchadnezzar.

The Babylonian king could not permit Jehoiakim's defiance to pass unnoticed. About 606 B.C. he sent a large army to lay siege to the city of Jerusalem and to punish Jehoiakim, the rebel king. In II Chronicles 36:6 we are told that Nebuchadnezzar "bound him in fetters to carry him to Babylon." We do not know whether this was actually done or not. It seems that on this campaign the Babylonian king did carry away to his native state a number of princes including Daniel, Shadrach, Meshach and Abed-nego. Some think that Jehoiakim "traded" these for his own freedom.

13. Jehoiachin.

The next king of Judah was Coniah, who took the name Jehoiachin. He was the son of Jehoiakim and was but eighteen years old at the time. He soon proved disloyal to Nebuchadnezzar and again the Babylonian army came to Jerusalem. Seeing that his case was hopeless, the king of Judah and his family surrendered and were taken, with a large number (10,000) of the others to Babylonia. Among these captives taken in 597 B.C. were the best workmen of the city. Ezekiel, the great prophet of the time, was also among those taken into captivity. The Babylonians probably carried with them also as much treasure as they could loot from the city of Jerusalem. King Jehoiachin was a prisoner in Babylon for thirty some years.

14. Zedekiah, Judah's Last King.

The Babylonians placed Mattaniah, who took the name Zedekiah, in charge of the depleted little kingdom. He was only twenty-one years old and faced the hard task of governing a group of poor people left without leaders. He had no one upon whom he could lean except the unpopular and stern Jeremiah. It was but natural, therefore, for him to give ear to the plea of Tyre, Sidon, Ammon, Edom and Moab to join them in coalition against Babylonia. It may be that Nebuchadnezzar heard of this and because of it called Zedekiah to Babylon for a reckoning. At least Zedekiah went to Babylon and, upon his pledge of continued loyalty, was allowed to return to his post in Jerusalem.

Zedekiah's loyalty to Nebuchadnezzar was short-lived. A new Pharaoh (Hophra-Apries) came to rule in Egypt in 588 B.C. He was ambitious and soon began plans for action against Babylonia. It was natural to covet the support of Judah in such an undertaking. There were many in Zedekiah's little kingdom who were favorable to such an alliance and they began to put pressure on their king. Jeremiah, the prophet, warned them against this treacherous policy, but Zedekiah yielded to the pressure and refused to pay his regular tribute to the king of Babylonia. It was up to Nebuchadnezzar now to settle matters in Palestine once and for all.

15. Destruction of Jerusalem.

The Babylonian king and his army came swiftly and with a vengeance. They besieged Jerusalem to the consternation of all its inhabitants. In terror they freed all their slaves, hoping by this gesture to win the saving favor of Jehovah. An Egyptian army now appeared in Palestine and the Babylonians withdrew from Jerusalem in order to stop the Egyptians. It is worthy of note that these slave owners in Jerusalem reclaimed their slaves as soon as the siege was lifted.

In the battle the Egyptians were defeated and the Babylonians again laid siege to Jerusalem. The beleagured inhabitants fought desperately, knowing full well their fate if they fell into the hands of Nebuchadnezzar. For more than a year they held out, but finally a breach was made in the walls and the enemy poured into the city. Zedekiah and his family managed in some way to escape and hurried down to Jericho. Here he was overtaken and seized. He was taken to Riblah on the Orontes river where he was made to pay for his treachery to Nebuchadnezzar. His sons and seventy others were slain. He was forced to look on, and with this picture of horror fresh in mind, was immediately blinded. He was then taken in chains to captivity.

Jerusalem was utterly destroyed. The patience of Nebuchadnezzar had been exhausted. The city must not rise again to trouble him. It was sacked and the temple was burned. "And he burned the house of Jehovah, and the king's house, and all the houses of Jerusalem." (II Kings 25:9.) All valuables of any consequence were taken back to Babylon. This once-proud city was utterly destroyed and stripped of all its treasures and, without walls for protection, was left in complete ruin. For more than a century it was to remain a desolation.

16. Captives Taken to Babylonia.

When the work of destruction was completed the best of the remaining people were taken away as captives. This was the third and last group of Judah to go to their new home in exile. It will be seen that the captivity was in reality not an event but a process. Three different groups were taken away in the years 605, 597 and 587-86 B.C. The kingdom of Judah was at an end!

17. People Left in Judah.

Only a small remnant of poor, discouraged and leaderless people was now left in Judah. To control them Nebuchadnezzar appointed a man named Gedaliah as governor. His headquarters were at Mizpeh, a little town a few miles north of Jerusalem. Jeremiah remained in Judah to do what he could to encourage this desolate remnant. He was the only steadying influence left. To the groups who went away into captivity he offered encouragement and hope. He boldly predicted that some day they would return to their homeland. Such a hope seemed so impossible and preposterous that few, if any, dared believe it.

It appears that insurrection soon broke out among those left in Judah. Gedaliah was murdered by Ishmael, a member of the royal family, and civil war resulted. Fearing the wrath of Nebuchadnezzar, the leaders fled to Egypt and took Jeremiah with them. What Nebuchadnezzar did about this is not known.

18. End of the Kingdom of Judah.

In this unhappy manner the once-glorious Hebrew kingdom ended. According to the Biblical record this was caused by the failure of the people to be loyal to Jehovah, their God. Their persistent policy of rebellion and wickedness resulted in this experience so filled with sorrow and humiliation. By way of summary we may say that at this time the Jewish nation was broken up into there or four groups. (1) Those taken into Babylonian captivity. (2) Those remaining in Palestine. (3) Those who fled to Egypt. (4) We may mention also those of the northern kingdom taken to Nineveh in 721 B.C. They "disappeared" so far as the actual historical record is concerned but we have good reasons for assuming that they did not become extinct. Of one thing we may be certain. We have come to the end of one period of the history of God's chosen people. But the future was not altogether hopeless. Out of the ashes and ruins of their material kingdom a new and better nation was to arise.

Chapter XII

THE CAPTIVITY AND THE RESTORATION

JEREMIAH, EZEKIEL, DANIEL, EZRA, NEHEMIAH, ESTHER, HAGGAI, ZECHARIAH, MALACHI

Section I — The Captivity.

1. Extent of This Period. 2. The Jews in Judah and Egypt. 3. The Jews in Babylonia. 4. Nature of the Captivity. 5. Disgrace of the Captivity. 6. Length of the Captivity. 7. Religious Crises for the Jews. 8. Ezekiel. 9. Jeremiah. 10. Daniel. 11. Predictions of Return From Exile. 12. Benefits of the Exile.

Section II — The Restoration.

1. Rise of Cyrus. 2. Policy of Cyrus. 3. Famous Decree of Cyrus. 4. Returning Groups. 5. The First Company. 6. Situation in Palestine. 7. Second Temple. 8. Haggai and Zechariah. 9. Queen Esther. 10. The Return of Ezra. 11. The Teaching of the Law. 12. Synagogues. 13. Nehemiah's Return. 14. Rebuilding the Walls. 15. Further Work of Nehemiah. 16. Malachi. 17. Close of the Old Testament.

The Captivity and the Restoration

JEREMIAH, EZEKIEL, DANIEL, EZRA, NEHEMIAH, ESTHER, HAGGAI,
ZECHARIAH, MALACHI

SECTION I — THE CAPTIVITY.

1. *Extent of This Period.*

The period which we are now to study begins with the fall of Jerusalem 587-86 B.C. and goes to the rather indefinite time of the close of the Old Testament, approximately 400 B.C. For the Jews it was a time, not only of humiliation and sorrow, but of radical changes in nearly every area of their lives. Experiences in a strange new world awaited them. Gone were the days of splendid material kingdoms. Their hope for the future lay in the realization of spiritual ideals and purposes. In these years "the dross was consumed and the gold refined."

This seemingly crushed and hopeless little group was to go on living. The great Babylonian empire which now wielded such power will ultimately fall. The proud Persians who will soon crush Babylon will flourish for awhile and then pass into oblivion. The kingdoms of Greece and Rome, too, will pass off the scene. But the little remnant of Jewish people shall not be destroyed.

2. *The Jews in Judah and Egypt.*

As stated in the preceding chapter, a group of Jews was left in and around Jerusalem after its destruction by Nebuchadnezzar. We have seen also that these were mostly the undesirable and irresponsible ones who would not be of any profit to Nebuchadnezzar in Babylon. After the rebellion of Ishmael, which resulted in the death of Gedaliah, most of the better class of those remaining fled to Egypt, probably to escape the wrath of the Babylonian king. This would leave a doubly undesirable group in Palestine. No doubt other governors were appointed to succeed Gedaliah. Apparently neighboring nations like the Philistines, Ammonites, Moabites and Edomites, took advantage of the weakened condition of this remnant and moved in to possess as much as possible. The Edomites moved west across the Arabah and up into Judah itself. Centuries later these Edomites, known in New Testament times as Idumeans, were incorporated in the Maccabean kingdom and many of them intermarried with the Jews. During all this time Jerusalem remained a ruined and desolate city. Back in the old homeland there was little to offer hope for another Jewish state.

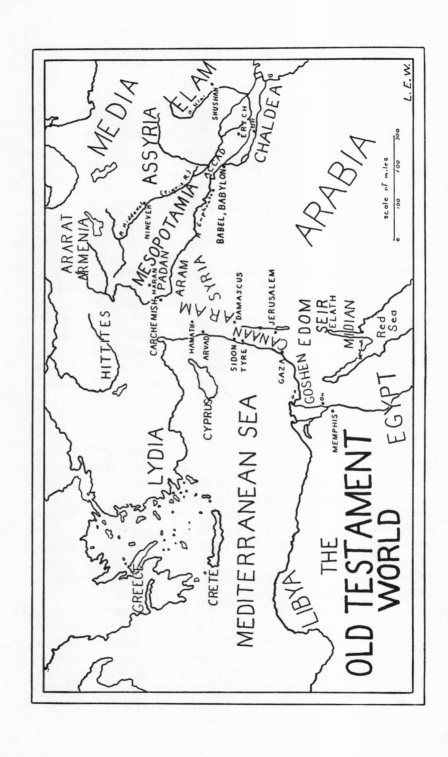

L.E.W.

MEDIA

ELAM

R. NIL

SHUSHAN

ASSYRIA

CHALDEA

ERECH

ACCAD

UR

scale of miles

0   100   200   300

ARARAT
ARMENIA

R. Hiddekel

MESOPOTAMIA

(Tigris R.)

NINEVEH

R.Euphrates

BABEL, BABYLON

ARABIA

HITTITES

CARCHEMISH

HARAN
PADAN

ARAM

DAMASCUS

JERUSALEM

EDOM
SEIR
ELATH

MIDIAN

Red
Sea

HAMATH

ARVAD

SIDON
TYRE

CANAAN

GAZA

GOSHEN

MEMPHIS

ON

LYDIA

CYPRUS

MEDITERRANEAN SEA

LIBYA

THE
OLD TESTAMENT
WORLD

EGYPT

GREECE

CRETE

The Jews who went to Egypt fared well. They were hospitably received and apparently prospered, though they probably lived in segregation in its large cities. They tried to transfer to their new home in Egypt many of their habits of life at home, especially in religious practices. In Elephantine they built a temple to Jehovah which was very similar to the old one in Jerusalem. However, not all were worshipers of Jehovah. Those who settled near the Nile river repudiated Jehovah altogether and became idolaters.

The Jews continued to live in Egypt even after those from Babylonia returned to Jerusalem. At the time of Alexander the Great's conquest of Egypt 333-32 B.C., and afterward, there were many Jews in such cities as Alexandria. Even though life was dominated by Hellenism after the Greek conquest they were anxious to remain loyal to their ancestral faith. It was in Alexandria that the first translation of the Old Testament was made. The Jews, desiring their Scriptures in the prevailing language so that their children might be able to read these, made the famous Septuagint about 275 B.C.

3. The Jews in Babylonia.

We have already noted that there were three different importations of these exiles into Babylonia (605, 597, and 587-86 B.C.). The total number of these can not be finally determined with accuracy. Probably the most frequent estimate of 50,000 is not far wrong. They represented the leading people from every point of view.

What kind of a world was this new home of theirs? Compared to the poor little country of Palestine it was a big, rich and prosperous country. Here the Jews found an advanced culture, big business and materialistic splendor. Babylon, the chief city, was one of great wealth and magnificence. It was the center of a vast empire including all of Mesopotamia and the highlands beyond, as well as Syria and Palestine. The city of Babylon was on the monotonous plains of the banks of the Euphrates river. Ancient writers describe it as a city surrounded by four walls, each fifteen miles in length. Twenty-four streets ran north and south and the same number east and west. In this way each street terminated at a gate in the wall (100 of these) and the city was thus made up of more than six hundred square blocks. It is said that in the center of each square was a garden. The city contained many elaborate and expensive buildings such as palaces and temples. To relieve the homesickness of his wife for her native hills Nebuchadnezzar constructed, at tremendous expense, the famous hanging gardens. In reality these were immense terraces placed on top of each other until they reached the height of the city walls. On these were planted beautiful shrubs and flowers. Even if this ancient description be exaggerated, we may be sure that this great city was one of the most beautiful and famous of ancient times.

Nebuchadnezzar was an able king. He not only erected famous buildings but developed agriculture and trade enterprises to bring great wealth to his kingdom. A system of canals furnished water to the fertile plains and insured rich harvests.

This kingdom was famous also for the advanced stage of culture and learning which its people had attained. The Magi were learned men with a wide reputation for wisdom. The people were skilled in astronomy and astrology. They had libraries and a well-developed literature. They were advanced in the art of making pottery and in textile work. In such a wealthy, cultured and prosperous kingdom the captive Jews were to make their home. The new world forced upon them the necessity of adjustment to new situations and of testing their own faith and ideals. How little and insignificant was their own poor kingdom back in Judah compared to the extent and wealth of this kingdom. Here also they were confronted with opportunities for attaining individual wealth. There is no doubt that many of them became so engrossed in these pursuits that they lost all interest in returning to Palestine. They preferred to live in this new land where they could enjoy the fruits of their labors and engage in the opportunities for accumulating wealth. It was in this period that the Jews developed their peculiar genius for merchandising.

4. Nature of the Captivity.

The Jewish exiles were placed in a rich plain on the river or canal, Chebar, which connected Babylon with Nippur (Ezekiel 1:1-3). Apparently they enjoyed great freedom in this new home, even though they appeared to have been segregated. It should be noted that they were not slaves, ill-treated and forced to do unbearable work, like their forefathers in Egypt. They were colonists with freedom to do practically as they chose, provided of course, that they were loyal to the Babylonian government. Generally speaking they were allowed to govern themselves and manage their own affairs. In religious matters also they appear to have had reasonable freedom. Their leading men were expected to conform to the religious practices of the kingdom as in the case of Daniel and his companions. But there is no record of the whole group being persecuted on religious grounds. It seems that some of them found strength in a new loyalty to Jehovah and even in this foreign land they read their Scriptures and prayed regularly to Jehovah, their God. Ezekiel the prophet was allowed to work among them and to keep alive their hopes of the destiny of their nation.

5. Disgrace of the Captivity.

One may ask then, in view of all the advantages they enjoyed in their new home, if there were any punishment in this period of exile. How did the Jews themselves feel about it all? Unquestionably there was homesickness, resentment and bitterness toward their captors. This feeling is vividly expressed in Psalm 137.

"By the rivers of Babylon, there we sat down, yea, we wept, when we remembered Zion. Upon the willows in the midst thereof we hanged up our harps. For there they that led us captive required of us songs, and they that wasted us required of us mirth, saying, Sing us one of the songs of Zion. How shall we sing Jehovah's song in a foreign land? If I forget thee, O Jerusalem, let my right hand forget her skill. Let my tongue cleave to the roof of my mouth, if I remember thee not; if I prefer not Jerusalem above my chief joy. Remember, O Jehovah against the children of Edom the day of Jerusalem; who said, Rase it, rase it, even to the foundation thereof. O daughter of Babylon, that art to be destroyed, happy shall he be, that rewardeth thee as thou hast served us. Happy shall he be, that taketh and dasheth thy little ones against the rock."

The disgrace of the captivity was in the loss of their freedom, the destruction of their government, in being a people without a country. They were subjects of another power; a strange people in a strange land. A people who have once tasted the privileges of an independent and free nation, even though it be small, could never be happy in captivity.

6. Length of the Captivity.

We have already noted that Jeremiah advised the people of Judah to accept the inevitable supremacy of Babylonia and to submit to captivity even before the awful disaster took place. He further predicted that they would ultimately be allowed to return to Judah. "For thus saith Jehovah, That after seventy years be accomplished at Babylon I will visit you, and perform my good word toward you, in causing you to return to this place." (Jer. 29:10.) Jeremiah further demonstrated his faith in this prediction by using his personal savings to purchase a field in Judah. It was only natural that most of the people would not believe such a prediction. It is probably that in the terrible disaster, with their city lying in ruins and having only the faint hope of mercy from their conquerors, that not one of those who started the long journey to Babylonia had any hope of ever returning.

According to Jeremiah's prediction they were to return after seventy years. Was this fulfilled? There are two ways of considering these dates both of which show that this prophecy was correct. The time from the captivity of the first group 607-06 B.C. to the time of the return of the first group, 536 B.C., would make seventy years. Also the time from the destruction of Jerusalem 586 B.C., and the taking of the last group of exiles, to the time of the completion of the temple, 516 B.C., would make seventy years. It is customary, however, for historians to speak of this period as fifty years from 587 B.C. when the city fell to 537 B.C. when the first group returned to Jerusalem.

7. Religious Crises for the Jews.

The years of exile produced a crisis for the Jews in their religious life. It was twofold in nature. Amidst the prosperity of Babylon with all its attractive opportunities for material gain many were tempted to drift away from the faith of their fathers. Here were the necessities of life in abundance; financial security and even luxury were available to them. What advantages did Jehovah worship have to offer, compared to these things? Then, too, had not their God forsaken them and allowed them to be captured and exiled? Did it pay to worship God anyway? No doubt many of the Jews gradually accepted this substitute for faith and came ultimately to lose interest in spiritual religion.

The many who genuinely desired to be loyal to their God also had a problem. Among all people of their day gods were thought of as tribal or national. The Edomites, Moabites and others had their gods which were supposed to be worshiped principally by their own nation in its homeland. No doubt many Hebrew people thought of Jehovah as a national God who could be worshiped only in Palestine. "How shall we sing Jehovah's song in a strange land?" Through Ezekiel and other prophets and teachers they had to learn that Jehovah their God could be worshiped anywhere. He is the one God who is near to all; indeed, the God whose presence none can escape!

8. Ezekiel.

The prophet Ezekiel has been called "The Star Figure of the Exile." His whole career belongs to this period and he was the most powerful man among the "captives at Chebar." The revelations of his mission and message began during the reign of Zedekiah, though his great work was done while in Babylonia. He was a quiet, humble man, but one endowed with great intellectual powers. He lived among the captives and served to keep many of them from being overcome by Babylonian paganism. In his work he used parables, visions, allegories and similitudes. He repeated the teachings of his predecessors and urged unfailing loyalty to Jehovah. He warned against injustice, immorality and idolatry. He preached a message of hope even in dark exile.

He is known chiefly for two great truths he constantly emphasized. He preached the doctrine of individualism with great force. The individual is morally responsible to God. He also helped the Jews to realize that Jehovah was their God, not only while in Palestine, but also in Babylonia. He is not only their God, but he is the God of all other people who will love and trust him. The ministry of this great prophet not only helped to save his immediate generation; it had a far-reaching influence on the future of Jewish faith and practice.

9. Jeremiah.

Much of the ministry of Jeremiah belongs to the days immediately preceding the captivity. But he also was a tremendous tower of strength to the people in the bewildering experiences of the exile. He preached courage and faith in God. He wrote letters to them in Babylonia giving hope and assurance of God's unfailing purpose for them as a nation (Chapter 29). He never went to Babylonia, choosing rather to remain at Jerusalem, but he never lost his concern for his fellowmen away from their native land. As stated in the previous chapter, he was taken, or as some think, went voluntarily, to Egypt. Here he remained faithful to his ministry even to the end, though his work may not have been outwardly successful. There is a tradition that he died a martyr's death in Egypt.

10. Daniel.

Among those taken in the first group of captives to Babylonia in 607-06 b.c. were certain selected young men of royal blood. Four of these were: Daniel, Hananiah, Mishael and Azariah. Their names were changed to Belteshazzar, Shadrach, Meshach and Abed-nego. Daniel was the leader of these four who were to be given special preparation for service in the court of Babylonia. The story of their steadfast loyalty to Jehovah and of their determination to maintain their ideals of personal chastity is familiar to every student of the Bible. They were found in the best of condition at the end of the three year period of preparation and were thus appointed to places of responsibility.

Daniel spent his whole career in captivity and was a man of remarkable influence, as will be shown by four miraculous occurrences. (1) He was able to interpret the disturbing dream of Nebuchadnezzar. Even though the interpretation of the dream announced the doom of his kingdom, Nebuchadnezzar paid the highest tribute to Daniel. He presented him with costly gifts, elevated him to the position of head of all his wise men and fell down on his face and worshiped him. (2) His three friends were miraculously delivered from the fiery furnace where they had been placed as punishment for their loyalty to Jehovah. (3) His visions concerning Babylonia, Persia, Greece and other countries. (4) His deliverance from the den of lions.

11. Predictions of Return From Exile.

In another connection we have noted that there were a number of specific predictions that some of these Jewish exiles would return to Palestine. The student may find these in the book of Isaiah, chapters 13, 14:21, 44-47, Jer. 28:4, 11, 29:10, chapters 50-52, Ezekiel chapter 27.

In Isaiah (chapters 44-48) the reasons for their return are given. Jehovah is superior to all pagan gods and is able to deliver his people from the power of all evil ones. He had delivered them in every great crisis in past years and will do so again. He had a great purpose for this nation who were his own people. They were to serve him in revealing God to other nations. Since they are his co-laborers he will forgive, restore and deliver them. Their years of suffering in exile have prepared them for their unique mission of sympathetic helpfulness to all mankind.

12. Benefits of the Exile.

The long, hard years of humiliation and sorrow in exile had some distinctly beneficial results in the life of the Jews. We shall enumerate some of the changes and developments that came during this time. (1) They were thoroughly cured of idolatry. This was the sin chiefly responsible for their experience in exile but they were so thoroughly weaned away from it that never since then have Jews been idolaters. (2) The synagogue came into existence. Back in Jerusalem they had their temple. This was not available in Babylonia so they built smaller houses which served, not only as centers of worship, but also as places for instruction in their law. The synagogue was destined to play a very important role in their lives in the next centuries. It was a prominent institution in New Testament times both in Palestine and in other places where Jews lived. (3) They did a great deal in the collecting of their literature during this time. (4) Religion for them became distinctly more spiritual and personal. They could not observe the elaborate ceremonies connected with worship in the temple but their faith was decidedly more spiritual in character. The doctrine of individual responsibility was so emphasized by Jeremiah and Ezekiel that their faith came to have much more of the personal element in it. (5) The law of Moses took on a new significance for them. In the fires of suffering the real value of this law came to be appreciated. Judaism was born in this period. (6) They became a people more genuinely united in ideals and purpose. Factional strifes and jealousies practically disappeared and they attained a unity which was highly desirable. They were a "separate" people who were able to stand together against outside influences. (7) They came into a new understanding and appreciation of their destiny as a nation. They came to be a people with a mission. They were to be spared in order to fulfill this high mission to other peoples. All in all, there were beneficial changes wrought in the years of exile.

Section II — THE RESTORATION.

1. Rise of Cyrus.

We come at this point to deal with the greatest statesman of this period of history; indeed, Cyrus may be regarded as one of the most remarkable men of ancient history. He played a big role in the life of the Jews; he determined the destiny of millions of people in this sixth century B.C. by bringing a new alignment of nations and by setting up a great empire which displaced the Semitic peoples in the role of leaders in southwest Asia. His entrance upon the scene opens a new era in history.

He appears as a man thirty years of age in the year 559 B.C. in the province of Anshan of Media. He was of royal blood and at once demonstrated unusual qualities of leadership. Within ten brief years he was the undisputed king of all Media. His kingdom soon came to include all Persia, the northern part of the Mesopotamian valley, Armenia and even Asia Minor. Within twenty years he was king of all the territory from the Indus river in the east to the Aegean Sea. In his expansion westward, however, he had bypassed ancient Babylon for the time. Now with his western boundaries established he returned in 539 B.C. to lay siege to Babylon.

Naturally we should expect this capital city to put up a vigorous defense against the invader Cyrus. This, however, was not the case. The city surrendered without a fight. We are told that the gates were voluntarily opened to him by citizens within. Why did this strange thing happen? Two reasons are given. The people who had been so abused by their kings were ready to submit to any other power in the hope of an improvement in their condition. It is likely also that the reputation of Cyrus, this new world figure, so strong and invincible, and yet so gentle and considerate and humane, had already preceded him. Be that as it may, the city surrendered in 539-38 B.C. and the new Persian kingdom now exercised undisputed control over all the vast expanse of southwest Asia.

Since the time of Hammurabi the Semitic race had dominated this historic territory. This Semitic control now ceased and was replaced by the Aryan race who were to control it for the next thousand years.

2. Policy of Cyrus.

This new ruler of the ancient world was indeed an unusual man. He was a master leader exercising a skill seldom excelled. He appears to have been friendly, frank and extremely considerate of his subjects. Friends and enemies seemed to have been captivated by him. The treatment accorded his subjects, so long in Babylonian captivity, illustrates this generous spirit.

In modern terminology Cyrus would be called a "Liberal." He was concerned with the welfare of his subjects and freely parted with tradition to accomplish his purposes. He soon discovered the large number of people who had been brought in by force from other countries and forced to live in Babylonia, many of them as slaves. Their restlessness and discontent probably encouraged him to do the daring and unexpected thing. He reversed all former policy by making it possible for all peoples who had been brought in by force and who wanted to return to their homes to do so.

3. Famous Decree of Cyrus.

This policy of leniency, which allowed them not only the privilege of returning home but which gave them protection and assistance as well as freedom of worship, was revolutionary. The generous nature of this famous proclamation is given in some detail in the book of Ezra. "Thus saith Cyrus, king of Persia, All the Kingdoms of the earth hath Jehovah, the God of heaven, given me; and he hath charged me to build Him a house in Jerusalem, which is in Judah. Whosoever there is among you of all His people, his God be with him, and let him go up to Jerusalem, which is in Judah, and build the house of Jehovah, the God of Israel, (He is the God) which is in Jerusalem. And whosoever is left, in any place where he sojourneth, let the men of his place help him with silver and with gold, and with goods, and with beasts, besides the free-will offering for the house of God which is in Jerusalem." (Ezra 1:2-4.)

The tone of this proclamation would naturally lead people to assume that Cyrus was a believer in Jehovah, the God of Israel. Scholars accepted this view until the inscriptions of Cyrus were deciphered. These inscriptions represent him as a polytheist who probably desired the favor of all gods. It is true, however, that this remarkable man was the agent of Jehovah to accomplish his purpose for Israel. There are a number of references in Isaiah to Cyrus as the servant of Jehovah, as for example: "That saith of Cyrus, He is my shepherd, and shall perform all my pleasure, even saying of Jerusalem, She shall be built; and of the temple, Thy foundation shall be laid." (Isa. 44:28.) And "Thus saith Jehovah to his anointed, to Cyrus, whose right hand I have holden, to subdue nations before him, and I will loose the loins of kings; to open the doors before him, and the gates shall not be shut . . . I am Jehovah, and there is none else; beside me there is no God. I will guide thee, though thou hast not known me." (Isa. 45:1, 4, etc.)

This famous proclamation issued in 538 B.C. made it possible for all the Jews who wanted to do so to return to their homeland. There were some who wanted to return and who did go back to rebuild the wastes of Judah.

4. Returning Groups.

We have no way of knowing how many Jews were in Babylonia at the time. It is probably safe to assume that the number was considerably larger than the number taken there from Judah. Whatever may have been the total number at the time, it is clear that not a large number manifested any great desire to return to the old homeland. Most of them appear to have been pretty well satisfied with their new home, especially since Cyrus manifested a very lenient attitude toward them as citizens. Doubtless many had become firmly established in profitable business ventures; numbers had formed strong friendships in Babylonia which led to marriages in considerable number with people in this adopted land. No doubt many of them lacked faith to leave a land where they were economically and politically secure and undertake the long journey of eight hundred miles back to the poor little country where their lives would be marked by hardships and limitations. As we shall see later according to the Biblical accounts, there were about sixty thousand altogether to return.

In all the Old Testament there is no problem of chronology more difficult to solve than that connected with the return of these groups of exiles, particularly with Ezra and Nehemiah. For our present purposes there would be no value in entering upon a discussion of this vexing problem. The first group was led by Zerubbabel and some time later other groups went back under Ezra and under Nehemiah. We may not be far wrong in assuming that these last two were not far apart.

5. *The First Company.*

Zerubbabel, a prince of the house of David, was the leader of the group which left in 537 B.C. to return to Jerusalem. He had associated with him Joshua, the priest, and Shesh-bazzar who had charge on the journey of the sacred vessels of the temple which Nebuchadnezzar had taken from Jerusalem at the time of its capture. In his account Ezra (Chapter 2) gives in some detail the number in this company. He states that there were 42,360 Jews who took along 7,337 slaves; about 4,000 of the priestly family, and about 7,500 animals, horses, asses, and camels. To bring this immense company of some 50,000 people with their possessions, the long journey of eight hundred miles was a big undertaking. It is said that they received voluntary assistance from friends and also that Cyrus made grants to them. Even with assistance all along the way it would require faith and real courage to undertake this venture. Cyrus and other friends, such as their Jewish brethren who prefered not to return, made substantial provisions for their support after their arrival in their desolate, poverty-stricken homeland.

The motive for this great undertaking was primarily a religious one. They wanted to restore the ancient temple in Jerusalem. They had pride in the God-given mission of their nation. Without the strong impulse furnished by religion it is doubtful if they could ever have started their journey or survived the hardships on the way and after their arrival.

6. *Conditions in Palestine.*

After the destruction of Jerusalem in 587-6 B.C. there was not much left either in people or resources. We have noted already that many of the Jews left there had gone down into Egypt and furthermore that the Edomites, Moabites and Ammonites had gradually pushed into the territory of ancient Judah. These invaders had intermarried with the few natives left and formed a sort of mongrel group which, from every point of view, must have been inferior and undesirable. In the meantime the Samaritans, occupants of the former northern kingdom, had moved southward to occupy as much of the territory as possible. Jerusalem, so thoroughly sacked by Nebuchadnezzar, was still in ruins. With the capture of Babylon by Cyrus the desolate little province of Judah came under Persian rule.

This was the discouraging situation which the company of Zerubbabel faced as they came home again. They probably had their choice of a place to live and would begin as soon as possible to set up housekeeping again. Only those well over fifty years old would remember much of the former city. There were some who could recall the glory of Solomon's temple and the splendor of Jerusalem. Most of them knew of it only by report. What they faced now was different. It would require not only careful planning but real courage to start all over again in the midst of the debris and ruins of the former city.

7. Second Temple.

They found their way to the site of the temple of Solomon and after repairing the altar, offered sacrifices. They determined to rebuild this temple, though it would have to be very different from the glorious one of Solomon. This rebuilding seems to have been the main objective of their return. According to Ezra (3:7) they secured masons, carpenters and other workmen for this enterprise. Also they secured workmen from Phoenicia to cut and transport to Joppa cedar wood from Lebanon for the temple. In the second year after their return they laid the foundations of this new structure with great ceremony and genuine rejoicing. It is to be noted that the older men in the group who knew of the ornate and glorious temple of Solomon wept as they saw how inferior their new house of worship would have to be. The general plan and the size were the same as Solomon's; the chief difference was in the quality. None of the costly and ornate furnishings and refinements of the former temple could be had for this structure.

Shortly after the laying of the foundation these builders faced a crisis. The mixed population of Judah came to offer their services and gifts in the undertaking. Their offer was promptly and firmly rejected. "Ye have nothing to do with us in building a house unto our God; but we ourselves together will build unto Jehovah the God of Israel, as king Cyrus the king of Persia, hath commanded us." (Ez. 4:3.) If this refusal seems unfriendly and unreasonable let us remember that these who offered their assistance were not Jews who were loyal to Jehovah but were idolaters and in all probability were not sincere in their proposal. Zerubbabel and other leaders, now thoroughly weaned from idolatry, saw in this proposal a dangerous opening that might easily lead to compromise and open idolatry. Naturally these neighbors reacted to this refusal and would now become their enemies and would seek to hinder them in their work. "Then the people of the land weakened the hands of the people of Judah, and troubled them in building, and hired counselors against them, to frustrate their purpose all the days of Cyrus, king of Persia, even until the reign of Darius, king of Persia." (Ez. 4:4-5.)

8. Haggai and Zechariah.

In the face of these frustrations the work of rebuilding was stopped for some fourteen years. About 520 B.C. a prophet named Haggai came to Zerubbabel and Joshua to rebuke the people for ceasing their work on the temple while at the same time they were building and beautifying houses for themselves. As punishment God sent a drought upon the people. Spurred by this rebuke the people resumed their work. They were to complete this new temple and not to be discouraged even if it did not compare favorably with the former temple. In a real sense this new temple shall be more glorious. "The latter glory of this house shall be greater than the former, saith Jehovah of hosts; and in this place will I give peace, saith Jehovah of hosts." (Haggai 2:9.)

Contemporary with Haggai was the young prophet Zechariah who also gave strong encouragement to the builders. Their enemies are to be broken. Zerubbabel will, through the aid of the Spirit, overcome all opposition and shall finish the task. Such preaching seems to have been effective. "And the elders of the Jews builded and prospered, through the prophecy of Haggai the prophet and Zechariah the son of Iddo." (Ezra 6:14.)

After four more years the building was completed and was dedicated in 516 B.C. with great rejoicing. This was a marvelous accomplishment which would have a stabilizing effect on the lives of the people. This temple would serve as a center around which they could build for the future. With homes of their own and a temple available for services, life in the homeland would be more hopeful. At least the future was not so dark as when they first returned.

9. *Queen Esther.*

The beautiful story of Esther belongs to this general period of history. We need not concern ourselves here about when and by whom it was written. The events recorded in this little book occurred in the reign of Ahasuerus of Xerxes of Persia about 483 B.C. The scene is laid in Susa of Shushan, the capital of this vast empire.

Since the time of Cyrus Persia had continued to expand as a world empire. Darius (521-485 B.C.) had enlarged his holdings as far east as India, west to Thessaly in Europe, and from Caucasus in the north to Egypt southward. The government was well organized and administered and was in a flourishing condition. It remained for two centuries the dominant power of the world. Darius died in 485 B.C. and was succeeded by one Atossa who took the name Xerxes. Darius had been defeated by the Greeks, so Xerxes made elaborate preparations to punish the Greeks. This war against Greece is not only a famous one, familiar to students of history, but it was most important in its indications of what should later happen in Greece. The armies of Persia, hitherto invincible, were disastrously defeated and all but annihilated 479 B.C. For a long time afterward Persian rulers were content to stay away from Greece. Xerxes lived his last years in dissipation and was finally assassinated by his servants in 464 B.C. Artaxerxes I, son of Xerxes, was the next king of Persia who ruled for a period of forty years (464-424 B.C.). This was a comparatively uneventful and weak reign. At his death Darius Nothus came to the throne to rule nineteen years (424-405 B.C.).

The setting for the story of Esther is at Susa or Shushan in the province of Elam. A mound of ruins, still called Shush, was explored by archaeologists some years ago. Here they found the ruins of an immense hall three hundred and forty-three feet long and two hundred and forty-four feet wide, which may be the very palace hall described in Esther.

The story opens with an account of a great feast for his nobles, made by Ahasuerus at his palace. He commanded Vashti, his queen, to be present, probably in a role which was inconsistent with her ideals of decency. She refused to attend and for this refusal was deposed. The king then ordered the gathering of a large number of the most beautiful maidens in his kingdom from which he would later select a queen. This is probably the first "beauty queen" contest in history.

Living in Susa at the time was a Jew named Mordecai who had no children of his own but who had adopted his cousin, Esther, a beautiful young woman. Among those selected as "candidates" for the queenship was Esther who had won the favor of the king. From all these maidens Esther was selected and became the queen. This naturally gave prominence to Mordecai who soon proved his alertness. He discovered a plot by the king's eunuchs to assassinate the king. He exposed the conspirators and they were promptly executed. A record of this service was made in the chronicles of the court but for a time this record escaped the notice of the king.

The villain in the story was a man named Haman, who with his strong ambition soon came into royal favor and was rapidly promoted to a high position. In this position he received the obeisance of everyone except Mordecai, the Jew. Haman, greatly angered by Mordecai's refusal to do him honor, sought means by which to avenge his hatred rival. Discovering that Mordecai was a Jew, he persuaded the king to approve a wicked scheme to destroy the Jews in the kingdom. He represented these people as wealthy and exceedingly dangerous to the kingdom and suggested that they be exterminated and their property confiscated by the court. This twofold appeal, which promised, not only security from a supposed enemy, but immense wealth as well, won the instant approval of Ahasuerus. The king gave Haman the authority to destroy all Jews in the kingdom and to confiscate their possessions.

Mordecai soon learned of this infamous decree which was now fully authorized. In great distress he counseled with Esther and suggested to her that the only hope for his people was through her intercession with the king. In his plea to Esther Mordecai used the often quoted words; "Who knoweth whether thou are not come to the kingdom for such a time as this?" and Esther's reply: "So will I go in unto the king, which is not according to the law; and if I perish, I perish."

All the Jews, at the suggestion of Esther, agreed to observe a fast of three days. She then presented herself before the king. This oriental monarch, captivated by the beauty of Esther, extended the golden sceptre and asked her to state her request. Her petition was a simple invitation to the king and Haman to attend a banquet. At this feast she asked only that they be present at a similar occasion next day.

In the meantime, Haman, now desperately determined to humiliate and destroy Mordecai, asked his family for suggestions as to an appropriate and impressive way of destroying his enemy. They suggested that a scaffold seventy-five feet high be built and that he secure the king's permission to hang Mordecai on this scaffold. That night the king, unable to sleep, called for the chronicles and as he read these he learned for the first time how Mordecai had saved his life. He learned also that Mordecai had not been properly honored for this service. Early next morning when Haman came to the court to request the death of Mordecai, the king asked him what ought "to be done unto the man whom the king delighteth to honor?" Naturally assuming that the king was planning to honor him, Haman suggested that the man (honoree) should be clothed in royal garments, crowned by the king, and escorted through the streets of the city by one of the king's noblemen. The king agreed and then commanded him to see that these honors were bestowed upon Mordecai. This Haman was forced to do.

At her banquet Esther recounted to the king the story of Haman's wicked plot to destroy all her people. In great anger Ahasuerus ordered that Haman be instantly hanged on the gallows he had erected for Mordecai. In the meantime the king's edict for the slaying of the Jews had been officially approved and was then being sent out into the various parts of the kingdom. According to the custom of the country ("The law of the Medes and Persians, which altereth not.") this law could not be rescinded. However, a new edict was issued which allowed the Jews to defend themselves against their enemies. We are told that they did this so vigorously that some 75,000 of their adversaries in the realm were slain. Thus the Jews were saved from extermination as had been planned by their enemies. To celebrate this deliverance a feast was inaugurated. This feast, known as Purim, is still celebrated by the Jews each year about the middle of March.

10. The Return of Ezra.

There are differences of opinion among scholars as to the date of Ezra and of Nehemiah. However, since their work is not affected by this question, we shall not attempt to discuss the problem here. We can be sure that the work of each of these came some time after that of Zerubbabel.

Ezra was a descendant of the high priest Seraiah and was both a priest and a scribe. His chief objective in returning to Jerusalem was to "teach in Israel statutes and ordinances." (Ezra 7:10.) He was primarily concerned in seeing the laws of Moses taught and observed back in the homeland. The Persian king gave him substantial financial help and full authority for his work. "Whosoever will not do the law of thy God, and the law of the king, let judgment be executed upon him with all diligence, whether it be unto death, or to banishment, or to confiscation of goods, or to imprisonment." (Ezra 7:26.) He gathered the group of those who were willing to return with him at the river Ahava, where they prayed unto God for protection and guidance. Special men were designated to go along with this company of some six thousand people to carry great amounts of gold and silver and precious vessels for the temple. In addition to this help the leaders were to call upon the local governor of Jerusalem for other resources that might be needed.

The journey to Jerusalem required about four months. Upon their arrival they gave thanks to God, offered sacrifices and presented themselves to the Persian government. In Jerusalem Ezra saw his worst fears realized. In the years since Zerubbabel the people had grown negligent of the law of Moses and had slipped into a state of religious lethargy. They had violated the law against marriage with idolaters to the extent that many of the most prominent families were involved. In great humiliation Ezra rent his clothes and wept. This sincere and zealous prophet then offered a fervent prayer unto his God, confessing the sins of the people and pleading for the forgiveness of their sins. This earnest prayer and his plea to the people caused many of them to confess their sins of the past. Many also took an oath to put away all their foreign wives and children. In the interest of convenience and efficiency a special court was set up to examine each case. Failure to carry out the order was to be punished by the forfeiture of all property. This court finished its work in two months. The book of Ezra closes with a rather long list of those who agreed to put away their foreign wives.

11. The Teaching of the Law.

Ezra's work went much further than his domestic reform movement. He was deeply concerned in instituting proper services of worship which involved the whole work of the priests and the ritual used in the temple. He was particularly desirous of seeing that the people were taught the laws of Moses. Assembling all the people he read to them the law slowly and distinctly. This reading was from early morning until midday and "the ears of all the people were attentive unto the book of the law." He and his helpers stood upon a pulpit of wood above the people and "they read in the book, in the law of God, distinctly; and they gave the sense so that they understood the reading." (Neh. 8:8.)

In addition to this work of oral teaching Ezra is credited with arranging and codifying the law of Moses and of having this reproduced in sufficient numbers to make it available for teaching. As a priest he doubtless did much to establish the regular work of the priesthood and to set the pattern for their services for many years to come. This literary work of Ezra was a magnificent contribution to his people and to religion.

12. Synagogues.

It was in connection with the activities of Ezra that the synagogue came into prominence. This institution was destined to play a very important role in the life of Jews for the next several centuries. The word synagogue literally means *an assembling together*. It is used frequently for the congregation of Israel and later as the house of assembly. It arose as a substitute for the temple. Jews who lived outside Jerusalem needed a building or an institution to serve them as the temple served those in the Holy City. The synagogue was commonly used for the purpose of worship, for education, and for the direction of the religious, social and civil life of the people. In the time of Ezra this institution was used also in Palestine, and even in Jerusalem itself where the temple was located. It is said that at the time of Jesus there were as many as four hundred in Jerusalem alone. Every Jewish community had one or more, depending on its size. Wherever the Jew went in these next centuries he set up his synagogue. Paul and his companions found synagogues in their travels in the Gentile world. These centers of community life were exceedingly important in the life of Jewish people. Archaeologists have uncovered the ruins of a number of these in Palestine.

13. Nehemiah's Return.

The third group of exiles to return from Babylon to the old home-land was under the general direction of a layman known as Nehemiah. He apparently came from a well-to-do family of Jews living in Susa or Shushan. He rose to the high position of cup-bearer of Artaxerxes, king of Persia. This influential position was also highly lucrative. Nehemiah doubtless was an able and distinguished man since every experience of his and all the references to him indicate distinction. He was also a man of genuine piety and of unquestioned loyalty to his people. His brother, Hanani, brought to him at Susa the distressing news of the needy condition of his people back in Jerusalem. The city was defenseless, the walls had never been repaired and the people were at the mercy of their enemies about them. This news depressed the spirit of Nehemiah to the extent that his very countenance revealed his anxiety and distress. The king, noting his distress, inquired the reason for it. Nehemiah then told his story and expressed his desire to visit the city and assist his people in their need.

The king graciously expressed his sympathetic interest by giving Nehemiah leave of absence to go to Jerusalem and in addition provided passports and letters to the officials in Palestine. He provided him also with a royal escort and with authority to secure materials for rebuilding the walls of Jerusalem. Thus it was that Nehemiah made the first of his long journeys of a thousand miles to the homeland of the Jews.

14. Rebuilding the Walls.

Upon reaching the city Nehemiah found it in even worse condition then he anticipated. The people were demoralized and there were active enemies all about them. Nehemiah displayed good business judgment, wise leadership, and great patience and determination in his undertaking. His first step was to get the facts in the situation. He secured this information in the quiet of night by riding entirely around the ruined walls and making careful notes of what must be done. When he had made his survey and had calculated the cost in materials, labor, and time, he was ready to "sell" the project to the people.

Acting as governor of the city, he organized the people for this gigantic undertaking. Specific sections were assigned to different groups of workmen under a supervisor. We should remember that while the city was exposed by the ruined walls, not all of the walls were down flat. Great gaps had been made and probably most of the wall had been wrecked but the foundations were still in place and much of the material originally built in the wall was still available. Even under such conditions the task was a tremendous one. This new undertaking aroused the suspicion and the active opposition of their hostile neighbors — the Samaritans, Ammonites, Arabians, and Philistines. Under the direction of Sanballat the Horonite, Geshem the Arabian, and Tobiah the Ammonite, determined efforts were made to stop the work of rebuilding and to defeat the undertaking. Many devices were employed to thwart the plans of Nehemiah. He was equal to all their threats and their efforts to stop him. Refusing to debate the matter, he drove his workmen to finish the job. The workmen themselves were armed with weapons, regular guards were stationed at crucial points and the entire wall was guarded day and night. Nehemiah himself remained constantly on the job to push the project. By almost superhuman efforts, against desperate opposition, the walls were repaired in the remarkably short space of fifty-two days. This accomplishment would give to the people a new sense of security and would enhance their chances of survival in their hostile surroundings.

15. Further Work of Nehemiah.

This unselfish and courageous leader served also in another capacity. His deep spiritual interests caused him to lead in a movement for the reform in social and religious practices of his people. His brother, Hanani, was made governor of the city and the government was reorganized for greater strength and protection. After some years, feeling now that his task was accomplished, Nehemiah returned to his post in the court of Susa. Still later he learned of other difficulties and abuses back in Jerusalem and made a second trip to the city. He found that Tobiah, the Ammonite, had secured through the high priest a special room for himself in the temple. Nehemiah acted at once to have him expelled. He found also that a goodly number had intermarried with foreigners, thus disregarding the law and violating their solemn pledge. He attacked this thorny problem of mixed marriages with courage and force. He was exceptionally zealous in this for he is quoted as saying: "And I contended with them and cursed (reviled) them, and smote certain of them, and plucked off their hair, and made them swear by God saying, Ye shall not give your daughters unto their sons, nor take their daughters for your sons or for yourselves." (13:25.) If this seems extreme we should remember that the future mission of the Jews depended upon keeping the race pure. The difference between the Jews and alien peoples must not be obliterated.

Nehemiah was instrumental also in correcting serious offenses of the well-to-do against the poor. He led in a crusade for the proper observance of the Sabbath day. He expelled all foreigners from the courts of the temple so the worship of Jehovah could be kept pure. He gave his influence to the renewed teaching of the laws of Moses. It is held by some scholars that Nehemiah returned the second time to Susa about 413 B.C.

The works of Ezra and Nehemiah are so closely related that scholars often consider their contribution as one (jointly). Whether we look at their work as one common enterprise or whether we consider each separately, we find that there is common agreement that Nehemiah is one of the really outstanding men in Old Testament history. A man of wealth, with high rank and unquestioned character, he devoted himself without reservation to a discouraging and apparently hopeless undertaking in the interest of the religious, social and economic welfare of his people. With almost superhuman energy. in the face of determined and clever opposition, he led the people in rebuilding the walls of their city. He showed his loyalty to the law of Moses by his religious reforms. For the sake of his nation's future mission he took his stand against mixed marriages. His concern for the poor among his people was evinced by championing their cause against the abuses by their wealthy brethren. His courage, born of confidence in his own integrity, is revealed in his famous reply to the threats of his enemies — "Should such a man as I flee?" The quality and the depth of his spiritual life is shown in the prayers recorded in his book. His unselfish and generous nature is shown by the fact that he gave all these years of devoted service to his people without any monetary compensation whatsoever. Without his magnificent contribution one wonders if this discouraged and struggling little colony could have survived. Nehemiah deserves a place among the greatest benefactors of his race.

16. Malachi.

The book of Malachi is the last book in the Old Testament. We know little about the author of the book. The word means *my messenger*. The setting and the contents of the book are such that practically all scholars place it in the time of Ezra and Nehemiah. The temple had been rebuilt but the priests were guilty of perverting sacrifices. The poor were oppressed by the rich. The people were withholding their tithes and offerings. Temple services were formal and without spiritual tone. Men were marrying pagan women; some were actually divorcing their Jewish wives in order to marry outside their race. There was a general air of worldliness and a declining interest in spiritual religion.

This messenger reproves the people for their sins, accuses them of robbing God and warns them of the time when the faithful shall be separated from the faithless. He speaks of the retribution of a future state. He urges the people to be faithful to the law and to await the Lord's forerunner who should come in the spirit and power of Elijah.

17. Close of the Old Testament.

We have now come to the close of the Old Testament record. It is about 400 B.C. The Jews are at home in Jerusalem, though they are still the subjects of the king of Persia. They are but a small group with but few resources and without anything comparable to the splendor and wealth of the old kingdom in the days of David and Solomon. But they are not to be extinguished. Their glorious spiritual mission is yet to be realized. Dark as it might appear, there were some faithful and devout souls who cherished the promises made to their forefathers and who by faith looked for the realization of these expectations.

Chapter XIII

THE PROPHETS

Section I — The Work of the Prophets.
1. Introduction. 2. Definition of a Prophet. 3. Distinguishing Characteristics. 4. Their Call. 5. Their Training. 6. Kinds of Prophets. 7. Nature of Their Work. 8. Chronological Order. 9. The Fulfillment of Prophecy. 10. Pointing to Christ.

Section II — Early Prophets
1. Introduction. 2. Joel. 3. Jonah.

Section III — Eighth Century Prophets.
1. Amos. 2. Hosea. 3. Isaiah. 4. Micah.

Section IV — Seventh Century Prophets.
1. Zephaniah. 2. Jeremiah. 3. Nahum. 4. Habakkuk.

Section V — Sixth Century Prophets.
1. Daniel. 2. Ezekiel. 3. Obadiah.

Section VI — Later Prophets.
1. Haggai. 2. Zechariah. 3. Malachi.

CHAPTER XIII

The Prophets

Section I — THE WORK OF THE PROPHETS.

1. Introduction.

Having completed our survey of Old Testament history we shall now consider briefly the work of a class of very influential men in the life of the Hebrew people. Even a brief survey of these men and their work will be helpful in understanding the life of God's chosen people.

The work of the prophets of Israel extends over a period of several hundred years, certainly from the time of the Judges to the close of the Old Testament. The period of greatest prophetic activity was during the time of the Kingdom, especially during the latter years of both Israel and Judah. These prophets, spokesmen for God, exercised a tremendous influence on the life of the nation, oftentimes actually helping to fix the policy and determine the course of Hebrew history.

2. Definition of a Prophet.

The prophets were powerful leaders of religious, social, and even political life in Old Testament history. They were men with a message from God. The very name prophet is a significant one. There are three Hebrew words translated prophet. The first two of these are from the verbs *Ro'eh,* used eleven times, and *Chozeh,* used twenty-two times. These words mean "to see" and convey the idea of a man of vision. Thus the prophet is called a "seer." This implies that he is able to obtain a knowledge of spiritual realities not available to others. The third word *Nabhi,* used some three hundred times, meaning to "announce" or perhaps to "bubble up," represents the prophet as a "speaker." Thus the prophet is one who has received in a special manner a vital message and who must declare or speak that message. During the course of Old Testament history other terms were applied to these religious leaders. They are known by such terms as "Watchmen," "Men of God," "Servants of Jehovah," "Messengers of Jehovah," "Interpreters," and "Men of the Spirit."

3. Distinguishing Characteristics.

There are several marks by which one may recognize the prophet:

(1) He was influenced and motivated by his "call" to speak in his day.

(2) He was conscious of God's authority and on this basis spoke courageously and uncompromisingly.

(3) He was a man of the spirit, spending much time in communion with God, often in solitary and lonely places.

(4) He was often a rugged individualist who would attract attention. He followed no prescribed order and was independent of ritual and popular custom.

(5) He was a faithful and often fierce denouncer of evil practices of the individual and the nation.

(6) Many of the prophets reveal in their discourses the future of the nation and of the Kingdom of God.

4. Their Call.

These prophets were men who considered themselves "called" of God to declare the message which they had received. This "call" came in various forms. In some instances it was by an audible voice. In other cases it came in a vision. The vision was usually accompanied by spoken words of invitation and command, as with the great prophet Isaiah (Isa. 6:1-13). But in each instance these men were convinced that they had been selected and commanded to give forth the message of God to the people of their time. They proclaimed their message with the assurance that it was the word of God. "Thus saith the Lord" is the refrain running through their deliverances.

5. Their Training.

We have but few details about their training for their work. Without doubt they were men of unusual ability, of wide observation and accurate understanding of their times, and men with great force of character. In some instances their work was preceded by periods of quiet meditation and deep study in some secluded place. For example, Amos was in the wilderness of Tekoa where he was prepared for his task. There are several references made to the "schools" of the prophets. As early as 1200 B.C. (the period of the Judges) they seem to have been organized into communities or schools. Gibeah (I Sam. 10:5, 10), Ramah (I Sam. 19-18), Bethel (II Kings 2:3), Jericho (II Kings 2:5), and Gilgal (II Kings 4:8) were centers where these groups gathered and from which their influence went out. Samuel was a leader of these schools of the prophets. Of the details of their training and the extent of their history we know but little. We do know, beyond question, that the prophet was usually a man well equipped for his task and a man of great force and influence.

6. Kinds of Prophets.

There were many prophets whose messages have not been preserved in book form. These men exerted a great influence and did not write books. Elijah and Elisha are good examples of this type. Others have left their books to be included in our Bible. There are sixteen books of prophecy in the Old Testament. These are called major (4) and minor (12) prophets. It should be pointed out that the terms "major" and "minor" do not refer to the relative importance of their work, but rather to the length or the brevity of their books. We do not know just how these writings were preserved. It is possible that some well informed person took notes on their deliverances and then put them in written form. It is more probable that these men themselves preserved their messages in written form, either before or after delivery.

7. Nature of Their Work.

We ought to get as accurate an understanding as possible of the nature of the work these men did. The word prophet means one who "speaks before." The idea seems to be that of one who stands in the presence of a person or a company and speaks forth a message. A prophet then is a servant of Jehovah who represents him before men.

These men were preachers of righteousness. Their mission was to declare the message of Jehovah to the people of their time. They were proclaimers of the will of the Lord. Their work related to the past, the present, and the future. The prophets were regarded as the historians of Israel. They traced the control of Jehovah over the fortunes of his people. They recorded and interpreted the work of the Lord with his people in the past.

They had a message for the present. They called the people to repentance and set forth the will and purpose of Jehovah for the people in their day, urging men to conform to his will. They gave practical advice to their leaders. They sought to give men a greater knowledge of God and to relate that knowledge to the present day.

And their work related to the future. They gave promises of reward for righteous living and threatenings of punishment for failure to practice the teachings of Jehovah. They proclaimed the divine purpose of God with Israel as a nation. They preached salvation in the fullest sense. They indicated the "advent of Jehovah Himself to be the redeemer of his people." They proclaimed the establishment of his kingdom upon the earth. Their preaching pointed to the future.

Let us guard against the view so often held by people of limited understanding that all their work was of a predictive nature. While some of their greatest teachings are in the field of prediction or foretelling, much of their work was for the situations of their own time.

Usually they were men called forth by a crisis or an emergency to declare the will of the Lord. They were prominent in the field of statesmanship. They were well informed students of the affairs of their day, both national and international. They gave their message or advice to the kings and statesmen of the day with all confidence and with the expectation that this would be heeded as the word of Jehovah. They stood forth as the revealers of the will of God in the great crises of Israel's history. The priest was to perform the routine duties in the services of the sanctuary. The prophet was the independent and authoritative voice to speak forth the message for the time.

8. Chronological Order.

It is well to have a general idea of the chronological order of the canonical prophets. Of course, the exact date and the circumstances under which each of these did his work are not agreed upon by all scholars. In general we can speak authoritatively of three periods in the history of the Old Testament that were productive of great prophetic messengers. The first of these periods was in the eighth century before Christ, the century of the Assyrian crisis. To this period belong some of the greatest of these religious leaders, such as Amos, Hosea, Isaiah and Micah. The second period, during the seventh century before Christ, was the time of the Chaldean crisis. In this century we can place men like Nahum, Zephaniah, Habakkuk and Jeremiah. The third period, the time of the Exile and the Restoration (about 580-400 B.C.) produced Ezekiel, Haggai, Zechariah and Malachi. While there is some difference or opinion among scholars on the exact date when these men worked, and consequently of the precise order in which they came, we shall give a listing which seems to us to be reasonable.

Early Prophets: Moses about 1300 B.C., Samuel 1100 B.C., Elijah 870 B.C., Elisha 850 B.C., Joel 840 B.C., Jonah 800 B.C.

Eighth Century (Assyrian Crisis) Prophets: Amos 760 B.C., Hosea 750 B.C., Isaiah 740-698 B.C., Micah 735 B.C.

Seventh Century (Chaldean Crisis) Prophets: Zephaniah 625 B.C., Jeremiah 625-585 B.C., Nahum 625 B.C., Habakkuk 610 B.C.

Sixth Century (Exilic Crisis) Prophets: Daniel 590 B.C., Ezekiel 590 B.C., Obadiah 585 B.C.

Later Prophets: Haggai 520 B.C., Zechariah 520 B.C., Malachi 435 B.C.

Naturally a full appreciation of the work of each prophet depends upon an intelligent understanding of the circumstances in which he worked. Nevertheless it is true that their messages are independent of time and have a distinct value for every age.

9. The Fulfillment of Prophecy.

There are few fields of Bible study which have been as widely misunderstood and as generally misinterpreted as that of the fulfillment of prophecy. Some of these interpretations are not only fantastic, but are actually erroneous and harmful. Kirkpatrick in his book, "The Doctrine of the Prophets" has one of the sanest and best statements on this subject. "Prophecy and fulfillment were once supposed to be related as the reflection in a mirror to the object reflected. The complete course of future events was thought to have been mapped out in a way intelligible to the prophet and his contemporaries. Prophecy was considered as being throughout 'inverted history.' But the fulfillment is related to prophecy rather as the plant with all its beauty of leaf and flower and fruit is related to the seed from which it is sprung. The connection can be traced: The microscope can detect the parts of the future plant wrapped up in the envelope of the seed; but it cannot foretell, apart from experience, what the full growth will bring, or how the minute and colorless rudiments will develop into rich variety of form and color. And so prophecy contains the germ which is to spring up in a new form in the fulfillment; the principle will in due time receive its legitimate development. It is the outline which will be filled in and take definite shape."*

When we insist on an exact literal fulfillment of all the words of the prophets we are doing violence to the very spirit and purpose of their work. We need to exercise great caution in our interpretations. As a further word on the fulfillment of prophecy we may observe that some of the predictions of the prophets have already been realized and some are yet to be fulfilled. As an example of the former we may cite the predictions of the downfall of Jerusalem and the Babylonian exile. To illustrate the latter we may quote the words of Isaiah: "And they shall beat their swords into plowshares, and their spears into pruning-hooks; nation shall not lift up sword against nation, neither shall they learn war any more," (Isaiah 2:4.)

*Kirkpatrick, H. F.: *The Doctrine of the Prophets*, pp. 15-16, Third Edition 1920, MacMillan & Co. Used by permission.

10. Prophecy Pointing Toward Christ.

There is a vital relationship between the prophets of the Old Testament and the work of Christ. "God, having of old time spoken unto the fathers in the prophets by divers portions and in divers manners, hath at the end of these days spoken unto us in His Son." (Heb. 1:1-2.) The voices of that long succession of men whom he raised up from time to time through a period of more than a thousand years were the voice of God. But in these later days he hath spoken to us through His Son. In him the many partial and fragmentary utterances are reconciled. He is the one supreme and final revelation of God. The Messenger is himself the message.

The messages of these preachers of righteousness are not out of date. In their time they cried out fearlessly against greed, injustice, immorality and apostasy. They made a distinct contribution to the life of their day. That contribution is not all in the past. Their messages, if properly presented, will make a great contribution to the solution of the problems and needs of the twentieth century.

SECTION II — THE EARLY PROPHETS.

1. Introduction.

The study of Hebrew prophecy is a vast field. Countless volumes have been written dealing with the general subject and an even larger number have been devoted to the life and work of individual prophets. Who could say, for example, how many books have been written on Isaiah alone? It is obvious, therefore, that any treatment we can give to this large field in this brief study will have to be very limited. It will be possible to give only a few facts about each prophet and his book, leaving for others the task of a more detailed study of each book.

We are considering these in their probable chronological order since it will save confusion and will make it easier for the student to follow the general narrative of Old Testament history.

Of the six prophets listed in the first group we will consider only two, Joel and Jonah, since the works of the other four (Moses, Samuel, Elijah and Elisha) have been studied in connection with the historical record of their respective periods.

2. Joel.

This is a brief book of three chapters having only seventy-three verses altogether. The word Joel means *Jehovah is God.* We know very little about the man Joel, and this is known indirectly from his book and not by any direct historical reference. He was probably a native of Jerusalem, as indicated by his familiarity with the temple and its services. From a study of his book one gains the impression that he was a man of courage, of sincere faith in God and of devotion to spiritual values.

There are two distinct schools of thought as to his date. Traditionally he has been placed in the 9th century before Christ, living in the day of Athaliah and Joash in Judah. Later scholars insist that he belonged to the post-exilic period. The value of his work does not depend upon dates but there seem to be good reasons for accepting the earlier date for this prophet.

His message was called forth by a national calamity. There had been a devastating plague of locusts which had left the land stripped of food. This was followed by a famine with resulting poverty and misery. These calamities created a situation that called for the sure word of Jehovah. Joel came forth to speak for God in this dark hour. It is probable that he spoke far more than is included in his book. The book itself has two distinct divisions. The first (1:1-2:27) is a call to repentance and prayer. In the second (2:28-3:21) Jehovah promises to hear the cry of his people, to remove the cause of their sufferings and to restore prosperity and enrich them spiritually. "And I will restore to you the years that the locust hath eaten, the cankerworm, and the caterpillar, and the palmerworm, my great army which I sent among you (2:25)." "And after these things I will pour out my spirit upon all flesh . . . and everyone who calls on the name of Jehovah shall be saved." (2:28, 32.)

3. Jonah.

This little book contains one of the most familiar stories in the Old Testament but one that is widely misunderstood. Unfortunately the very mention of the word Jonah provokes a smile, or even a sneer, because of his strange experience with the great fish of the sea. Indeed, the word Jonah has become for many people a sort of synonym for hard luck or misfortune. To many readers the beauty and the significance of the story are missed because of these popular notions.

It should be said at the outset that there are various interpretations of the book. There have always been those who take it as actual history. To these, Jonah was a real man whose actual experiences are recorded. There are others who regard it as pure fiction — an imaginary person with imaginary experiences. There are still others who favor the allegorical interpretation. These scholars hold that the story is a parable intended to teach a great lesson, namely, Jonah is a type of Israel and the fish represents the captivity of the Jews.

We cannot present here the arguments for and against these three interpretations. It is to be observed that the advocate of each view holds that the value and purpose of the book is best understood by accepting his particular interpretation.

In II Kings 14:25 the writer states that Jonah, the son of Amittai, lived in the days of Jeroboam II in Israel, that is about 800 B.C. He came from a little village not far north of the present city of Nazareth. Times were prosperous, money plentiful, and the spirit of nationalism or patriotism was running high. The kingdom of Israel had been expanded and the people were proud and confident. Jonah was a prophet of God sent to speak to the people in these circumstances.

Jonah was commanded of God to go to Nineveh, the capital of Assyria, which was the rising power in the northeast, and to preach to the city, urging the people to repent. Unwilling to do as commanded, he went westward to the seaport town of Joppa and purchased passage on a ship going to Tarshish, probably in Spain. (Some one has said that at least, he was honest enough not to use his clergy permit!) During the voyage a severe storm arose and the seamen questioned Jonah, who admitted that he was fleeing from Jehovah and was probably responsible for the storm. Thereupon, at his own suggestion, Jonah was thrown into the sea. God had prepared a great fish — not a whale — which swallowed the prophet. At the end of three days the fish deposited Jonah on the shore of his native country. Again Jehovah commanded the prophet to go to Nineveh. This time he proceeded at once to do as he was commanded.

Through all the streets of Nineveh he went to give the warning of Jehovah and to call on the people to repent. His words reached even the king himself, who "arose from his throne, and laid aside his robe from him, and covered himself in sackcloth, and sat in ashes." (3:6.) The king called upon his people to fast and humble themselves before Jonah's God. Their cries for mercy were heard and God spared this wicked city of 120,000 people "who could not discern between their right hand and their left." The book closes with an account of Jonah's apparent disappointment at the sparing of the city to which he had proclaimed the message of Jehovah.

The one unmistakable message of the book is the concern of Jehovah for all peoples, regardless of race or nationality. We have here the message of "Foreign Missions" eight hundred years before the birth of Christ. As George Adam Smith says: "The truth which we find in the Book of Jonah is as full a revelation of God's will as prophecy anywhere achieves. That God has granted to the Gentiles also repentance unto life is nowhere else in the Old Testament so vividly illustrated. This lifts the teaching of the book to equal rank with the second part of Isaiah, and nearest of our Twelve to the New Testament."*

Section III — THE EIGHTH CENTURY PROPHETS.

1. Amos.

Amos, the uncompromising prophet of righteousness, lived in the reign of Jeroboam II of Israel, about 760 B.C. The student will recall that this was an era of great national expansion accompanied by almost unparalleled national prosperity. Assyria (Nineveh) which had been spared by the preaching of Jonah was now rising up, preparing to reach toward the Mediterranean in a program of conquest. In less than forty years after Amos began his work the northern tribes (Israel) were captured and taken into exile in Assyria. Despite this threat the people of Israel, enjoying their material prosperity, allowed themselves to descend into a state of moral corruption and spiritual decay that threatened their very existence. Amos came forth with his message to save them from disaster. In his condemnation of their wickedness he mentions almost every sin conceivable — immorality, drunkenness, theft, greed, injustice, disregard of the poor, defrauding the helpless, neglect of spiritual duties and forsaking of Jehovah, their God. Outwardly the people were religious, taking pains to attend the proper ceremonies, observe the technical regulations and make required offerings. Inwardly, however, they were selfish, cruel, wicked and worldly-minded.

Amos came from the little town of Tekoa, about twelve miles south of Jerusalem. In this lonely wilderness region he grew up to become a shepherd and a keeper of sycamore trees. In the quiet semi-desert area he had time to meditate and to learn the truth. Unquestionably, he was acquainted with men and affairs in the kingdom, probably through his periodic trips to the markets and in business transactions. He had a strong body, an alert mind, and a sensitive spiritual appreciation. In some way not revealed to us, God spoke to him, calling him for his high mission. He came under the strongest

*Smith, George Adam: *The Book of the Twelve Prophets,* p. 348 — Harper Brothers.

conviction that he must go up from his home to Bethel, a city in the southern part of the northern kingdom, to declare the word of God, to denounce the sins of Israel and to warn them to prepare to meet God. He went to this religious shrine and faithfully discharged the duty which Jehovah had laid upon him. We do not know how long he remained in the city, though we are told that he refused to leave when commanded to do so by Amaziah the priest. Using a clever device to secure attention, he began by denouncing the surrounding nations for their sins. In his denunciation he came ever nearer to Israel, even denouncing their neighbor, Judah. With every person in the great crowd now alert to hear his word, he poured forth the judgment of God upon Israel for their sins.

The book of Amos is one of fine literary quality. Just how and when it was produced we may not know, though it seems reasonable to assume that he should put these addresses in order upon his return from the mission to Bethel. The nine chapters of the book fall naturally into three sections. (1) Chapters 1-2 recount the judgments of God against the surrounding nations for their wickedness. (2) In the next four chapters (3-6) we have three messages against the sins of Israel. (3) The last division (7-9) gives five visions of the prophets — locusts, fire, the plumb-line, the basket of summer fruit, and the desolate sanctuary.

The book has many distinct values, two of which we mention briefly. It is an authentic picture of internal conditions in Israel in one of its most important periods. It has value also as an illustration of the message of a great prophet and the manner in which he worked. The key statement of his message may be found in 5:24 "Let justice roll down as waters and righteousness as a mighty stream."

2. Hosea.

This prophet may be considered a contemporary of Amos, though he probably did his work some ten years later. He lived under Jeroboam II of Israel and under Uzziah, Jotham, Ahaz and Hezekiah of Judah. Conditions in general were the same as in the time of Amos. The international situation was growing steadily more threatening with the Assyrian doom coming nearer. In Israel rapid changes came after the death of Jeroboam II. Within twenty years six kings had occupied the throne at Samaria. Internally conditions were no better. Apparently the faithful ministry of Amos had not produced any permanent reformation. The same sins blighted the land and Israel seemed unaware of danger and unresponsive to the gracious mercies and proffered guidance of Jehovah their God.

We know but little of the background of Hosea. He was a native of the northern kingdom and in this kingdom he did all his work as a prophet. The first chapters of his book tell the tragic story of his marriage to a woman named Gomer. "Jehovah said unto Hosea, Go take a wife of whoredom and children of whoredom." (1:2.) How can this be explained? Did God thus put his approval on immorality? There are three interpretations of his marriage, all of which have vigorous advocates. There are some who claim that this account is literal history, that Hosea married an adulteress. Other scholars hold that this is an allegory, that the story was invented to illustrate the idea of God's love for men. A third view is that Hosea actually married Gomer, who at the time was a clean woman but later became impure. The last interpretation seems by far the most reasonable one and hence is held by a majority of students.

The story is that Gomer bore to him three children "Jezreel" (vengeance), "Lo-Ammi" (not my people) and "Lo Ruhamah" (unpitied). Later his wife became entangled in sin, was guilty of unfaithfulness, and still later she went out to sell herself. What must have been the anguish of soul experienced by the sensitive and devoted husband! In due time God commanded Hosea to go out into the city to redeem or buy back his unfaithful wife and bring her home, forgive her, restore her fully and love her freely.

This bitter tragedy did something for Hosea that nothing but suffering and sorrow can do. He was forced to drink deeply of the cup of woe as well as of the spring of joy. This experience enabled him to understand something of God's immeasurable love for his people. It enabled him also to plead with his people effectively to return to their God who loved them. The entire experience came to be a sort of living analogy of God's relation to Israel. Just as Hosea had loved Gomer with his deepest devotion, and she, despite this, had deserted him and must be brought back by redeeming love, so God had loved Israel who had forsaken him for other gods. Thus the message of Hosea is one of the tenderest and most appealing of all the prophets. For pathos and beauty is is unsurpassed. Amos preached to the conscience; Hosea was a prophet of real repentance.

The heart of his message may be found in a number of selected statements from his book. "How can I give thee up, Ephraim?" "How can I let thee go, Israel?" "My heart is turned within me, my compassions are kindled together." (11:8.) "Return, O Israel, to Jehovah, thy God; for thou hast fallen by thine iniquity. Take with you words, and return to Jehovah. Say to him, remove altogether iniquity, and receive us graciously and we will render the fruit of our lips." (14:2.) "I will heal their backsliding, I will love them freely; for my anger is turned away from them." (14:4.)

3. Isaiah.

Isaiah belongs at the head of all lists of the prophets. In him prophecy reaches its perfection. He has come to be the standard by which all the others are measured. As one enthusiastic critic has put it — Isaiah has all the great qualities of all the prophets. In the length of his service, in the critical issues he faced, in the content of his message, in the effectiveness of his work and in the quality of his written messages he excels them all.

In the chapter on the southern kingdom we have already dealt with his work as a statesman and prophet. In this connection we must be content merely to mention the leading facts in his life. He was of an aristocratic family, the son of Amoz, who is said to have been the brother of king Amaziah. His ministry extended from 750 to 698 B.C., during the reigns of Uzziah, Jotham, Ahaz, Hezekiah and Manasseh. He received his call (Chapter 6) in the year that Uzziah died, and for some fifty years lived and served in Jerusalem. He was married and had two sons who were given symbolic names, "Shear-Jashub" (a remnant shall return) and "Maher-Shalal-hash-baz" (the spoil speeds, the prey hastens). Nothing is certainly known of the life of Isaiah after the crisis of Sennacherib's invasion. The tradition that he was sawn asunder by the wicked king Manasseh is probably without a factual basis.

The prophet lived in the critical days of the Assyrian domination. Within the first twenty-five years of his ministry the Assyrians captured Samaria and ended the northern kingdom (722 B.C.). Twenty-one years later the same pagan foes stood at the gates of Jerusalem and would have captured the southern kingdom also but for the miraculous intervention of Jehovah through Isaiah, his messenger. The greatest problems faced by Judah were not military. This Assyrian invasion raised many racial and religious problems which called for the courage and wisdom of the great Isaiah. He stood firm against idolatry and every other sin which threatened to overwhelm the little kingdom of Judah during these critical years. This brilliant, cultured and consecrated servant of God, the trusted counselor of kings, worked for fifty years at the very heart of the life of the nation. Perhaps no statement about the prophet summarizes better his magnificant qualities than that made years ago by Valeton: "Never, perhaps, has there been another prophet like Isaiah, who stood with his head in the clouds and his feet on the solid earth, with his heart in the things of eternity and with mouth and head in the things of time, with his spirit in the eternal counsel of God and his body in a very definite moment of history." (Quoted in the Cambridge Bible.)

The book of Isaiah likewise stands at the head of all books of prophecy. Purely from the standpoint of literature it is unexcelled, indeed, unequalled! It has practically all the essentials of good literature. Perhaps its outstanding characteristic is its wealth and brilliancy of imagination. Isaiah's wide store of knowledge is no more astounding than his power of graphic and picturesque description. It is oratorical in style and is "plain, noble and rapid." The entire book is illumined by the brilliant fire of a genius.

The book of Isaiah is the noblest in prophetic literature if not in all the Old Testament. It is most like the New Testament and is far more frequently quoted in the New Testament than any other. The reader who spends most of his time in the New Testament will be surprised to discover how much of its meaning, and even its language, is taken from Isaiah. The book is a long one of sixty-six chapters.

The question of Deutero-Isaiah, that is the authorship of the second part of the book (40-66) is perhaps the best known problem in Biblical criticism. For the past century an increasingly large number of scholars have come to the conviction that this second section was not written by the Isaiah of the 8th century B.C., but was produced by some man living in the time of the Babylonian exile, since this section is clearly intended as a message of comfort and hope to those exiles. There are still many others who hold to the unity of the book, that is, that Isaiah is the author of the entire book. There are lengthy and involved arguments on each side and it is not possible to present these in the limits of this study. Happily, however, the value of these messages are not involved in this complicated question.

The book easily falls into two general sections with the following natural divisions.

I

1. Promises and rebukes for Israel and Judah, 1-12.
2. Prophecies against foreign nations, 13-23.
3. Prophecies of general judgment, 24-35.
4. Historical section dealing with the Assyrian invasion, 36-39.

II

1. Messages of comfort for the exiles, 40-48.
2. The Servant of Jehovah, 49-55.
3. The future glory of God's people, 56-66.

Even the briefest study of this great book should include careful consideration of chapters one, six, forty, forty-nine, fifty, fifty-two, fifty-three, fifty-five, and sixty-five.

4. Micah.

Micah *(who is like Jehovah)* was a contemporary of Isaiah and, therefore, lived under the same conditions and faced the same problems. Isaiah did his work in the city while Micah seems to have worked with people out in the country. He came from the little village of Moresheth on the borders between Judah and Philistia, a distance of about twenty-five miles southwest of Jerusalem. His home was on the main highway between Jerusalem and Egypt and because of this the young prophet had opportunities to learn of big events taking place in his time. We know almost nothing of his family or of his home life. His work indicates that in some way he had an unusual knowledge of social abuses and civic corruption. He had a vital knowledge of the elements of real religion and he had courage to declare the truth as he understood it. Speaking of his mission he declares: "But I am full of power by the Spirit of Jehovah and justice and might to declare to Jacob his transgression and to Israel his sin." (3:8.) He championed the cause of the poor against the oppressions of the rich. He loved his country, but was especially devoted to his own poor and oppressed people. He preached righteousness and justice with flaming words. His words were effective because the reasons for his passionate proclamations were so evident: "Pinched peasant faces peer between all his words."

He denounces corruption, injustice and false standards of religion. His book of sermons is arranged logically. The seven chapters fall into three natural divisions. (1) The doom of Jerusalem and Samaria (chps. 1-2), (2) The transgressions of religious leaders (3-5), and (3) Jehovah's controversy with his people (6-7).

Some of his statements are quite familiar because they are frequently quoted. "Woe to them that devise iniquity and work evil upon their beds." (2:1.) "But in the latter days it shall come to pass, that the mountain of Jehovah's house shall be established on the top of the mountains, and it shall be exalted above the hills; and peoples shall flow unto it." (4:1.) "And they shall beat their swords into plowshares, and their spears into pruning-hooks; nation shall not lift up sword against nation, neither shall they learn war any more. But they shall sit every man under his vine and his fig tree; and none shall make them afraid; for the mouth of Jehovah of hosts hath spoken it." (4:3-4.) "But thou, Bethlehem Ephratha, which art little to be among the thousands of Judah, out of thee shall one come forth unto me that is to be ruler in Israel; whose goings forth are from old, from everlasting." (5:2.) "He hath showed thee, O man, what is good: and what doth Jehovah require of thee, but to do justly, and to love kindness, and to walk humbly with thy God?" (6:8.)

SECTION IV — THE SEVENTH CENTURY PROPHETS.

1. Zephaniah.

This prophet, unlike Micah, was of aristocratic lineage. Some scholars hold that he was related to Josiah, who at the time was king of Judah. If so this background enabled him to speak effectively on the sins of his time.

He lived at a crucial time in international affairs. The Assyrian rulers, who for more than a century had dominated southwest Asia, were now declining in power. Babylonia, under Nabopolassar, was soon to gain the supremacy in this area of the world. Although Nineveh did not fall until 612 B.C., Babylonia was the dominant influence as early as 625 B.C., the date of Zephaniah. To be a witness of the transfer of world power from one kingdom to another was an exciting experience for this alert man.

It will be recalled that the chief event in the reign of Josiah, king of Judah, was his reformation. This was a nation-wide movement backed by the deepest conviction of the young king. It is likely that Zephaniah, Jeremiah, and even Habakkuk and Nahum, supported the reforms of Josiah. The discovery of the book of the law in the repairing of the temple and the deep religious enthusiasm that followed must have furnished an inspiring situation for the work of a young man like Zephaniah. The young prophet had accurate knowledge of conditions in the city of Jerusalem where he probably lived all his life. His stern denunciations of the sins of the people and his impassioned cries for repentance have given him the name "puritan." He took a dark view of the situation and offered only one hope, namely, turning to Jehovah, the God of Israel.

His book is a short one, having only three chapters with a total of fifty-three verses. It is made up largely of dark pictures but expresses the conviction that there is always hope and even joy for those who fully trust Jehovah. "Sing, O daughter of Zion; shout, O Israel; be glad and rejoice with all thy heart. O daughter of Jerusalem. Jehovah thy God is in the midst of thee, a mighty one who will save; he will rejoice over thee with joy; he will rest in his love; he will joy over thee with singing." (3:14, 17.)

2. *Jeremiah.*

The prophet Jeremiah, whose name means *exalted of Jehovah,* lived the latter part of the seventh century and part of the sixth century before Christ. His ministry of some forty years is usually dated about 625-585 B.C. The student will recognize this period as the time of the last years of the kingdom of Judah and the early part of the Babylonian captivity. It was his hard lot to live through those tragic years, to witness the death of a nation and the discouraging prospect of exile in a foreign land. He was called to the unhappy task of condemning the corrupt life and practice of his people, of warning against the consequences of sin, of pleading with his brethren to turn to their God and save themselves. In later years he had to kindle their hopes and undergird their faith when they faced the certainty of exile. Still later he must encourage and keep together as far as possible the remnant of those left in Jerusalem in the confusion and desolation of a ravaged community. He did not go with the exiles to Babylon, though he wrote them and sought to encourage them in the hope of mercy in the future. He lived among the people in the ruined city until forced to go with them into Egypt. We have no record of his latter years, though the tradition is that he died as a martyr in Egypt. Another tradition says that he was taken to Babylon where he died.

He was by all means the chief figure of his time, towering above every man in the period. He was a patriot, a prophet and a statesman, a wise counselor of kings and a courageous foe of wickedness and sin. By nature he was sensitive, timid, and melancholy. He had no home, no family, and much of the time, no friends. His life was practically that of a martyr but he bore his sufferings without complaint or bitterness. He has frequently been called the "weeping prophet." However, when we remember the circumstances and understand fully his courage and the difficult situation in which he had to labor, we can see the injustice of such a designation. In reality he was one of the strongest and bravest of men who knew how to stand for the truth without pitying himself. It took a man of the greatest strength to stand uncomplainingly as did Jeremiah.

The book of Jeremiah is a long one with fifty-two chapters and is made up of biography, history, and prophecy. The book is difficult to understand since the events and chapters do not appear in proper chronological order. The first chapter gives an account of the call of the prophet. Chapters 2-35 contain his prophecies relating to Jerusalem and Judah. Chapters 36-45 are made up of biographical accounts. In chapters 46-51 there are several brief prophecies concerning foreign nations. Chapter 52 is a historical appendage dealing with Zedekiah.

Jeremiah made two distinctive contributions to religious truth. (1) True religion is essentially spiritual in nature. (2) Personal responsibility is inescapable. These contributions constituted a mighty step forward.

3. Nahum.

This prophet belonged to the same period as Zephaniah and Jeremiah. We may assume that his date was not far from 625 B.C. George Adam Smith thinks 640 B.C. would be better, while a number of other scholars place him much nearer to 612 B.C., when Nineveh, the capital of Assyria, fell to Babylon. This city, so famous in the two preceding centuries, never recovered after 612 B.C. Up to this time it had been impregnable. The city with its walls one hundred feet high and wide enough for three chariots to drive side by side on its top had remained unconquered for more than a century. It is said that outside this massive wall was a moat one hundred and forty feet wide and sixty feet deep, dominated by some twelve hundred defense towers. This proud and cruel city had been involved in the sufferings of multitudes of people. She was to be repaid for all her sins. The judgment of God was to come upon her.

The word Nahum means *compassion*. Some students claim that his home was on the banks of the Tigris river, others, that he came from southwest Judah. Still others think that he was from Galilee, a native of Capernaum (City of Nahum).

His hatred for the cruel Assyrians can be detected in almost every sentence of his book. A holy and just God could not let this city live. Nahum's righteous indignation flashes like lightning in poetic utterances. God's wrath and vengeance are not to be thought of as the petty blunderings of men. "God is the master of his wrath and uses it." When God is angry it is because of principle and not caprice. This city, guilty of cruelty, harlotry, brutality, oppression and rebellion against God, must reap the awful consequences. Nineveh mocked God and died. Such teaching is not inconsistent with the holiness of God.

4. Habakkuk.

We know but little about the man Habakkuk except by inference from his book. It is generally assumed that he lived and worked in Jerusalem. We know that he lived in the eventful years at the close of the seventh century before Christ (610-600 B.C.). He could see the passing of Assyria and the coming of Babylonia to the place of supremacy in his world. He probably was an eye witness to the first ravages of Jerusalem by the armies of Nebuchadnezzar. His spirit was deeply troubled by these momentous events. How could God permit so much suffering and death? How could God punish his own people, even though they had sinned, by a nation that was even more wicked? He was sincere in raising these questions; he really wanted an answer since he was a man of reverent spirit. He was an honest seeker of the truth who went directly to God for the answer.

This book of only three chapters consists of three general divisions. The first of these (1:1-2:4) is the dialogue between Jehovah and the prophet. The second (2:5-20) is a series of woes against the Babylonians. The third (3:1-19) is a beautiful ode or anthem of praise.

There are several familiar statements which will give a general idea of the contents of the book:

"Thou that art of purer eyes than to behold evil, and that canst not look on perverseness, wherefore lookest thou upon them that deal treacherously, and holdest thy peace when the wicked swalloweth up the man that is more righteous than he?" (1:13.)

"He stood and measured the earth;
He beheld, and drove asunder the nations;
And the eternal mountains were scattered;
The everlasting hills did bow;
His goings were as of old." (3:6.)

"For though the fig tree shall not flourish,
Neither shall fruit be in the vines;
The labor of the olive shall fail,
And the fields shall yield no food;
The flock shall be cut off from the fold,
And there shall be no herd in the stalls;
Yet I shall rejoice in Jehovah,
I will joy in the God of my salvation." (3:17-18.)

Section V — PROPHETS OF THE SIXTH CENTURY.

1. Daniel.

In the preceding chapter we have given some attention to the work of Daniel among the Babylonian exiles. There are two views regarding the authorship of the book of Daniel. The view held by many scholars is that this book was written by the Daniel of the Babylonian exile some time between 600-533 B.C. There are others who believe that the book was composed by some man or group of men living in the second century before Christ.

The name Daniel means *God is my Judge*. Daniel was probably born in Jerusalem and was among those first taken into Babylonian captivity (600 B.C.). He was selected for special service by Nebuchadnezzar and served with distinction in the government. In all his experiences he never compromised his convictions nor wavered in his loyalty to Jehovah his God. He lived through the entire period of the exile and probably died in Babylon.

By his example and teaching he was a mighty influence among the Jews in exile. He believed and taught that God would deliver his servants. He was confident of the final triumph of the Kingdom of God.

The book is apocalyptic in nature, containing visions that are variously interpreted. There is much in it that can be understood by all who studiously read it. The book contains two very obvious sections: Daniel's personal experiences (1-6) and his visions of the Kingdom (7-12).

2. Ezekiel.

The name Ezekiel means *God will strengthen*. This prophet was a priest in Jerusalem and was taken to Babylonia as a captive in the second group of exiles in 597 B.C. During the exile he lived by the river Chebar which was a large canal running from the Euphrates river above Babylon in a southeasterly course through Nippur to the Tigris river. He was probably well acquainted with Daniel, who lived in Babylon, and it is probable that they worked together. It is possible that he knew Jeremiah back in Jerusalem before going into exile. Some students think that as a young man he was a disciple of Jeremiah.

As a priest Ezekiel would receive special training and would be well acquainted with the formalities and rituals of religion. From the book of Ezekiel we are able to know something of his character and his work. His work as a prophet differed somewhat from that of most of the other prophets. He did not so much predict or forecast events, but rather had visions of these. In his book there are many symbols, visions, parables and allegories, some of which are concerned with future events and some with existing facts and conditions.

The student should read carefully the story of Ezekiel's dramatic vision and call in the first three chapters of the book. His mission was chiefly to destroy the false hopes held by so many exiles of an early return to Jerusalem. God had a purpose in the exile; they were to remain in Babylonia a long time to learn this lesson. They must rethink their faith and learn the larger spiritual mission of their race. Ezekiel was to serve as their spiritual guide, to warn against apostasy, to console, to stimulate and to enhearten them. For twenty-two years he worked at his discouraging and difficult task. The people of Israel and the entire world are more deeply indebted to this faithful and unselfish "watchman" and interpreter than we will ever know. Without him the faith of Israel might not have survived the hard years of captivity.

His book, when properly understood, is a significant literary and religious volume. Along with the visions and parables and allegories, which are subject to different interpretations, there are powerful addresses and appeals which are very practical and are easily understood. It is very easy to outline the book as follows: (1) his call (1-3), (2) the destruction of Jerusalem (4-24), (3) predictions against foreign countries (25-32), (4) predictions concerning the restoration (33-48).

3. Obadiah.

Obadiah, with its one chapter of twenty-one verses, is the shortest book in the Old Testament. The name means *servant of Jehovah*. We know nothing of the author except some general impressions gained from his book. He was probably a native of Judah. He lived at the same time as Ezekiel and Jeremiah, hence was an eyewitness of the destruction of Jerusalem by Nebuchadnezzar. He was deeply offended by the lack of sympathy and even the delight which the Edomites exhibited in the destruction of Jerusalem by the Babylonians. The Edomites, living south of Judah, were the descendants of Esau, hence relatives of the Jews. For many centuries they had been neighbors, though the relations between Edom and Judah had been strained, and even bitter, much of the time. These "relatives" should have shown sympathy in the destruction of the kingdom of Judah; instead, they rejoiced in the ill fate of their neighbors. The book of Obadiah is an oration directed against Edom for this unbrotherly behavior. Edom was destroyed in 582 B.C. The book of Obadiah apparently was written between the destruction of Jerusalem and Edom, hence the date is usually given as about 585 B.C.

The theme of the book is the coming destruction of Edom. Nothing can save them from the judgment of Jehovah for their brutal treatment of the Israelites fleeing from the ruined city of Jerusalem in 587 B.C. Edom is doomed but Israel shall be restored and blessed because "the saviours shall come up on Mt. Zion to judge the Mount of Esau; and the Kingdom shall be Jehovah's." (Vs. 21.)

SECTION VI — LATER PROPHETS.

1. Haggai.

This prophet belongs to the latter part of the exile in Babylonia. He was born in Babylon and was in the company of Zerubbabel which returned to Jerusalem under the decree of Cyrus to rebuild the temple. He began his ministry during the rebuilding and was the first prophet in Jerusalem after the return. He worked about 520 B.C.

His chief objective was to stimulate and encourage the Jews in their big undertaking of reconstructing the temple and of re-instituting their worship. This undertaking was a heroic one and oftentimes the people grew discouraged and were prone to lose hope. The prophet contends that their crops were poor and their general condition depressing because they had neglected God's house and had been forgetful of their duties to Jehovah. They were weary and despondent in spirit and had not peace and happiness because of wrong relationship with God. Their other leaders apparently were not able to move the people to action, so God called the prophet Haggai to speak his message to the ruler, the priest and the people.

The little book of two chapters is made up of four brief oracles or discourses, each definitely dated. These came between August and the last of December in the year 520 B.C. In the first chapter Haggai makes his appeal and then tells of the preparations for rebuilding. In the second chapter he describes the glories and blessings of the new temple and its services and then closes with a message of hope to Zerubbabel to the effect that he would be spared in the destruction that would come to the surrounding nations. Israel was to endure because of her imperishable mission.

2. Zechariah.

This prophet was contemporary with Haggai, hence the background of his work is the same. He was probably a much younger man. He stood with the older prophet and gave his strength and energies to the same great objective. The name Zechariah means *he whom Jehovah remembers.* He has been called the prophet with "the soul of an artist and the eye of a seer."

His book has fourteen chapters and is made up of three obvious sections. (1) The first (1-6) is a series of visions intended to encourage the people to rebuild the temple. (2) The second (8-9) is an appeal to practical activity. (3) The third (10-14) is a "disclosure of destiny," a revealing of the future of Israel. There is a critical problem connected with the authorship of the last section. Critics are almost unanimous in holding that this section was written much later and perhaps by another author. Be that as it may, the general value and purpose of these last six chapters is not affected.

3. Malachi.

The last of the prophets, Malachi, *my messenger* or *messenger of the Lord,* lived and labored in the restored community of Jerusalem. While there are differences of opinion as to the date of his ministry, it seems reasonable to place him around 435 B.C. Many changes had occurred since the times of Haggai and Zechariah. The people had grown indifferent to their spiritual obligations, had neglected the temple and were worldly, restless, and in danger from their enemies about them. Crops were poor, the priests were corrupt and the people refused to pay their tithes and offerings. Worship had degenerated, social abuses were widespread and home and family life were decaying. Nehemiah had come back to Jerusalem to rebuild the walls and to help his brethren in their plight but he needed the support of a prophet. Malachi was called to serve in this crisis.

While we have but few facts about this man we know that he was a vigorous, courageous spokesman, filled with zeal for the cause which he represented. He must denounce their lethargy, rebuke their sins, and stimulate them to reform.

His book, composed of only four chapters, contains severe denunciations of social evils, strong rebukes for the hypocrisy of the priests, as well as prophecies of deliverance and of better days ahead. The book may be analyzed as follows: (1) Jehovah's love for Israel 1:1-5. (2) Israel's failure to love Jehovah, as proved by their polluted offering, the sins of the priests and their heathen marriages 1:6-2:16. (3) God's coming to judge his people 2:17-4:6.

The prophet insists that God's acceptance of men's offerings and service is conditioned upon the sincerity and purity of the life of those who make them. The people had robbed God not only in tithes and offerings, but they had withheld from him their loyalty and their love. If the people gave to God what rightfully belonged to him, abundant blessings should follow. It demanded, however, not only formal offerings, but purity of heart and sincerity of spirit.

"Bring ye the whole tithe into the storehouse, that there may be food in my house, and prove me now herewith, saith Jehovah of hosts, if I will not open you the windows of heaven, and pour you out a blessing, that there shall not be room enough to receive it." (3:10.)

"And all nations shall call you happy; for ye shall be a delightsome land, saith Jehovah of hosts." (3:10, 12.)

Chapter XIV

THE POETICAL LITERATURE OF THE OLD TESTAMENT

Job, Psalms, Proverbs, Ecclesiastes, Song of Solomon, Lamentations

Section I — Introduction.
1. Time of Writing. 2. Poetry in the Old Testament.
3. Parallelism. 4. Kinds of Hebrew Poetry. 5. Golden Age
of Hebrew Poetry.

Section II — The Book of Job.
1. Introduction. 2. Date and Authorship. 3. Nature of
the Book. 4. The Prologue. 5. The Arguments. 6. The
Epilogue.

Section III — The Book of Psalms.
1. Introduction. 2. Nature and Purpose of the Psalms.
3. Divisions of the Book. 4. Date and Authorship. 5.
Variety of Moods. 6. Range of the Psalms. 7. The Perfect
Manual of Devotions. 8. Some Immortal Psalms.

Section IV — The Book of Proverbs.
1. The Use of Proverbs. 2. Date and Authorship. 3.
Divisions of the Book. 4. General Contents.

Section V — Other Books of Poetry.
1. Ecclesiastes. 2. The Song of Solomon. 3. Lamentations.

CHAPTER XIV

The Poetical Literature of the Old Testament

Job, Psalms, Proverbs, Ecclesiastes, Song of Solomon, Lamentations

Section I — INTRODUCTION.

1. Time of Writing.

At the beginning of our studies we saw that the materials in the Old Testament belonged to three general classifications: (1) history, including the Mosaic laws, (2) prophecy, and (3) poetry. The first two of these we have already considered. The closing chapter of our Old Testament studies will be devoted to a brief survey of the poetical books.

Some of these are collections of writings by different authors over a period of several hundred years. Others, like Job and Ecclesiastes, were the work of one writer. While each of these six books has its own particular message and value all of them are worthy of study.

2. Poetry in the Old Testament.

There are six books in the Old Testament usually classified as poetry: Job, Psalms, Proverbs, Ecclesiastes, Song of Solomon, and Lamentations. However, Hebrew poetry is not confined to these books. The student using an American Revised or any later translation of the Bible will easily discover many brief poems outside these books. These poems are found in the earliest books such as Genesis 4:19-23, Numbers 21:14-15, Judges chapter 5, and so on. The earliest literature of the Hebrews, like that of all other peoples, was poetry. There are probably several reasons for this. Among early peoples emotion usually was expressed in impassioned song. Again, special occasions such as marriages, and victory in war, usually were celebrated with song and dance.

It is well to remember that we do not have in our Bible all the poems written and used by the Hebrew people, since in general only religious poems found their way into the Old Testament. Biblical writers refer to collections of poems called the "Wars of Jehovah" (Numbers 21:14) and the "Book of Jashar" (Josh. 10:12). There are at least thirteen synonyms in the Hebrew language for the word *song,* indicating that lyric poetry was very popular among the Hebrews in Old Testament times.

Poetry of the Old Testament is quite different from ordinary poetry in that it has neither rhyme nor metre. Hebrew poetry resembles our free verse and consequently suffers but little in translation.

3. Parallelism.

The distinguishing characteristic of Old Testament poetry is what is usually termed parallelism. By this we mean the repetition of the same idea in the second verse in slightly different phraseology. There are four different types of parallelism: (1) Synonymous, in which the same idea is repeated, though in slightly different words. The prayer of David in Psalm 5:1 will illustrate this type:

> "Give ear to my words, O Jehovah,
> Consider my meditation."

(2) Antithetical, in which a contrast of two ideas is made. For example, the familiar statement in Proverbs 10:1.

> "A wise son maketh a glad father;
> But a foolish son is the heaviness of his mother."

(3) Synthetical or progressive, in which the second line supplements and completes the thought of the first. An example of this may be found in Psalms 29:1.

> "Ascribe unto Jehovah, O ye sons of the mighty,
> Ascribe unto Jehovah, glory and strength."

(4) Comparative, in which ideas are compared. This may be illustrated by Psalms 42:1.

> "As the hart panteth after the waterbrooks,
> So panteth my soul after thee, O God."

4. Kinds of Hebrew Poetry.

Generally speaking there are four kinds of poetry found in the Old Testament.

(1) Lyric. This is the poetry of sentiment. It is "emotional verse of song like form." The Psalms are the most familiar lyric poems in the Old Testament.

(2) Dramatic. This is poetry with drama the chief thought. Job illustrates this type.

(3) Gnomic or proverbial. This type is in the form of sayings or proverbs. The book of Proverbs is the best example of this type.

(4) Elegiac. "A meditative poem with a sorrowful theme." Lamentations illustrates this kind of Hebrew poetry.

The poems of the Old Testament, particularly the Psalms and Proverbs, are known and loved by millions of readers. No other poems are so cherished and so continuously studied and appreciated as the works of the singers of Israel. Many scholars hold that the poetry of the Old Testament is the most significant contribution of the Hebrew people to the literature of the world.

5. *Golden Age of Hebrew Poetry.*

There are good reasons for holding that the period of the United Kingdom was an era in which much of the great poetry of the Old Testament was written. (1) This period followed the important reforms and constructive leadership of Samuel who was able to stir the fires of religious patriotism among the Hebrews. He established schools of the prophets which promoted spiritual and literary activities and studies. Unquestionably these schools were well organized, were attended by many young men and were influential in cultivating music and poetry. Under his leadership a start had been made in producing poetry. (2) David, through his victories and conquests, had enlarged the limits of the kingdom, had established a substantial government and had created a sense of national unity and pride. Under his reign and that of Solomon it was natural for this fine art to flourish. We may compare this period to the Elizabethan period of English literature. In the time of Solomon an acquaintance with learning was an accepted requirement of court life. (3) The setting up of the Ark in Jerusalem, making this their holy city, the center of their worship of Jehovah, would logically stimulate the writing of great religious hymns.

Without attempting any discussion of the complicated question of the dates of the various Psalms and of other books of Hebrew poetry we may well consider at this point in our studies the leading books of poetry in the Old Testament. Accordingly, we shall give consideration to: (1) The book of Job. (2) The Psalms. (3) The Proverbs and (4) The other books of Hebrew poetry.

SECTION II — THE BOOK OF JOB.

1. *Introduction.*

This is one of the most remarkable books ever written. It is not easy to read or to understand since it deals with some of the profoundest problems of life. It is dramatic poetry, conversation and argument, in dignified and exalted language. For centuries literary critics have marvelled at its perfection and beauty. Victor Hugo once remarked that "the book of Job is perhaps the greatest masterpiece of the human mind." There is a story of Thomas Carlyle, the great English critic and philosopher, who on one occasion was a guest in the home of his friend Lord Tennyson. In the evening Tennyson asked Carlyle to read a passage from the Bible for evening worship. The family had gathered and Carlyle opened the Bible and began to read from the book of Job. He became so absorbed in this classic that he read chapter after chapter, unaware of the passing of time. The members of the family quietly slipped away to retire and left him reading. In the morning the maid discovered him still reading, utterly absorbed in the conflict of soul experienced by the servant of God who lived in the land of Uz. The story may or may not be true, but fortunately we have Carlyle's evaluation of this great book: "I call this book, apart from all theories about it, one of the grandest things ever written. Our first, oldest statement of the never-ending problem — man's destiny, and God's ways with him here on the earth. There is nothing written, I think, of equal literary merit." This is high praise coming from a man like Carlyle.

2. Date and Authorship.

Strangely enough we know neither the time of writing nor the author of the book. So far as scholars can determine there is no way of discovering either of these facts, though there are various opinions on it. The date of its writing has been variously placed all the way from Moses to the Exile, or even afterward. Limits of space will not permit any discussion of the arguments for different dates of writing. However, one or two statements may not be out of place in this connection. The setting and the atmosphere of the book would indicate that Job lived about the time of Abraham. However, the writer of the book could easily have lived at a later time since writers often use some epoch or period in the past as the setting for novels or dramas. It seems reasonable to suppose that some writer living in the Golden Age of Hebrew letters (1000-700 B.C.) should have written this immortal book. Moses, Elihu, Elijah, Solomon, Hezekiah, Jeremiah, Ezra, Isaiah and other Old Testament characters are believed by various scholars to have been the author. Some critics hold that it has a composite authorship. But we do not know. Happily, however, the interest and the value of the book are absolutely independent of all problems of authorship and date of writing.

3. Nature of the Book.

There are three well defined divisions of the book: the prologue (Chapters 1-2) in prose; the main body or the arguments (Chapters 3-41) in exalted poetry; and the epilogue (Chapter 42) in prose. As will be seen from the foregoing analysis, the major portion of the book is the poetical section, consisting of the speeches of Job and his so-called comforters, Eliphaz, Bildad, Zophar and Elihu, and the words of the Almighty. This is "polished" poetry and naturally is not to be considered a verbatim report of their conversations since these lengthy speeches would not be carried on in such elevated poetry.

The book deals with one of the profoundest and most puzzling problems of human life. "Why do the righteous suffer?" The purpose of this book seems to be to disprove the theory that suffering or misfortune is a sign of divine displeasure and is always brought upon men by their own sins.

4. The Prologue.

The writer first gives an account of Job's righteous life and prosperity, picturing him as the ideal man. The next scene, laid in heaven, relates the conversation between Jehovah and Satan in which Jehovah speaks of the piety of Job. To this Satan replies that Job is good because it pays. Satan asserts that Job would renounce God if he should lose his possessions. Jehovah gives Satan permission to test Job in this way. However, Job is not apprised of this. Then follows the story of one calamity after another upon the good man. All his possessions are taken including even his seven sons and three daughters. Job bows submissively but does not renounce God.

Satan next contends that Job will renounce God if his bodily sufferings are severe enough. Physical pain will do it. "Skin for skin, yea all that a man has will he give for his life." Jehovah gives Satan permission to afflict his servant, only not to kill. Job is afflicted with some horrible disease — boils, black leprosy or some other. His plight is now most pitiable. In his terrible suffering even his wife advises him to curse God and die. However, he remains loyal to Jehovah.

Hearing of his great distress, his three friends visit him to comfort him. They rend their clothes and sit with him seven days and nights in silence.

5. The Arguments.

This main section of the book is really made up of three parts. First are the long arguments between Job and his three friends. Next come the speeches of a pompous young man named Elihu, and finally the climax, which is the answer of God to Job out of the whirlwind, and Job's reply.

The first cycle of discussion with Eliphaz, Bildad and Zophar (Chapters 3-14) is mainly their charge that Job is guilty of some great sin and consequently is being punished. Job vigorously denies their charge. In the second cycle (Chapters 15-21) these friends insist that his claim of innocence is an added proof of his guilt. In the third cycle (Chapters 22-31) the three "comforters" argue that his afflictions are the type that would come to a man guilty of the sin with which they have charged him. In these three cycles they speak in the same order each time. Job replies to each argument in turn.

Elihu, the confident and boastful young man, shows how Job claims to be innocent himself but really accuses God wrongly. He insists that suffering may help one to be righteous and prevents one from sinning.

The two addresses of Jehovah are given at this point to instruct Job. God appears suddenly and overwhelmingly out of the whirlwind. In the first speech the creative power of God is shown to Job and he is rebuked for answering God whom all animals fear. In the second address Job is shown that before he or any other criticizes the Almighty for the way he rules the universe he should know better than God how to do it. Job declines to reply to the Almighty, but he repents in dust and ashes (38:1-42:6). In this experience Job's faith is not only strengthened but is reinforced and illuminated. "I have heard of thee by the hearing of the ear; but now mine eye seeth thee." This faith is all sufficient and does not "need nor ask a sure and certain answer to the sad questions of this earth."

6. The Epilogue.

This last section in prose closes the story. It gives Jehovah's rebuke to the three friends and his vindication of Job. This faithful servant is rewarded with even greater prosperity than he formerly enjoyed. He became also the father of seven other sons and three other daughters known above all other maidens of the East for their beauty.

SECTION III — THE PSALMS.

1. Introductory

The most frequently read, and consequently, the most familiar part of the Old Testament is the book of Psalms — or parts of it. The average reader who may not have the time nor the inclination to study the books of history or law or prophecy will find himself reading in the book of Psalms frequently. This is true partly because these are poems which can be read quickly and easily. Perhaps the real reason is that he finds in these great poems the thing which he needs. They are devotional poems and as such they satisfy the desire of the Christian for ready and genuine fellowship with God.

2. *Nature and Purpose of the Psalms.*

The book is a collection of poems which covers a long period in the history of Israel. As we shall see later, one of these is ascribed to Moses, thus going back to early days of Hebrew history, and some probably were written during the last years of Old Testament history. They are poems composed and used for a wide variety of occasions or purposes. Many of them are hymns which were used in worship. No doubt many of these were set to music and were used in the liturgy of temple worship, though naturally the music has not been preserved. They correspond to the hymns or songs of worship used by Christian groups today.

3. *Divisions of the Book.*

In the Septuagint and in the Hebrew the 150 chapters of the book are grouped into five divisions. Each division closes with a doxology. In fact, the last Psalm in each division is itself a doxology. The divisions are as follows: (1) Psalms 1-41. (2) 42-72. (3) 73-89. (4) 90-106. (5) 107-150.

These Psalms naturally vary in length and form. The shortest is 117, with only two verses. This is also the shortest chapter in the entire Bible. The longest Psalm is 119. It contains twenty-two sections of eight verses each, a total of one hundred and seventy-six verses. Each section is given (in the American Revision) the name of a letter in the Hebrew alphabet — Aleph, Beth, Gimel, etc. This chapter is likewise the longest in the Old Testament.

4. *Authorship.*

The authorship of these poems is a question on which there is the widest difference of opinion among scholars. In the titles or superscriptions seventy-three are ascribed to David, twelve to Asaph, eleven to the sons of Korah, two to Solomon, one to Moses and one to Ethan. Exactly fifty are anonymous.

Some scholars reject these superscriptions as altogether worthless with the claim that they are not a part of the original text but were added later by some editor. This view is supported also by the contention that in the Hebrew language the same preposition may be translated "to," "of," or "for." To illustrate, a Psalm of David may mean that it is one which he wrote, or one which he owned, or one that was dedicated to David, or one written "for" David.

This is too complicated a question to attempt to discuss adequately in this connection. However, most scholars agree that these super-scriptions should not be discarded as altogether worthless. We may never be able to determine the authorship of certain of these Psalms, but fortunately it does not matter so far as their meaning and value are concerned.

Traditionally David is given credit for the writing of a great number of Psalms. The exact number of these may never be agreed upon but for the average reader this is not important. There are good reasons for believing that David was the author of enough to make him the leader of Psalmody and to place him among the front ranks of the poets of the world.

For our purpose we may dispose of the question of authorship with the statement that these poems are a collection of the best writings of the Hebrew people covering hundreds of years of their history. In general their value is the same regardless of when and by whom they were written.

5. Variety of Moods.

One of the characteristics of the Psalms is their expression of every emotion of the human heart. As some one has said, "they are lyrical poems which voice all the varying aspirations of the soul of man, in all the varying circumstances and conditions wherein man can be found, but suffused and influenced throughout by the consciousness of God and a sense of the intimate personal relation with the Divine." Martin Luther called the Psalms "A Bible in miniature."

There are expressions of thanksgiving, triumph, praise, adoration and confidence on one hand. Contrasted with these expressions one finds the revelations of discouragement, desolation, penitence and humiliation. The Psalmist cries out of distress for deliverance. He expresses his deep, abiding love for the law of Jehovah, his joy in meditation upon it. He expresses his patriotism in thrilling verse. He speaks of the brevity and frailty of human life. He exults over his enemies — the enemies of the Lord. He contrasts the ultimate end of the wicked with the righteous. He expresses his conviction of the certainty of God's eternal purposes for his nation and for all his people. Indeed, these songs express all the varying emotions of the human heart.

6. Range of the Psalms.

There are various ways of classifying the contents of the book of Psalms. Without attempting any detailed classification we may point out some six or seven types of poems contained in the Psalter.

(1) Those that deal with nature. It is surprising to note the variety of references to the world of nature which are contained in the book. Sun, moon, sky, stars, the tempest, thunder, waterfalls, the north wind, the trees, the falling leaves, the green fields, the pastures, woods, hills, valleys, the wild creatures, birds, flowers and others are mentioned.

(2) Patriotic songs, battle hymns, triumphal odes, and prayers for victory. The Hebrews, like all contemporary peoples, identified their God with battle, hence they prayed for victory and when victorious they gave credit or thanks to their God. This note is found frequently in the Psalter.

(3) Songs of adversity are rather frequent. The fugitive in despair seeks comfort from God, the desolate heart buffeted by adversity, holds on to his faith. God is the source of strength and light when men are weakened and in despair.

(4) Songs of citizenship and patriotism. The abuses of citizenship, and the vices of ungodly men are vividly portrayed. The Psalmist describes the godly man as one who walks uprightly, speaks the truth, slanders not, keeps his promises, pays his debts, and keeps his own heart pure and clean. Good religion is good citizenship.

(5) Songs for special occasions. There were certain special occasions that called forth poems in celebration of the event. Banquets, sheep-shearings, gathering of crops, entertainment of guests, and wedding feasts, all were celebrated by special songs.

(6) The meaning of life. The poets of Israel, like all other thoughtful people, sought the answer to this old, old question. In the Psalms there are many references to it. The Hebrew poets were impressed by the brevity of life and used many figures of speech to portray it — like the dew of the morning, the short-lived grass, the night watch, a tale that is told. Their conclusion was that wisdom lay in clean living and right relation with Jehovah.

The Psalmists also pondered the problem of death and what lies beyond. "The paths of glory lead but to the grave." But this is not the end. Beyond the grave, behind the shadow is the bright light of immortality, for the soul shall not be left in the grave and "He will not suffer His holy one to see corruption." Unquestionably there are positive declarations of immortality in these songs of Israel.

(7) Psalms dealing with personal religious experience. This number is very large. How often he speaks of the struggle of the soul with doubt, fear, wickedness, agony, despair and remorse. In victorious vein he speaks of the joys of forgiveness, the peace of soul, the confidence of restored fellowship. All of these may be found in the great penitential poem, Psalm 51, which was probably written in connection with David's great sin. Such poems are not "pretty rhetorical phrases designed to catch the ear of the congregation"; they are the sincere pleadings of a broken and a contrite heart.

7. *The Perfect Manual of Devotion.*

The book of Psalms has done more to mold the language and form of public worship and private devotions than any other book. In Old Testament times these songs were the models of worship, of prayer and adoration, of penitence and hope, of praise and thanksgiving. Even to the present time no one has improved on these. So the Psalter has become the text book of Christian devotion. As Dr. Hastings says, "It has molded and colored the best men's best feelings, and given words to their most ardent prayers. Its voice has blended with the battle-cries and cradle-songs of Christendom. What passionate confessions and petitions and thanksgivings have found utterance in its verses! What multitudes of the dying have spent their last breath on its syllables — since the day when Jesus Himself died with a text out of the Psalms upon His lips."*

8. *Some Immortal Psalms.*

Every one of these Psalms is worthy of serious study, but some of them are especially valuable and precious to Christian people. Perhaps no two people would select out of this collection the same list of favorite ones. However, there are some of these which are all but universally accepted as immortal poems, which have been read and re-read and memorized by countless thousands of devout people through the centuries. We are, therefore, venturing to suggest a number of these with the recommendation that the student shall master them — even memorize them.

Psalm 1 — The classic contrast of the wicked and the righteous man.
Psalm 8 — The glory of man as God has made him.

*Hastings: *The Speaker Bible*, Volume I, Psalms, p. 254.

Psalm 15 — The ideal citizen.

Psalm 19 — The glory of God's creation and his law.

Psalm 23 — The immortal shepherd Psalm, the most famous of all.

Psalm 32 — The blessedness of forgiveness and of trust in God.

Psalm 51 — The penitential prayer for forgiveness.

Psalm 90 — God's eternity and man's transitoriness.

Psalm 103 — The greatest poem of praise ever written.

The Psalter is the great book of devotion for the human heart in its hunger for satisfying fellowship with God. We may agree with W. E. Gladstone, the great English statesman, who said: "All the wonders of the Greek civilization heaped together are less wonderful than the simple book of Psalms."

Section IV — THE PROVERBS.

1. The Use of Proverbs.

A proverb is a short, pithy saying. It is an axiomatic statement. It is a "maxim which contains the wit of one but the wisdom of many."

As a form of literature it is very old and universal in use. Every people and nation and tongue has used these. In our own country we have a great many of these sayings which have come to be a part of our thought and speech. From Benjamin Franklin's "Poor Richard's Almanack" have come many of the most familiar ones which all of us use today. We are constantly making and using new ones.

This type of literature was especially beloved by Oriental people, including the Hebrews. These sayings crop out here and there in the prose sections of the Bible. "As is the mother, so is her daughter" (Ezek. 16:44). "The fathers have eaten sour grapes and the children's teeth are set on edge" (Ezek. 18:2). We are told (I Kings 5:29) that Solomon "spake three thousand proverbs, and his songs were a thousand and five."

2. Date and Authorship.

The book of Proverbs is not the work of one man but is rather a collection of proverbs covering a long period. Indeed, some scholars speak of the book as a collection of collections of such sayings. Just when the book was completed in its present form we are not able to say, but again this does not matter. Competent scholars still hold that Solomon was the greatest maker of proverbs in Hebrew history and that he was the author of more of the proverbs in the book than any other one man. The collection of sayings in Proverbs 10:1 to 22:16 is specifically ascribed to Solomon and it is possible that he is the author of other parts of the book as well.

3. Divisions of the Book.

The book as we have it contains some five distinct sections or divisions. (1) The superiority of wisdom 1-9. (2) The practical proverbs of Solomon 10:1-22:16. (3) Words of the wise 22:17-24:22. (4) The proverbs of Solomon which were copied by the scribes of Hezekiah, chapters 25-29. (5) A general section containing the "words of Augur," and the "words of Lemuel," and a description of or tribute to a worthy woman, chapters 30 and 31.

4. General Contents.

The book is not theoretical or speculative, but is exceedingly practical in nature. It is concerned with conduct, behavior or wise living. It has been called "A Business Manual for Young Men" since its constant appeal is to young men. The object seems to be to inspire young men to honesty, purity, and industry.

The first section is devoted to the praise of wisdom. This begins with a right relation to God. "The fear of Jehovah is the beginning of knowledge." The young man is warned against such vices as treachery, violence, miserliness, laziness, discord, drunkenness, and especially against the strange woman. Constant emphasis is placed on personal purity.

The second section is made up of brief proverbs on a wide variety of subjects. Among these are many pungent sayings extolling the virtue of *industry* and condemning the habit of *indolence*. This section contains many classic statements on proper *business relations* such as debts, notes of security, and so forth. One of the most familiar topics treated in this section is that of the use of the *tongue*. Improper and inconsiderate speech is the cause of endless strife, suffering and ruin. The young man is warned also against *drink*. No stronger statements against this social evil can be found anywhere. The virtue of *friendship* is exalted. A true friend is one's greatest possession, but one can have only a few real friends. Friendships should be formed carefully and then studiously cultivated and preserved.

The closing poem, praising a worthy woman (31:10-31), is one of exceptional beauty and significance. In this poem each of the 22 verses begins with a letter of the Hebrew alphabet. In Proverbs as in other Old Testament books, the position of woman is an honored one.

Her power for good or evil is fully recognized and the good woman is to be given her just praise.

SECTION V — OTHER BOOKS OF POETRY.

Having considered briefly the three best known books of Old Testament poetry, it will be well to say a word about the other poetical books which are not so familiar to the general reader. Two of these, Ecclesiastes and the Song of Solomon, are usually classed as poetry while the third one, Lamentations, is sometimes included among the prophets.

1. Ecclesiastes.

The Hebrew word translated Ecclesiastes means *preacher* or *proclaimer,* and signifies one who calls together and addresses an audience. Traditionally the book is regarded as the work of Solomon. However, most scholars hold that it is the work of a writer who lived in the latter years of Old Testament history. The name of this later writer, who puts himself in Solomon's place and writes as if he were Solomon, is not known. It represents the experience of a man who had the best of everything — wealth, rank, honor, fame, and pleasure and who, at the end, was disillusioned. He felt the emptiness of all such so-called blessings and concludes that all was "vanity and vexation of spirit" — "vanity of vanities, all is vanity."

The purpose of the book seems to be to show that self-gratification and successful worldliness do not bring satisfaction to the human heart. Life without a knowledge of and fellowship with God is empty and meaningless. Man has a destiny which calls for co-operation with God in some worthy enterprise, and in this he finds abiding peace of soul. The book ends with the familiar injunction: "Fear God and keep his commandments; for this is the whole duty of man." (Eccl. 12:13.)

2. The Song of Solomon.

This little book is sometimes called the *Song of Songs,* as well as *Canticles.* It is a love song, or perhaps a collection of love songs, which were greatly admired by Oriental peoples. It abounds in metaphors and enters freely into the description of physical beauty and charm. To some Western people it appears offensive to good taste because of its emphasis on the intimacies of love, but this was in good taste among Orientals and should not be regarded as vulgar or sordid.

The book has been variously interpreted. There have always been those who insist that it refers to the mutual love of Christ and his

Church. Others insist that no such interpretation was intended, that this poem was written to celebrate the strength, the beauty and the constancy of human love. Those who hold this view contend that the importance of a strong, clean love between man and woman, on which the home is built, is sufficient justification for placing this book in the list of inspired writings in the Bible.

3. Lamentations.

This book, which is an elegy or a funeral dirge over the desolation of Jerusalem after its destruction by Nebuchadnezzar, was written by Jeremiah and was at one time a part of the book of Jeremiah. The prefix in the Septuagint states: "And it came to pass after Israel was led into captivity and Jerusalem laid waste, Jeremiah sat weeping and lamented this lamentation over Jerusalem, and said . . ." For this reason the book is sometimes placed among the prophets.

The book has a unique structure. It is really a poem each verse of which begins with a letter of the Hebrew alphabet in proper order. Thus there are twenty-two verses in each chapter, except the third which contains sixty-six verses.

The book describes vividly the miserable and wretched condition of the wasted city, together with the horrors of its siege. The writer holds that the cause of their desolation is their sins against Jehovah. Sin blinds and destroys men and grieves the heart of God. Only God can triumph over sin.

> "Thou, O Jehovah abidest forever:
> Thy throne is from generation to generation." (5:19.)

Chapter XV

THE INTER-BIBLICAL PERIOD

Section I — The Jews Under Persian and Greek Rule.
1. Importance of This Period. 2. Sources of Study. 3. Divisions of the Period. 4. The Jews Under Persia. 5. Rise of Greece. 6. Philip of Macedon. 7. Alexander. 8. The Jews Under Alexander. 9. Division of Alexander's Empire. 10. The Jews Under the Ptolemies. 11. The Septuagint. 12. Significance of Hellenism. 13. The Jews Under the Seleucids. 14. Antiochus Epiphanes.

Section II — Hebrew Independence.
1. Maccabean Dynasty. 2. Mattathias at Modein. 3. Achievements of Judah. 4. Worship Restored. 5. Jewish Independence. 6. Successors to Judas. 7. Pharisees and Sadducees.

Section III — The Jews Under Roman Rule.
1. The Roman Empire. 2. Pompey Conquers Palestine. 3. Struggles for Power. 4. Antipater in Palestine. 5. Herod the Great. 6. The Birth of Christ.

CHAPTER XV

The Inter-Biblical Period

Section I — THE JEWS UNDER PERSIAN AND GREEK RULE.

1. Importance of This Period.

The Old Testament closed about four hundred years before the birth of Christ. This period between the close of the Old Testament and the beginning of the New is known as the Inter-Biblical period. Thus we have no record in the Bible of the experiences of the Jews during this time. Nevertheless it is a very important period since such vast changes in social, economic, political and religious life took place during this time. It is impossible for the student to understand the life of Jesus and other New Testament events without some acquaintance with the happenings during these four hundred years.

The Old Testament points to Jesus and is fully appreciated or understood only in the light of the New Testament. For this reason we feel that a study of the Old Testament should include all the significant events and developments in Jewish life up to the actual time of the birth of Jesus Christ. We are, therefore, including this chapter in our study of Hebrew history.

2. Sources of Study.

Since the Bible itself contains none of the history of these four hundred years the student naturally asks, What are our sources of study for this important period? There are three chief sources: secular history, the works of Josephus, and the Apocryphal writings.

The history of Persia, Greece and Rome furnish a great deal of information for the period. The eminent Jewish historian, Josephus, while not always reliable, gives full consideration to the history of the Jewish people during this period.

There are fourteen books of Jewish writings which belong to this general period and are known as the Apocryphal ("secret" or "hidden") books. These writings, historical and religious in nature, are not included as a part of our canon of the Bible, though there has been frequent debate and difference of opinion on this matter. Even though they are not included in the list of inspired books they have great value in the understanding of Jewish history and life of this period. Because of their value we are giving the list of these books. They are: I Esdras, II Esdras, Tobit, Judith, Esther (additions), The Wisdom of Solomon, Ecclesiasticus, Baruch, The Song of the Three Holy

Children, The History of Susanna, The History of the Destruction of
Bel and Dragon, The Prayer of Manasseh, I Maccabees and II
Maccabees.

From these three general sources the student is able to learn the
important facts in the life of the Jewish people in the Inter-Biblical
period.

3. Divisions of the Period.

This history between the Testaments is made up of four distinct
divisions which we shall consider in proper order in this chapter. These
divisions are: (1) Persian, 538 (400)-332 B.C. (2) Greek, 332-167 B.C.
(3) Hebrew Independence, 167-63 B.C. (4) Roman 63 B.C.-70 A.D.

4. The Jews Under Persia.

In the preceding chapter we have dealt with the story of Persia's
gaining control over the Jews by their conquest of Babylon in 538 B.C.
The Jews, being captives of Babylon, naturally became the subjects of
Cyrus the Great. Under Cyrus and succeeding rulers the Jews were
given many privileges and were accorded many favors. Cyrus not only
permitted them to return to their homeland but gave them great
assistance in these undertakings. Protection in travel and special
monetary grants were provided for them. So far as the record goes the
Jews were treated fairly by the Persian rulers, both in Persian territory
and in Palestine. Naturally they were not free but so long as they
recognized the supremacy of Persia and observed the laws governing
them they were not molested or abused.

When the Old Testament closed about 400 B.C. the Jewish people in
Judah were still the subjects of Persia. This continued, apparently
without any outspoken resentment on the part of the Jews, until the
Persian power began to wane and finally came to an end with the swift
conquests of Alexander the Great of Greece.

5. Rise of Greece.

It has not been possible to recount the story of Persia's expansion
after the time of Cyrus into a great world power. Suffice it to say that
under vigorous leadership her armies advanced ever further westward
until they reached the Aegean Sea, the western boundary of Asia. Not
content with this they even crossed the sea to enter Europe (Greece)
where they maintained a slight foothold for a little time. However, here
they met their strongest opponent, the Greeks, who challenged them
and drove them out of Europe and ultimately conquered all of the

territory once held by the proud Persian forces. This contest between the powerful Persian empire of the Orient and Greece, the dynamic new power in the West, was one of the most significant in all history. Had Persia won in this contest the course of history for centuries might have been different.

To appreciate the significance of the expansion of Greece and the conquests of Alexander the Great it is not necessary to give any detailed account of the early years of Greek history. This vigorous race, destined to affect so deeply the course of history, began to emerge as a nation several centuries before Alexander the Great. They occupied the south-eastern fringe of Europe and some of the Aegean isles — the territory still called Greece. The very mention of the word Greek brings to mind some of the glorious achievements of this remarkable race. They excelled in almost every area of human activity. Ancient Athens was the intellectual center of pre-Christian history. Here all the arts flourished and reached the heights of attainment. The Greeks developed the most effective language the world has known. In philosophy, literature, sculpture, architecture and other liberal arts they made a contribution unequalled by any other people. They gave to the world such men as Thucydides, Aristophanes, Xenophon, Socrates, Plato, Aristotle, Diogenes, Alexander, Demosthenes and many others. In the fourth century before Christ their culture was to be taken by zealous apostles far east into the Orient itself.

6. Philip of Macedon.

Macedonia was one of the chief states of Greece. Philip, the father of Alexander, was king of Macedonia until the time of his death in 334 B.C. His two great ambitions were to see Greece attain a place of leadership in the world, and to prepare his son to realize this dream. Both these ambitions were to an unusual degree attained. Philip was able to give to his people a conception of their possibilities as a nation and he inspired in his son an ambition to rule the world.

7. Alexander.

This man, destined to affect the lives of millions of people and scores of nations, began his career in vigorous fashion after his accession in 335-34 B.C. In his brief reign of twelve years he accomplished more in conquest than any man before him.

He defeated the Thebans in several decisive battles. Crossing into Asia, he met and defeated the forces of Darius in the two famous battles of Granicus and Issus. He then moved through Syria and Palestine to

Egypt. Tyre defied his armies for several months before falling. On his way to Egypt he approached Jerusalem, which he took apparently without difficulty. There is a tradition that he was met outside Jerusalem by a company of Jewish priests who impressed him so favorably that he granted them very reasonable terms for their holy city. One story has it that among these priests who met him Alexander recognized one who had previously told him that he should conquer the world.

From Jerusalem he went to Egypt which soon fell completely into his hands. On the northern shore of this ancient country he founded a great city to which he gave the name Alexandria. This city still stands after having played a prominent role in world events during these twenty-three centuries.

Not yet satisfied, he led his army back through Palestine and Syria to meet the forces of Darius at Arbela on the plains of Assyria. This battle was decisive and brought to its end the empire of Persia. All Persian territory now belonged to Alexander but this ambitions conquerer was not yet content. The fabulous wealth of far eastern countries beckoned to him. He continued his march eastward finally moving into India itself. Here his soldiers rebelled and his career of conquest came to an end.

Intoxicated by his phenomenal achievements, Alexander surrendered his ideals so that his character underwent a complete change in his last years in the Orient. He became vain and unreasonable and yielded to the temptations by which he was surrounded. He drank to excess and contracted a fever which brought on his death in Babylon in 323 B.C. He died at a very young age, but in a few short years he had "made history."

We may not agree that Alexander deserved the appellation "the great," but we must agree that he was a strong man. While he was not without fault, at the same time his character was far above that of most conquerors. As a student of the philosopher Aristotle, he became a passionate disciple of Greek culture and believed that he was under obligation to spread this culture over the ancient world.

8. The Jews Under Alexander.

Throughout his career Alexander seemed to be partial to the Jews. He admired their excellent qualities and granted to them in Alexandria and in other cities the privileges of citizenship. Apparently they were never the victims of discrimination as long as he lived. No doubt he would insist on their accepting Hellenistic philosophy but there is no record of his forcing them to renounce their faith in order to do this. After his death, however, the Jews entered upon an era of the bitterest suffering in their long history.

9. Division of Alexander's Empire.

When Alexander died in 323 B.C. there was no man strong enough to succeed him and to hold together this vast empire he had molded. Accordingly the kingdom was divided in 323 B.C. among four of his generals — Ptolemy, Lysimachus, Cassander and Seleucus. These divisions are usually called; the western or Greece proper; the northern or Armenian; the eastern or Syrian; and the southern or Egyptian. We need not give attention in this connection to the western and the northern divisions since the Jews were not involved in either of these. The Jewish people were very much affected by the other two. The Syrian or eastern section under Seleucus lay directly north of Palestine. The southern or Egyptian section under Ptolemy lay southwest of the Jewish homeland. In reality Palestine was sandwiched between these two powers and was passionately coveted by both the Seleucids and Ptolemies.

10. The Jews Under the Ptolemies.

Shortly after the division of Alexander's kingdom Palestine fell to the Ptolemies in Egypt. Ptolemy Soter was the ruler and at first was very severe in his treatment of the Jews. Later, however, he came to appreciate their good qualities and treated them with consideration. Numbers of Jews were given places of authority and prominence. Soter was succeeded by Philadelphus, who likewise gave fair treatment to them. He was a very able ruler and was responsible for many achievements. He built the famous lighthouse, called Pharos, at the mouth of the Nile. Even more notable was his erection of the great library in Alexandria which was the important center of culture and learning in the Mediterranean world for several centuries. It was burned by the Mohammedans in the seventh century after Christ.

11. The Septuagint.

During the reign of Ptolemy Philadelphus, the famous Septuagint was produced in Alexandria. This was the translation of the Scriptures from Hebrew to the Greek language. Hellenism had come to dominate the Mediterranean world to the extent that the Jews themselves were ceasing to speak the Hebrew tongue, and instead were using the Greek language. Devout Jews saw that if their children were to continue to study their scriptures these must be put in the Greek language. This was a most significant event, since with this translation available every person who spoke Greek could read the scriptures. It made the Old Testament with all its predictions of a Messiah available to hundreds of thousands of people who otherwise might never have had the opportunity of reading the Jewish scriptures.

12. Significance of Hellenism.

In order to appreciate the real problem which the Jews faced in this era the student should understand something of the meaning of Hellenism (the philosophy of the Greeks) which was now confronting them at every turn. Hellenism was a way of life which was radically different from that of the Jews or any other Oriental people.

The civilization of Greece was essentially a city product. It developed in cities and must be propagated by city communities. In the Orient cities were collections of houses and peoples without much plan and were ruled by a tyrant, since the people were little more than slaves. On the other hand among the Greeks cities were well planned and artistically built. The people elected their officers, discussed public affairs and participated in their government.

To the Greek, life was good and should be enjoyed. Health was at the foundation. The gymnasium was a popular institution where the young men met for physical exercises and social activities. Activities of all kinds — games, contests, sports, dancing, music, poetry — were emphasized. Greek communities had a stadium for athletic contests, a hippodrome for chariot racing, a theater for dramatic presentations.

Literature and art occupied a prominent place in their lives. Being intellectually alert, they had their schools, their philosophical discussions, their training centers for students of art and sculpture. Every building must be adorned with sculpture. These adornments were statues of the gods, of prominent citizens, of philosophers and athletes. To the Greeks a city without art was unthinkable. They developed the most beautiful language of any people in history. It was an instrument of such beauty, precision and refinement that any other language seemed barbarous in comparison with it. No wonder that the Greek language conquered the world in a short time after the conquests of Alexander.

Manners and customs of living also were vastly different from those of Orientals. Their dress was gay, even gaudy, with mantles and broad brimmed hats. Their emphasis on proper styles and the attention they gave to proper personal appearance would impress the Jews as frivolous, vain, useless and even wicked.

Pleasure of all kinds was not only legitimate but desirable. Life should be enjoyed today — tomorrow we may not have. No wonder Epicureanism became the accepted standard of thought and behavior for most of the Greek people. Religion, particularly as it related to future life, had but little place in their thoughts.

The problem facing the Jews under Greek control was, Could they accept Hellenism and remain loyal to the faith of their fathers? Some felt that they could, and hence a few openly accepted it. The big majority, however, felt that they could not become Hellenists without betraying their faith. This heathenism must be resisted even unto death.

13. The Jews Under the Seleucids.

While the Ptolemies succeeded in getting control of Palestine in 323 B.C. this control was never securely established. The Seleucids and the Ptolemies were frequently at war with each other and the outcome of these struggles was almost always in doubt. Within twenty-five years after Alexander's death Jerusalem changed hands seven times. During the one hundred twenty-five years (323-198 B.C.) that the Ptolemies had nominal control of Palestine there were so many wars that an exact count cannot be made. Finally in 198 B.C. at the battle of Banias the Ptolemies were defeated ,and the Seleucids assumed control of the little country which had been between the upper and nether millstones for so long. The Jews thus came under the control of another race of conquerors.

Antiochus III, called "The Great," (223-187 B.C.) was the ruler of the Seleucid kingdom when Palestine was taken from the Ptolemies in 198 B.C. He endeavored to conquer Egypt itself from the Ptolemies but was unsuccessful. We know but little of his treatment of the Jews, though it probably was not too harsh. Seleucus IV came to the throne in 187 B.C. and ruled until 176 B.C. There were no outstanding events in his reign. The hard years for the Jews came with Antiochus Epiphanes who succeeded Seleucus IV.

14. Antiochus Epiphanes.

Antiochus IV, the grandson of Antiochus the Great, had two nicknames. By some he was known as "Epiphanes" (the brilliant one); by others as "Epimanes" (the dullard). There were reasons for both, since, in some ways he was a very brilliant ruler, and yet in other respects he was unbelievably stupid. He was a passionate devotee of Hellenism and his ruling ambition was to enforce this philosophy on all his subjects. The Jews thus had to face one of the most critical situations in all their history.

Shortly after he became king Antiochus Epiphanes got into difficulties with the people of Jerusalem by the appointment of a high priest
which the Jews would not accept. The same experience was repeated
a short time later with the result that very unhappy relations developed
between the king and his subjects. In 169 B.C. Antiochus was on a
campaign in Egypt when the report came to Jerusalem that he had been
killed. The Jews proceeded at once to celebrate, only to learn later that
the report was false. When Antiochus returned to Jerusalem he
wreaked his vengeance on the city and plundered the temple. Disorder
and bitterness increased. Antiochus now devoted himself with fanatical
zeal to bringing the Jews under absolute control. Some Jews in
Jerusalem had accepted Hellenism and were persuaded by the king to
join in his efforts to make all Jews conform. Many orthodox Jews were
imprisoned, forty thousand were slaughtered and an equal number were
sold as slaves. Still later he sent emissaries to all the synagogues where
the people were assembled on the Sabbath and massacred thousands of
men, women and children.

He was determined to destroy the worship of Jehovah. The temple
was plundered and all feasts annulled. The Jews were forbidden to
read their scriptures, to observe the Sabbath or to perform the rite of
circumcision. Two Jewish women defied his edict and had their boys
circumcised. When apprehended, they were led through the streets with
their children fastened to their necks, and were thrown headlong over
the steepest part of the walls. To show his contempt for the faith of the
Jews, he sacrificed a sow on the altar of burnt offering, cooked the
meat, and then poured the broth over all the building. He caused an
altar to the Greek god, Zeus, to be erected on the temple area. These
desecrations were the chief cause of the revolt of the Jews. At first Jewish
resistance was passive, but later, in desperation, this resistance became
a burning flame. The illustrious Antiochus underestimated the devotion
of the Jews to their faith. Under the circumstances it appeared that their
cause was absolutely hopeless, but such was not the case. Though they
could not foresee it, they were on the threshold of one of the most
glorious epochs in their history.

SECTION II — HEBREW INDEPENDENCE.

1. Maccabean Dynasty.

One of the most unusual ruling families in the long history of
the Jewish race was the Maccabean with which we are now concerned.
The father of this family was an aged priest, named Mattathias, who

lived in the little town of Modein, west of Jerusalem near the Philistine border. He had five sons, John, Simon, Judas, Eleazer, and Jonathan. He led the revolt which put his family to the forefront as rulers of the Hebrew people. The family is sometimes called Asmonaeans, a title derived from Asmoneus, one of their ancestors. They are more frequently called Maccabeans. There are various explanations given as to the origin of this name, though it probably was a sort of nickname meaning "hammerer." For several generations this dynasty was to exert a tremendous influence on the life of the Jewish nation.

2. Mattathias at Modein.

During the darkest days of the Antiochan persecution (167 B.C.) an event took place at Modein which started the revolution. An emissary of Antiochus appeared in the village to test the loyalty of the people to the king. He built an altar to Zeus and commanded Mattathias and his sons, as the leading citizens, to offer sacrifices to the pagan god with the promise of a large reward and the favor of the king. The aged priest refused to obey. When a younger man stepped up to obey the order, Mattathias, unable to control his anger, rushed forward and slew the young man, then turned and killed the emissary of the king. Realizing that the die had been cast the priest made an appeal to all loyal Jews to join him He and his five sons, together with a number of other zealots, then fled to the hills to declare open war against Antiochus.

When this bold stand had been taken larger groups of Jews took courage and joined the forces until a formidable army was recruited. This task of leadership in this uprising was too strenuous for Mattathias, who was already an old man. From his five strong sons he selected Judas to take the leadership of the new movement. The new leader was admirably suited for this difficult undertaking. He could inspire confidence, he could plan, he could fight and he had courage. He was intrepid and bold, a skilled strategist who appeared and disappeared swiftly. He was thoroughly familiar with the contour of the country; he knew the ravines, mountains and caves. In his bold undertakings he had the loyalty and unqualified co-operation of his patriots. Judas Maccabeus became the most spectacular military man of his race. A man of lesser stature could never have won independence from the merciless Seleucids.

3. Achievements of Judas.

To give the details of his wars with the Seleucids is obviously impossible in the limits of this chapter. We shall tell briefly of four of his victories. The Seleucid General Appolonius was sent first to crush these rebels led by Judas. Somewhere near Samaria Judas met the Syrian general and his army and completely routed them, gaining a store of supplies and much needed equipment. Next a large Syrian army was led by Seron, who planned to get to Jerusalem through the valley of Beth-horon. Judas trapped the army and almost annihilated it in the valley. Again he gained much booty. The third attempt to crush Judas was led by three generals whose combined forces numbered fifty thousand. They attempted to go through the passageway south of Mizpah. With only six thousand men Judas attacked them at dawn and took them by surprise. They fled in utter defeat. The fourth army to come up against Judas was led by Lysias, the commander-in-chief. His forces numbered sixty thousand. Just north of Hebron Judas attacked them with only ten thousand men and utterly defeated them. The Syrians withdrew, not to return until after the death of Antiochus Epiphanes two or three years later.

4. Worship Restored.

Taking advantage of the absence of the Syrians, Judas and his forces entered Jerusalem and cleaned up the temple court. They wept as they saw the desecration and wreckage before them. They destroyed all pagan altars and gods, then set up an altar to Jehovah, repaired the temple and put the city in order. On December 25, 165 B.C. the temple was rededicated to the worship of God. This occasion was memorialized by the "feast of the dedication." (John 10:22.)

Judas next proceeded to make war on several neighboring peoples who were sympathetic with the Syrians. He defeated the Idumeans in the south, later capturing Hebron, and then crushed the Philistines. He crossed the Jordan to administer defeat to the Ammonites as far north as Damascus. With the close of these campaigns he had gained possession of much of Palestine.

5. Jewish Independence.

Antiochus Epiphanes died of a loathsome disease while breathing out threats and slaughter against his enemies. Lysias now came against the Jews with a still larger force — one hundred thousand infantry, twenty thousand cavalry and thirty-two war elephants. Realizing that he was completely outnumbered Judas elected not to fight. He withdrew to Jerusalem to defend himself. Lysias besieged the city in his determination to crush Judas. A report of serious trouble back at Antioch caused Lysias to withdraw. However, before leaving, he came to terms with

Judas and guaranteed to all Jews the privilege of religious freedom. Judas had won what Mattathias had prayed for. The Jews could now worship their God without molestation. However, they were not yet politically free.

The Hellenists did not keep their agreement and new conflicts arose. The brave Judas was forced again to fight the Syrians, and died on the battlefield in 161 B.C. This greatest general and leader in Jewish history had achieved the seemingly impossible. Against overwhelming odds he had saved his people and their religion in their greatest peril. His name, even though the same as that of the most ignominious character in Jewish history, continues to shine with undying glory.

6. Successors to Judas.

At the death of Judas his brother Jonathan held a place of leadership for awhile. He was murdered by a Syrian general who hoped to gain the throne. However, Simon, another brother of Judas, moved swiftly and took charge. Demetrius II, king of Syria, needed the support of Simon and in order to get it bargained with this son of Mattathias. By the agreement reached Simon was recognized as Jewish high-priest, and the payment of all tribute of the Jews to Syria was stopped forever. This pact made in 143 B.C. began a new era in Jewish history. At long last they had gained political independence. The subsequent reign of Simon was one of great prosperity. "They tilled their land in peace, and the land gave her increase, and the trees of the plain their fruit . . . Simon provided food for the cities and furnished them with the means of fortification . . . and he strengthened all the distressed of his people, he was full of zeal for the law, and every lawless and wicked person he banished. He made the sanctuary glorious, and multiplied the vessels of the temple." (I Mac. 14:8-15.)

Simon was assassinated in 135 B.C. along with a group of his friends, by Ptolemy his son-in-law, who planned to seize the throne. However, John Hyrcanus, Simon's son, out-maneuvered Ptolemy and became the ruler. Under John Hyrcanus (135-105 B.C.) there was a period of rapid expansion. He annexed Idumea, Samaria and Perea to Judea. He beautified Jerusalem. He was the first Jewish ruler to issue coins. As high-priest he offended the strict Pharisaic party and later identified himself with the Sadducees, the rival religious party of the Jews.

7. Pharisees and Sadducees.

During this period which we are now considering the Pharisees and the Sadducees emerged as the two strong religious parties of the Jews.

They were opposed to each other at almost every point and the rivalry between them was keen and often very bitter.

The patriots who stood by Judas Maccabeus desired religious freedom and were willing to die for it. They were known at first as Hasidim. As soon as religious freedom was won they stopped fighting since they had no political ambitions. Out of this group came the Pharisees. The word means "separatists" and is usually interpreted as meaning separation from unclean things and persons. Gradually they came to be regarded as conservatives, those who held steadfastly to the law of Moses and the traditions of the fathers. They represent the common people, and especially in New Testament times, were the majority party and were very influential.

There were some Jews who saw the good in Hellenism and who believed that they could accept it and still be loyal to their own faith. These were largely of the aristocratic class and, while not nearly so numerous as the Pharisees, they were very influential in national affairs. They were of the priestly class and were considered by the Pharisees liberal and even anti-religious. They are known as Sadducees.

The antagonism between these two strong parties became so bitter that it ultimately wrecked the Maccabean kingdom and forfeited the political freedom of the Jews. John Hyrcanus died in 105 B.C. and was succeeded by Aristobulus I who ruled for only a year. He was succeeded by Alexander Janneus, who lived until 78 B.C. Both these were Sadducees. Janneus was vicious in his actions and was very severe in his treatment of the Pharisees. Janneus was succeeded by his wife, Alexandra, who was strongly pro-Pharisee. Under her rule the Pharisees were merciless in their treatment of the Sadducees.

When Alexandra died in 69 B.C. an era of civil war broke out between her two sons, Hyrcanus II and Aristobulus II. This bitter struggle for supremacy dragged on for six years, neither one being able to gain a decisive victory. In 63 B.C. Pompey the Roman general came upon the scene, and with his advent the period of Hebrew independence came to an end.

Section III — UNDER ROMAN RULE.

1. The Roman Empire.

The important place which the Roman people occupied in the history of the world is known, to some degree at least, by every student. The little city which sprang up on the banks of the Tiber river in Italy some seven centuries before the birth of Christ expanded until its dominion covered the entire basin of the Mediterranean and spread northward into Europe and eastward far into the Orient. For centuries it dominated the civilized world. Its contribution to civilization and its influence on the thoughts and lives of men have been surpassed by few other governments.

It was in this Roman world that Jesus Christ lived and did his work. "In the fulness of times" — when conditions were just right — the Jewish Messiah made his advent. Palestine, the home of the Jews, was a part of the Roman empire. The Jews were subjects of Rome and, like all their neighbors, were governed by Roman officials. They resented this domination, chafed under its restrictions and frequently rebelled against it, but to no avail. Their rebellion against Roman authority finally brought their national destruction. When Titus burned Jerusalem and scattered them aboard in 70 A.D. they were so completely crushed that they were never able to come together again. Their existence as a nation ended with this futile struggle.

2. Pompey Conquers Palestine.

The triumphant Roman army under Pompey moved eastward into Syria in 63 B.C. With the conquest of Syria Pompey paused to await developments in Palestine. We have seen that at this time the Jews in Palestine were deadlocked in a hopeless civil war between Hyrcanus II and Aristobulus II. Each of these claimants, feeling that he could not succeed without outside assistance and realizing that Pompey was now ready to move into Palestine, resolved to appeal to this Roman general. Each laid his case before Pompey, offered his resources and pled for his support. In his favored position the Roman general could take his time. Finally he announced his preference for Hyrcanus. Aristobulus hastily prepared to defend Jerusalem against the advances of Pompey. After a siege of three months Pompey captured Jerusalem and seized Aristobulus whom he sent, along with some of his supporters, to Rome as a prisoner.

When the Roman general had seized Jerusalem he horrified the Jews by entering the "Holy of Holies," as well as by other profane deeds. Having disposed of Aristobulus, he now set up Hyrcanus as ruler in Palestine, but without a crown. He also laid upon the Jews a heavy annual tribute to be paid to Rome. Jewish independence was at an end. The Roman ruled the Jews.

3. Struggles for Power.

The next fifty years were filled with intrigues, revolts, bloody battles and changing fortunes for the Jews. Pompey had sided with Hyrcanus

II, but Aristobulus II, whom he had sent to Rome, managed to escape and returned to Palestine. This was the beginning of renewed civil war among the Jews. Pompey had made Antipater of Idumea (ancient Edom) the adviser of Hyrcanus II. He proved to be a powerful influence and ultimately assumed authority for Rome in the troubled affairs of Palestine. He was a strong supporter of Pompey who had placed him in power.

In the meantime affairs in the Roman empire had resolved themselves into a life and death struggle between Pompey and Julius Caesar for the place of supremacy. The contest was finally settled in the battle of Pharsalus in 48 B.C. In this battle Pompey was killed. Julius Caesar was now the undisputed master in Rome.

Antipater, who had supported Pompey, was clever enough to convince Caesar of his loyalty to him. Caesar, therefore, placed him in the position of Procurator of Judea, a position above that occupied by Hyrcanus. In the meantime Caesar manifested a very lenient attitude toward the Jews, not only in Palestine, but elsewhere in the empire. He granted them special favors, among which was full religious liberty.

4. Antipater in Palestine.

With the full support of Caesar, Antipater became at once a powerful political figure in Palestine. He was thoroughly loyal to Rome and at the same time seemed to be genuinely interested in the Jews. The Jews hated him, however, since he was an Idumean, and thus a descendant of their bitter enemies in former years. Antipater had two sons — Phasael and Herod, who later became procurators of Judea and Galilee. Antipater was poisoned after only a year in his position. Three years later Caesar was assassinated in Rome.

5. Herod the Great.

Herod, the son of Antipater, was born in 74 B.C. and died in 4 B.C., a short while after the birth of Christ. In his career as a politician and ruler he more than any other man, represented the Roman government in dealing with the Jews.

After the death of Julius Caesar the Roman empire was divided among three triumvirs, Octavius, Antony and Lepidus. Syria and the East fell to Antony. On the whole, Antony was favorable to Herod and this friendship with Antony aided him greatly. Herod further strengthened himself by his marriage to Mariamne, granddaughter of Hyrcanus, and one of the most beautiful women of the time. This marriage identified him with the Maccabean line. About this time civil strife broke out anew among the Jews, and Herod hurried to Rome to confer with Antony. He persuaded Antony that he alone could preserve order in Palestine, so Antony appointed him ruler over Judea.

The story of the disgraceful flirtation of Antony with Cleopatra, queen of Egypt, is known to every reader of history. During this time war broke out between Antony and Octavius. In the decisive battle of Actium Antony was defeated. About a year later Antony and Cleopatra committed suicide in Egypt. Octavius now became Emperor of Rome under the title of Caesar Augustus.

In the meantime the crafty and unprincipled Herod was strengthening his position in Judea. This was done largely through intrigue and murder. To recount the record of murders committed by him during his reign would be a huge task. Suffice it to say that no one under suspicion escaped. Many members of his family fell at his order. Even Mariamne, whom he loved most devotedly, was killed upon his command. After her death his remorse was so great that he came near losing his mind. His was literally a reign of terror.

Despite all this Herod was an able ruler and did much for his country, though the Jews hated him with intense bitterness. In his saner moments he honestly sought to be helpful to the Jews and seems to have genuinely coveted their good will. His greatest service to them was the rebuilding of their temple. He hoped that this generous gesture would cause them to feel more friendly toward him, but apparently it failed in its object.

Historians tell us that his last days were indescribably horrible. Stricken by a foul disease of the flesh he lay on his death-bed a rotting mass. He suffered the most excruciating bodily pains, which were perhaps less torturing than the memory of crimes committed and the consciousness of the bitter hatred held by all who knew him. He died in 4 b.c. "dispensing death with one hand and crowns with another."

6. The Birth of Christ.

A few months before the death of Herod momentous events, though unrecognized by many, had been taking place. Four hundred years of silence at last had been broken. God had spoken again to the faithful of his people. The angel Gabriel had announced to a maid in Nazareth the coming of the Messiah, the real King of the Jews. While Herod lay on his death-bed in his palace at Jerusalem, Mary brought forth her first-born son and laid him in a lowly manger at Bethlehem. This new born babe was Jesus Christ, the King of the Jews.

With the birth of Jesus Christ a new era began. It was a new era, not only in the history of the Hebrew people, but in the history of all humanity as well. Though no one even dreamed of it at the time, this event was to become the dividing point in history. Several centuries later a calendar was made which began with his birth. Henceforth time was to be designated by B.C. and A.D.

The task of recounting the story of the Hebrew people up to this signal event has now been completed. The story of the wondrous life of Jesus and its influence on the world belongs to another volume. However this other volume can be appreciated fully only by those who know the story contained in the book which we have now completed.

A BRIEF BIBLIOGRAPHY

Adams, J. McKee: *Ancient Records and the Bible.*
Adams, J. McKee: *Biblical Backgrounds.*
Bailey and Kent: *History of the Hebrew Commonwealth.*
Barton, George A.: *Archaeology and the Bible.*
Blaikie and Mathews: *A Manual of Bible History.*
Calkin, John B.: *Historical Geography of Bible Lands.*
Duncan, J. G.: *Digging Up Biblical History.*
Francisco, Clyde T.: *Introduction to the Old Testament.*
Grant, G. M.: *Between the Testaments.*
Kent, Charles Foster: *The Historical Bible,* 5 volumes.
Kirkpatrick, H. F.: *The Doctrines of the Prophets.*
Knopf, Carl Sumner: *The Old Testament Speaks.*
Knott, Laura A.: *Student's History of the Hebrews.*
Maclear, G. F.: *A Class Book of Old Testament History.*
Mould, Elmer W. K.: *Essentials of Bible History.*
Price, Ira M.: *The Dramatic Story of Old Testament History.*
Sampey, John R.: *The Heart of the Old Testament.*
Schofield, J. N.: *The Historical Background of the Bible.*
Smith, George Adam: *The Book of the Twelve Prophets.*
Smith, George Adam: *The Historical Geography of the Holy Land.*
Tidwell, J. B.: *Introducing the Old Testament.*
Tidwell, J. B.: *The Bible Period By Period.*
Tribble, Hill, Yates: *Old Testament Biographies.*
Yates, Kyle M.: *Preaching From the Prophets.*